Reflections:
A Memoir

Reflections: A Memoir

Relatives
The Mourning After
Observations From Over The Hill

Davida Rosenblum

Library of Congress Control Number: 2008901226
ISBN: Hardcover   978-1-4363-2178-5
                  Softcover   978-1-4363-2177-8

To order additional copies of this book, contact:
Xlibris Corporation
1-888-795-4274
www.Xlibris.com
Orders@Xlibris.com
46446

Contents

Observations From Over The Hill

For Augusta
who nourished,
For William D.
who knew it all the time,
For Emily and Paul
who grace my life,
And for Ralph.

Acknowledgements

Memory, like other translations, is metaphor, and as such, may be more emotionally than literally true. Therefore, if I've misremembered any of the events depicted in this book, I plead translator's license and beg the indulgence of those who may remember them differently.

I have changed most names and some details in order to avoid causing anyone embarrassment or hurt. However, my daughter Emily, my son Paul and my late husband Ralph asked that their real names be used, thereby demonstrating their understanding and their trust.

Thanks are due Joyce Johnson for her expert editorial contributions to the first section; Pat Sylvia for her indispensable contributions to the last, and agent Phillipa Brophy for her unflagging encouragement during the writing of the last two. I am forever in their debt. Many thanks also to Christine Amarger for permitting me to use her etching, *Mon Cherie,* on the cover, and to David J. Bookbinder for the author's photograph and that of the etching.

Relatives

Sunday Dinner

I am sitting across from my mother, looking across a great oval table at a multitude of noisy, gesticulating people. The white tablecloth is dotted with crumbs and specked with gravy, its surface nearly hidden by platters of small doughy cakes and delicate porcelain teacups. The faces are featureless; none will emerge as separate entities until I am older.

Fully extended, as it is every Sunday, Grandma Gottfried's dining table fills the entire middle room of the parlor floor of the brownstone house in Brooklyn, making it nearly impossible to get out when once seated. At least eight people have to move if someone at the far end has to go to the bathroom. Therefore, anyone with a weak bladder learns to sit near the door. My cousin Shirley often moistens the cane of her spindle-back chair because she comes to the table late and has to settle for an inside seat.

It takes nothing more than the odor of chicken livers or the taste of a Hungarian sweet-and-sour sauce heavy on the lemon for me to be transported instantly back to that dining room on Hampton Place with its massive furniture, worn oriental rug and dark oak flooring showing around the rug's perimeter. Every Sunday, my father drives us there for dinner, not because he particularly likes Grandma Gottfried's cooking, but because it is unthinkable for him not to go. My father, by far the most powerful man in the world, is so intimidated by that tiny old woman that week after week he makes the journey against his own desire.

Each Sunday, on our way, he attempts to counteract any negative influence the forthcoming visit may have on our developing characters. We have nothing in common with any of our relatives, he reminds my brother and me repeatedly. We may be *from* this family of commoners, but not *of* it. We aren't like the rest, who care only about what they can make in the marketplace, whose only recreations are squabbling and poker, whose women spend their lives in the kitchen with children hanging onto their skirts. My father claims spiritual kinship with Spinoza, Mendelssohn and Marx, men of vision, who spent their lives inventing new philosophies, creating great works, changing the destinies of whole countries. As evidence, he cites my mother's talent as a pianist and his own love of music; somehow he is capable of listening at the same time to a Beethoven symphony and a Brooklyn Dodgers baseball game and of discussing the progress of either at any given moment. Defensive about his devotion to baseball, his only plebeian enjoyment, he points out that he also reads biographies of famous men and never fails to tune in every week to hear Father Coughlin deliver his fascist sermons, even though he disagrees with them violently, explaining that it's a clever man who keeps abreast of his enemies. By the time we reach our destination, my father has worked up an enormous appetite based mainly on an excess of bile, and devours the food of his childhood with a relish he never shows for my mother's pot roast.

I am now old enough to have a seat of my own and to be horrified by the delight my relatives take in argument: in my father's house the only emotion permitted expression is brotherly love. The Gottfrieds can never agree on anything. There is not a marriage, a pregnancy or the purchase of a funeral plot that isn't subject to a tribunal. They argue about the future disposition of my grandmother's silver, and just as passionately about the exact year my Uncle Jake opened his printing shop or the price of coal the previous winter. Two of my uncles once came to blows over whether or not Rudy Vallee was a better singer than Al Jolson. I sit and watch them all, primed by my father with the secret uncomfortable knowledge of our superiority, carefully keeping my distance from the vehemently expressed feelings that rage back and forth.

There, at the head of the table ever since my grandfather died, sits my grandmother, spectacles shading her intense, deep-set eyes. She is ladling out the steaming chicken soup, nectar with matzo balls, into wide, flat-rimmed bowls so shallow that the thumbs of those who pass them are scalded by the hot broth.

"Don't drop," she warns as she hands each soup plate to her only daughter, who stands beside her. Fanny, my father's sister, is helping to serve, assisted by her husband Moish. Fanny is sullen, quick to anger; Moish is meek and good-natured—a monument to the attraction of opposites. To Moish's right, their backs to the mahogany highboy lined with pewter plates and ornate silver spoons of many patterns, sit my Uncle Dewey, not yet married, and my Uncles Jake and Manny with their wives. Manny and Dewey are cab drivers. For me those names so embody their calling that some fifteen years later I will experience a faint jolt of surprise when the driver of my first cab is named something else.

I have taken a seat next to Uncle Jake, the only grownup among the Gottfrieds who talks to me. He whispers funny comments into my ear about the others, who glance at us suspiciously as we giggle together. On my other side sits my brother Bo, a sad, undersized child a year younger than me, who never plays with any of the other children and discomfits me with his odd, distant look. When he isn't slyly knocking my elbow as I raise my spoon to my lips, he's staring off into space, oblivious to the cacophony around him, or having slid off his seat onto the floor after dinner, lies fast asleep under the table, hidden behind the folds of the tablecloth. Beside him, urging him to eat more, is my mother, her gentle, worried eyes observing the progress of his meal and occasionally lighting on me with a smile that warms my insides as much as my grandmother's soup.

My six cousins fight and whisper, jabbing each other with the tines of their forks; their squeals furnish a treble counterpoint to the shouting baritones and altos of their elders. My cousin Shirley is dressed exactly like her mother, who spends her evenings making matching mother-daughter dresses, mostly in large floral prints with satin belts and short, puffed sleeves. At the moment, Shirley is crying because Aunt Rose won't let her leave the table to play with her jacks. My cousin Roy has lined up his remaining peas and is flipping them across the table like miniature missiles. His sister, Anita, is leaning further and further back in her chair, trying to see how far back it can go without falling. Sometimes, reaching the point of no return it tips and hits the wall, leaving her with her legs in the air, her Mary Janes kicking vainly against gravity. Uncle Jake's two sons are rolling a rubber ball back and forth across the table, just missing my water glass every time it passes. My oldest cousin, Jeffrey, is playing with one of the many practical jokes on which he spends his entire allowance. Last week it was an inflatable tube hidden under his plate that caused it to lift mysteriously off the table; right now it's a glass bubble in the shape of a teardrop that he inserts into one nostril, prompting my Aunt Fanny to shout at him to blow his nose for God's sake. Each time she reprimands him he snorts obediently into his handkerchief, only to have the bubble reappear instantly, this time in his other nostril.

My father is aloof from them all. He sits on my mother's right, trying to ignore all the activity around him and motioning at me every once in a while to sit up straight. Occasionally, a fleeting expression of anger softened by pain breaks through his mask of indifference, and my stomach tightens in visceral communion.

My Father

It is only now, when I am older than most of my Gottfried relatives were in those days, that I can begin to appreciate their richness, their color and their fierce sense of family. I suppose it was my loyalty to my father in his struggle to remain apart that prevented me from developing a feeling of connection with any of them except one—my Uncle Jake, who with his humor was able to cross the barrier I'd set up against the others. Throughout my childhood I permitted myself to see only what was most negative about my father's family: their Hungarian volatility, their vulgarity, their materialism and the absence of those things I'd been taught to value above all else: goodness, grace, and classical music, with the accent on Bach.

In a dramatic rejection of his origins, my father had turned his eyes westward to the Rosicrucians, an organization composed of the similarly estranged. It was based, of course, in California—the land, as my Uncle Jake referred to it before anyone else did, of the fruits and the nuts. An avid reader of Popular Mechanics, my father had seen their advertisement among the displays of chamois cloths and hand drills and had been instantly attracted. The Rosicrucians, who themselves looked toward the East, propounded a religion based loosely on Egyptian theology, Buddhism and Buck Rogers. At my father's urging, my mother had also become a member, but she never attained his level of conviction.

Our mailbox began to bulge with plain brown envelopes that contained thick, mimeographed pamphlets whose covers bore drawings of interlocking triangles, sphinxes and pyramids. These tracts, as promised, revealed the secrets of the ages, which included such things as complete descriptions of the process of reincarnation, the effects of cosmic rays on agriculture and instructions on how to uncover one's previous existences, improve the status of one's ever-evolving soul, and when necessary, make contact with the Higher Intelligence for guidance.

By the time I was six, our house had become the site of the biweekly meetings of the local membership. These gatherings were a cross between symposia on the Great Ideas of Eastern Man and gypsy séances, with candles providing the only illumination. The Rosicrucians were mostly a gentle group, with a disproportionate number of them handicapped in some way: I remember a couple in leg braces, a man in a wheelchair and a woman with a face that seemed to be spilt in two—one side normal enough, the other side bloated and loosely resting on her shoulder. At night from my bed I would listen to discussions on the subject of the latest mailing and sometimes even wander half-asleep into the room. I was never sent back to bed; on the contrary, my father was delighted to see me taking an interest, and encouraged me to stay.

He used suppertime to educate my brother and me to the guiding principles of Rosicrucianism, admonishing us to live exemplary lives to avoid being reborn into a lower stage of purification, and presenting death as a cozy passage to the next life. Words like "Karma," "Innate Goodness," and "Brotherly Love" (all spoken in capital letters), became as much a part of the dinner experience as the presence of the food itself. My mother would listen, looking slightly embarrassed, not completely convinced herself, but intimidated into silence by the force of my father's persuasiveness, a talent that years later he would use to his advantage in the selling of insurance.

If I had to characterize my father in just a few words, I would choose vain, ambitious and absurdly optimistic. His optimism took many forms, the most pervasive of which was the belief that all personal misfortunes were tests sent by whichever Egyptian god was in charge of that particular area, and that the individuals passing the tests would inevitably come to a happy end, with fame and fortune their reward. In other words, be patient, because everything happens for the best.

One sign of my father's personal vanity was his snub nose. Early photographs show him with a nose, while not as extreme as that of his mother, was still identifiable as a Jewish product. How then had it come to its present *goyishe* state? His story to me was that as a child he'd fallen off a swing in the back yard of his family's Brooklyn brownstone, breaking his nose so cleanly that it had miraculously healed into the thing of beauty that presently adorned his face. It wasn't until after his death that my mother told me his secret—that with the first money he'd earned after completing high school, he had talked a surgeon into removing the offending piece of bone, having decided that he didn't wish to live any longer with the nose nature had given him. In 1914, when he was eighteen years old, nose jobs were virtually unheard of, which illustrates the lengths to which he would go to get what he wanted. For all I know, he may well have been responsible for starting the beautification trend that would later transfigure the over-endowed noses of middle-class Jewish ladies everywhere. But mostly, his vanity expressed itself through his immediate family. Aside from his nose, my father's vanity wasn't of the usual type, nor was his ambition, for both applied less to himself than to his wife and children. It was important to my father than anything associated with him be the best. And so he set out first to win my mother and later to shape his children into the best possible specimens of humanity so that their excellence would reflect back onto him and make him shine in return.

My mother was no prize by Eastern Parkway standards. She was stout (the polite way in those days to refer to overweight) and her upper body, neck and jaw were slightly out of alignment due to a childhood bout with tuberculosis of the spine. By no stretch of the imagination could she be called pretty, but she had a goodness and a modesty of kind that my father must have found exotic in contrast to his wily and argumentative family. Her speaking voice was melodious and warm and her speech free of New Yorkisms despite her lifetime residence there, the antithesis of the harsh and nasal Brooklynese of his mother and sister. Above all, she was talented.

My father had somewhere picked up the idea that being able to play an instrument, sing, write a book, paint a picture—none of which he could do himself—placed a person somewhere on a scale halfway to God. My mother was a fine and sensitive pianist; as a bonus, she was able to turn this talent into money, another thing my father lacked, by giving piano lessons to children in the neighborhood. Their marriage, when he was almost thirty and she twenty-three, marked him as a *meshugenah* in the eyes of his family, who could not see past my mother's flawed body and into her spirit.

My father inspired in me a mixture of fear, love, hatred, self-confidence and deep feelings of inadequacy, all of which were constantly at war in me for supremacy. I found it difficult to believe him when he told me that I was the most beautiful girl-child in Brooklyn, when in the next breath he would add, "But if you wore your hair in braids (bangs, straight, curled), you'd be even more beautiful," or when he responded to my playing of a Bach prelude with, "Not even Horowitz could have played it better," only to cancel the compliment in the next breath with a lecture about not practicing enough to make the grade as a concert pianist, or proudly telling everyone within hailing distance about my perfect report card, leaving out the one B in arithmetic) and later scolding me roundly for not making straight A's.

He was always buying me extravagant gifts, which I would usually lose or break soon after, thereby incurring his wrath and adding another ounce or two to my growing store of guilt. When I was nine, I started to write copious amounts of poetry. The appearance of this hitherto unsuspected talent gave him such pleasure that, despite the fact that he was then in his third year of Depression-caused unemployment, he bought me a Waterman fountain pen with which to write my poetry. I can still feel the terror that nearly immobilized me as I walked home for lunch one spring day thinking that perhaps I should run away instead, because somehow the pen had disappeared from my pencil case. Years later, my husband bought me an expensive Cross fountain pen, which, in an unconscious replay of my childhood, I managed to lose. Again I felt the waves of shame more appropriate to my nine-year-old self than to a woman in her thirties, and the same paralyzing fear that made me wait months before I could tell him of my loss.

My brother and I were punished often—me for using profanities like "lousy"; my brother for not standing up for himself when he was bullied in school; both of us for not practicing our instruments (my father labored for years to turn my brother from a music-hater into a cellist). My punishment was my father's verbal anger, which would set the air to rocking and pressed against my body with such force as to take my breath away. This was always followed by a silent treatment that would last until, desperate for him to love me again, I had demonstrated my remorse and rehabilitation sufficiently by practicing five hours instead of three for the next few days and apologizing fervently enough for him to recognize my true repentance for whatever transgression I'd committed. But my brother got the worst of it. Coming home every day with bruises inflicted on him by children who sensed and exploited his vulnerability, he would be exhorted by my father to fight back, and taunted with the epithet "sissy" whenever he cried. Sometimes my father, out of his own deep frustration, would respond to Bo's crying by beating him with his belt, shouting as he did so, "Maybe this will put some courage into you".

It must have been terribly painful for Bo to witness the obvious pride my father took in me, and he fought back with the only weapon he had: a finely honed ability to harass me to the point of tears. To do my homework, I often had to lock myself in the bathroom. Forced to abandon the rib poking or the finger snapping he'd been doing near my ears, he would resort to rattling the knob of the locked door. At these times my mother was giving piano lessons in the living room, and I early understood that under no circumstances short of a fire was I to disturb her. On the days when my brother had been especially upsetting, I'd greet her when she was finished with a tearful shower of complaints, which she would transfer onto my father the moment he returned from his daily job-hunt. The shouting and the screaming would follow.

The intensity of my father's reaction so horrified me that it wasn't long before I complained to my mother about Bo only when I couldn't help myself, when my rage overcame my reluctance to subject him to the terrible punishment I knew he'd receive. And so I suffered, mostly in silence, my brother's unremitting assaults on my privacy, my feelings of fury and frustration growing more and more intense as I grew older.

My father's pride in me grew inversely to his disappointment in my brother. But this didn't stop him from constantly trying to improve what he so often proclaimed was already perfect. I was a plain, round-faced, somewhat dumpy child with glasses, straight brown hair, crooked teeth and a slightly recessive jaw, but with a nose that looked surprisingly like his post-operative one, and gray-blue eyes like my mother's, framed by lashes that were uncommonly long. Relatives and friends would invariably remark on my beautiful eyes—a sign to me that they didn't think much of the rest of my looks. All the time that my father was telling me how beautiful I was, a message that I never took seriously, he was arranging for changes: permanent waves every six months from the time I was twelve, braces throughout my entire adolescence, a back brace to straighten out a tendency I had to slump ("Posture!" he would shout angrily whenever I began to droop. "For God's sake STAND UP STRAIGHT!"), and for my seventeenth birthday he arranged to have my hair dyed ash blond.

My poor posture was the source of my single most excruciating moment. There was a children's radio program in those days in which a treacly avuncular type, appropriately named Uncle Don, would announce each evening the names of children whose birthdays fell on that day, send them scurrying to some remote spot in a bedroom where they would find a birthday present hidden, and then add something personal, such as, "Uncle Don wants to congratulate you for winning the spelling bee last week" or "My secret friend tells me that you have the prettiest curly hair he ever saw." I listened to Uncle Don every night, trying to figure out how he knew things like curly hair and spelling bees about children he had never met, and especially how he knew just where presents lay hidden if he'd never visited their homes.

On my sixth birthday, a few of my relatives had been invited over to celebrate. I had received lots of presents, but nothing yet from my parents. Just as the guests were getting ready to leave, my father said, "Wait, everybody. Let's listen to Uncle Don. Maybe he knows about Davida's birthday." We all drew close to the radio so that we could hear over the static, and sure enough, just before the end of the broadcast, Uncle Don said, to a great leap of my heart, "There's a little girl in Brooklyn named Davida who is celebrating her sixth birthday today, and if she looks under her bed she'll find a beautiful present there. But Davida, before you get your present, Uncle Don has a very special message for you. STAND UP STRAIGHT!"

My father's unslakeable thirst for self-improvement led him to leave his position as an agent with the Metropolitan Life Insurance Company just after the 1929 stock market disaster and a couple of years later invest borrowed money in a candy store in Brooklyn. The store remained open twenty hours a day and required that my mother relieve my father for a few hours each afternoon so that he could eat and catch up on his sleep. She was not happy with this arrangement. Always in frail health, she had to take her turn behind the cash register in addition to running the house, caring for her children, and teaching piano on the side.

To me, however—at least for the first few months—the candy store seemed a paradise. I especially loved the glass case with the sliding doors in which were stacked penny candies of every variety: chocolate babies, candy corn, tootsie rolls, orange candy bananas and colored sugar dots on long strips of white paper. Whenever my father was busy mixing a malted or giving change for a newspaper, I would sneak behind the candy case and break a sugar dot off one of the paper strips, popping it quickly into my mouth before he could see. I started out with only the pink ones, but soon, in the grip of an addiction, I became indiscriminate and would take any color. At first, I was careful not to break too many off any one strip, since a certain number of them would have fallen off naturally anyway; one more or less out of twenty-four wouldn't be missed. But as my passion for them grew, I became more and more careless until one day, my father pulled a strip from the middle of the pile to sell to a child who was standing before the case clutching his penny and found himself holding a long narrow band of paper with only a couple of dots remaining on its surface. His lips, always thin, became two steel wires, and his eyes flashed fury at me. But he said nothing. I spent the next two hours in a panic of guilt and fear waiting for the moment when he would confront me. When my mother came by to collect my brother and me for dinner, my father told her to watch the store for a minute, took me into the storeroom and asked me bluntly whether I had been stealing the dots. I had expected to be reprimanded, but his use of the word "stealing" shocked me. I had only been giving in to a blind appetite; it had never occurred to me that I had been engaging in an activity about which he'd delivered many stern lectures whenever he caught any of the neighborhood children doing it. *Me, stealing?* It came as a stunning realization that by indulging my passion for dots, I had entered the ranks of the criminal and been marked forever as a thief, perhaps forced to pay for my dishonesty even into my next reincarnation. Able to think only of how I had thrown away all of my futures, and in the fearsome knowledge that I would have to carry my many wrongdoings, beginning with the dots, throughout the lifetime I was then living and into the next, I took my beating almost gratefully, hoping it would erase some of the bad karma I had already accumulated.

Fulfilling all family predictions, the candy store went bankrupt after only two years. It came as a blow to my mother, although I imagine she was pleased to end her indentured service. But my father saw the demise of the store with the same optimism with which he saw every thing—as a blessing in disguise. It released him from the terrible hours, freed him to look for something better, but best of all, left him with a ten-year supply of pens, pencils, rubber bands, paper clips, and other essentials that he had illegally removed from the store just before declaring bankruptcy. All of the stock remaining should rightfully have been left on the premises to be divided among his creditors. But he was able to rationalize his act with the argument that the reason he'd gone bankrupt in the first place was because his creditors hadn't trusted him enough to wait a little longer, and therefore deserved to be done out of some of the stock.

The day after he removed the stationery items, he arrived home carrying a tremendous brown box, which he quickly hid on the top shelf of our only closet behind my mother's hatboxes. I was curious to know what it was that he had spirited away so quickly. All he would tell me was that it was something for me, but I'd have to wait until my birthday to discover what was inside. For months I was wild with curiosity, but my experience with the candy dots still fresh in my mind, I was afraid to peek.

The day I turned seven he took down the box and with great ceremony and a rendition of "Happy Birthday" opened it. There lay a dozen dolls of various sizes, all dressed magnificently in lace gowns and bonnets tied with satin ribbon. Some had moveable arms and legs, some had eyes that opened and closed, and one even had a tiny glass bottle with a rubber nipple attached to its wrist. This, when filled with water, could be inserted into a hole between her lips, the water immediately emerging in a stream from a hole between her legs. In a gesture of defiance to his creditors, my father had salvaged this magnificent hoard for me. I had never felt so privileged and so loved. But my joy was somewhat dampened when he told me that all of them weren't to be my present this year. I was to select the one I liked best, and the rest would be returned to the closet for future birthdays. I had no difficulty choosing—I picked the one that peed.

For each of the next five years this ceremony was repeated. By the third year the thrill had worn off; it hadn't taken me long to realize that each year the choices were becoming less and less desirable, since I'd chosen the best ones first. Somehow that never occurred to my father. He always seemed puzzled by my lack of enthusiasm when each year he would present me with the shrinking cache. I was twelve before my mother was able to talk him into giving the rest of the dolls to some younger cousins. That episode was my first lesson in the law of diminishing returns.

In the seven Depression years during which my father didn't work at all, my mother supported us by giving private piano lessons and doing a three-year stint with the WPA Arts Project. Even though there was never any change in our financial status, we moved every year in order to take advantage of the then current practice of giving what was called a "concession" to new tenants. Landlords weren't in great shape either, and to attract tenants, were offering three months without rent in exchange for a signed lease for the balance of the year. It was usually the last three months that would be rent-free, in order to prevent a kind of musical chairs wherein destitute and desperate families would move in and out of each other's apartments every couple of months without having to pay any rent.

This constant moving played havoc with my social life and gave rise to the annual horror of being forced to stand in front of a new class every October to be introduced. At those times I felt that the children were massed into a solid front against me. They would giggle when they heard my strange first name and stick their tongues out at me when I walked to my seat, and I would wonder each time, already knowing the answer, if I'd ever be accepted as one of them.

Half the time, the moves were to better neighborhoods and more spacious living space to take advantage of temporary improvements in our finances; the other times they would be to smaller, less desirable apartments as accommodations to bad years. I can still remember the acrid odor of ammonia and another chemical, which I've never been able to identify, which permeated some of those apartments on the day we moved in. The fumes would come from the empty Frigidaire, causing my eyes to tear painfully and my lungs erupt into spasms of coughing. Because of this, I much preferred apartments that came with the old-fashioned iceboxes, unaware that these represented the worst years for my father: it was only when our finances were at their lowest that we were forced to do without the latest conveniences, such as a refrigerator and a bathroom inside the apartment instead of in the hall.

In 1936, my father, who could, as he often boasted, sell gloves to a man without hands, talked a landlord who must have been new to the business into putting the rent-free concession up front. We moved in in October and out again in January. I remember that apartment well because it was the only one we ever lived in that couldn't accommodate our most important piece of furniture, my mother's piano, an ebony Mason & Hamlin baby grand with a tone as sweet as Hershey's milk chocolate. The piano had been hers from the time she was a little girl and had followed her into her marriage as a gift from her stepfather. My mother had begun to give me piano lessons a couple of years before, and despite the pressure that I was beginning to feel from my father to be a prodigy, I derived enough honest pleasure from it myself to love that piano with a passion I have felt for no inanimate object since. In a burst of childish anthropomorphism and bad punning, I had named it Toney. With each move Toney had come along with us, though sometimes its legs had to be removed so that it could be carried up several flights of stairs to the top floor apartment my father invariably liked the best; often doors had to be taken off their hinges before it could be maneuvered into its position in the new living room; sometimes, rarely, it had to be raised by pulley because the staircase was too narrow, all of us standing in the street below, holding our breaths while it was passed through a window tall and wide enough to allow its entrance. But this particular walkup had so many bends in the five-flight staircase that despite the efforts of three sweating moving men, we finally had to concede defeat. Toney was loaded back into the truck and taken to a storage warehouse in the bowels of Canarsie, never, I feared, to be seen again.

I was inconsolable over its loss. I sat on the cracked concrete steps outside the building and cried for hours, refusing to come upstairs even for dinner. I must have fallen asleep there because I awoke in my bed the next morning with no memory of how I'd gotten there. I repeated this performance every night for a week. It was because of the piano that my father had no trouble justifying our clandestine nighttime move out of that apartment on the eve of the first rent due. Despite the rigid moral code he usually applied to his own actions, he felt the landlord deserved no better since, apparently desperate for our tenancy, he had assured my father that the piano would make it up the stairs. In my father's eyes the original sin had been the landlord's, not his own. I heard him say to my mother on the night we stealthily crept away—my brother fast asleep on my father's shoulder, me trembling with terror that we'd be caught and sent to jail, that after all, fair is fair: an eye for an eye, a tooth for a tooth and three months concession for one beloved piano made inaccessible by greed.

My grief over the temporary loss of the piano had pleased my father greatly. He saw in my tears a promise of concert tours, critical acclaim and reflected glory. At the age of fourteen I began to take singing as seriously as I did my piano studies. This made my father even happier—he figured that now he had double indemnity against obscurity. For several years after that I sang folksongs, accompanying myself at the piano, at local public school assemblies, church functions and American Labor Party rallies. This last especially pleased him because by this time he'd given up Rosicrucianism for socialism. I seldom permitted my father to come to my performances, despite the pleasure I knew they gave him, because when he was there I would see my performance through his eyes and find it wanting in some way.

Once, when I was nineteen, feeling that it was about time I tried to deal with my father's attitude, I invited him to the performance I was to give that night in the auditorium of a local public school. Despite the glasses I had to wear to compensate for my nearsightedness, I felt unaccustomedly pretty. My hair, with unusual cooperativeness, had fallen quickly and with a minimum of patting and pushing into a flattering frame for my face; the outfit I wore, a long, brown mohair skirt and a blushing pink blouse with a peekaboo opening directly over my cleavage, looked absolutely smashing, and I experienced the unfamiliar and heady sensation of being a good-looking and talented young woman about to give a beautiful performance that would earn me a standing ovation from my audience and the post-concert attention of the best-looking boy in the crowd, who would turn out to be a Yale senior, very rich, and a virtuoso clarinetist so that we could play duets together during our long and happy union.

I was actually a singer of some talent. My voice was light and pure, though of limited range, but more than that, I knew I had what my singing teacher always said was far more important than a beautiful voice, something she called with great reverence, musicianship. I was among those few young singers, she assured me, who communicated every nuance of meaning in the lyrics of a song. She told me that when I sang of the killing of Lord Rendall by his sweetheart, she could see my listeners' eyes fill in sympathy for his mourning mother. When I sang "Black Black Black", she said, their expressions would grow pensive with memories of love.

That night, feeling confident and glamorous, I awaited my introduction with less nervousness than usual. When my name was announced, I floated on the applause to the piano that was set in the middle of the audience on a small raised platform about twenty feet in front of the stage. I smiled, bowed, sat down and prepared to begin the opening selection. Just as I was about to strike the first chord, I saw from the corner of my eye an urgently waving hand. Turning my head in its direction, I saw my father sitting on a folding chair just below the platform, the familiar frown of disapproval on his face. "Take off your glasses," he stage-whispered, "they look terrible". I felt as though I were singing the first song through clenched teeth, and knew that I would never invite him again.

Around that time, under the professional name of Davee Alan, I had managed to promote a summer radio program on a local station singing folksongs that I'd arranged into a loose story line. That first Saturday afternoon, I appeared at the radio station on Flatbush Avenue so nervous that my hands were wet with perspiration, making my fingers slip and slide on the keys and my voice to shake with a tremolo it had never possessed before. As a result, I wasn't too happy with my performance. Therefore, when I arrived for my second show, I was astounded when the station manager, looking slightly surprised himself, handed me about fifty letters. The first one I opened commended the taste of the station's personnel in presenting such a brilliant and talented singer and promised to listen to WLIB day and night for as long as I continued to sing under its auspices. I was delighted by the volume of mail, having had no idea that so many people were interested in listening to English folksongs in the middle of a summer weekend afternoon, especially in Brooklyn. But before I'd read very many more, something disturbing began to filter through my rapidly expanding ego. First of all, each letter expressed virtually the same sentiments, and even more suspicious, they all bore a Queens postmark. Once I'd noticed their place of origin, it didn't take much imagination to figure out what had happened.

My father, now working once again at the Queens branch of the insurance company he'd been trying to get back into throughout all of the years of his unemployment, had organized his coworkers, clients, and even his immediate superiors into a claque, and had seen to it that they wrote to WLIB whether they'd heard my program or not. He had provided them with my professional name, the address of the station and the libretto. Once again, my father had demonstrated the extraordinary effectiveness of his salesmanship.

Having expected only thanks, he couldn't understand my anger when I arrived home that afternoon. It was one of the few times I'd ever lost my temper with him.

"How could you embarrass me like that?" I shouted at him after telling him what I'd discovered.

"I thought it would help you professionally," he replied, surprised and hurt by my reaction.

"Well, all it did was make me feel like a fool. Whatever made you think it would *help*?"

I stormed out of the room. Behind me, in a sheepish tone I'd never before heard him use, he unknowingly spoke the punch line of a Yiddish joke about the efficacy of an enema in reviving a dead actor:

"It couldn't hurt."

My father sold a lot of insurance in his last twenty years, but this never seemed to reflect in his cash flow. I remember my mother pleading with him for a bigger allowance so that she could buy an extra pair of stockings or some underwear without having to ask him for extra money and have him ask her the invariable question: "Where does all the money I give you every week disappear to?" Because she couldn't stand up to him, she never did have any spare cash, and so wore torn stockings, safety-pinned bloomers, and blouses worn through under the arms. However, my father managed always to own a car even in our worst years. He loved cars. Second to cars he loved gadgets. He was always buying things like exotically shaped cookie cutters (my mother never baked), oven roasters with special surfaces (my mother never used the oven—she braised), and vegetable peelers of a complexity that would confound a master mechanic (my mother used an apple corer for everything).

My father was among the first in New York to own a Presto recording machine. I can still conjure up the smell of the acetate as it was being peeled off the disc by the recording needle. Somehow he remained forever unable to master its intricacies and never produced a single usable recording. This dashed his hopes of leaving the insurance business and setting up a recording service some day, one of his many plans for the future, and it is also the reason why I have no recordings of my radio shows, although each week he would attempt to record them off the air. After carefully setting all the dials, he would always forget to do one last thing like turn up the volume, push the record button or plug in the radio jack Later, when he owned a Leica (he bought only the best), planning to leave the insurance business someday to open a photography studio, he'd forget to take the lens cover off or would frame the picture in such a way that some crucial element of the composition, such as somebody's head, would be omitted. But like the optimist who, upon finding the horse manure in his Christmas stocking, rejoiced in his new horse, my father never lost his pleasure in the recording machine or the camera or his many other visionary purchases. He held fast to his faith that all mechanical obstacles would somehow melt away, and he would eventually emerge as the brilliant technician and artist he knew he had it in him to be.

This penchant for the rose-colored view extended itself later to my husband ("Someday he'll be a famous director"), my son ("Someday he'll be a famous violinist"), my daughter ("Someday she'll be one of the great beauties"). He even attempted to draw on his eternal hopefulness in regard to his son, who, for several years had begun to show signs of the mental illness that would later hospitalize him and render him nonfunctioning. But the best he could manage about my brother was a wistful "Well, it could be worse. At least he's not a criminal".

What he'd planned for his eagerly awaited retirement was to buy a trailer and, with my mother, make an extended trip throughout the United States, much of which he had never seen. He looked forward to it with such anticipation that my mother, who disliked automobile travel, was nevertheless prepared to go along without complaint, simply because she didn't have the heart to deprive him of something he had been planning with such enthusiasm. One morning at 2:00 A.M., just a few months before his dream was to come true, my father woke suddenly, complaining that he felt strange, but not appearing to be in pain. My mother later told me that it was the terror she saw in his eyes that made her throw on a robe and run downstairs to awaken the doctor who lived on the ground floor. By the time they arrived back in the apartment, my father's look of fear had changed to one of confusion. Less than five minutes later, he was dead of a massive stroke, his heart, to the bewilderment of the doctor, continuing to beat vigorously until the very last moment into the stethoscope pressed against his chest.

"Poor fellow," my mother said when she called me to tell me of his death. "I never saw him look confused before. He always seemed so sure of himself."

I was less shocked at the unexpectedness of his death than at the fact that he had died at all. I'd always thought he was immortal.

When I called to tell my brother, at first there was a long silence. Then he became oddly animated, telling me in a voice that was usually reserved for good news that he felt nothing. Nothing at all.

I did not grieve for my father. Neither, I think, did my mother. To me he had been the tyrant who attempted, even in my adulthood, to mold me to the image he had of me, which I rejected after my marriage when it was safe to do so, by giving up music entirely. To my mother he was the husband to whose standards and way of life she had submitted with loyalty, but not, I believe, with love.

It was my children who mourned my father, and deeply. My son tells me that even to this day he thinks of him often. For with them my father was able to do what he could not do with his own children, that is, love them totally, uncritically, and as they were. I would watch him reading to them, helping them blow soap bubbles into the wind, holding their little bodies with such tenderness that tears of envy would sting my eyes. I never knew his tenderness, only his pride. I never felt his love, only his ambition. And my children got from him what I myself could never give them as fully as I would have wanted, because in the end I am very much my father's daughter, and despite my best efforts, his faults are also my own.

Uncle Jake

There wasn't much laughter in Grandma Gottfried's house when I was there. Sunday afternoons were for eating, scolding and arguing, all serious business. What humor there was, was provided by my Uncle Jake, who'd been dubbed "The Joker" by my aunts because of his good-natured teasing and his magic tricks. He was a joker, however, only with children; with other adults he was courtly and somewhat formal. There were many times when I wished that he were my father instead of the one I had, thoughts I never dared speak aloud.

Uncle Jake could always be counted on to mispronounce my name, doing so each week, his eyes full of mischief as he greeted me.

"Ah, here's my favorite niece Vadeeda. Come give your Uncle Jake a kiss,"

I fell for it every time, and I would answer with the next line of a dialogue that never varied from week to week.

"My name isn't Vadeeda, it's *Davida,*" I would state firmly when he finally lowered me from just below the ceiling, where he'd held me for a long and deliciously scary time.

"But I can't say Davida," he would answer. "That's why I call you Vadeeda."

"But you just said it," I'd reply with exasperation. "You just said that you can't say Davida, but when you were telling me that you can't say it, you said it right."

That would get me nowhere, so I'd abandon that tack and try another.

"Say *Duh*," I'd begin.

"Duh," he would dutifully repeat.

"Now say *Vee*".

"Vee."

"Now say *Duh* again."

"Duh." By now I could smell victory.

"Now say *Duh-vee-duh*."

He would then pause as if pulling himself together for the big effort.

"Vadeeda!" he would explode triumphantly—then sadly, "I told you I couldn't say Davida."

I was ten before I caught on, but I kept it up for another couple of years because I didn't want to hurt his feelings.

I've come not to mind my name so much anymore, although I still don't like the sound of it, except when it's pronounced by someone with an accent. Then it will take on an exotic quality that momentarily eclipses its old associations. In recent years it has become a useful conversational gambit at parties when my partner of the moment has run out of topics. And before that, when I was in college, it even contributed its share of mild humor to the educational process. For instance, one semester I received a change-of-program card in the mail shortly after having registered for my courses, and a week later found myself green-bloomered and red-faced in a men's gym class because a sharp-eyed registrar, catching what she thought was a mistake, had switched me over. And once I was sent a stern notice from my local draft board threatening me with immediate incarceration unless I could explain to their satisfaction why I hadn't registered on my eighteenth birthday. Around the same time, a series of official-looking letters began to arrive, urging me to join the regular air force where I could be a man among men, or the navy, where I could see the world. How can I fault any of them for mistaking my gender when even after fifty years of an intimate, sometimes tearful, relationship with Con Edison, my electric bills still continued to arrive month after month addressed to some fictional character named David A. Rosenblum?

Amusing, yes, to my adult sensibility, but as a child my name caused me no end of embarrassment. When my teachers pronounced it "David" with a swallowed "uh" at the end, I felt my very sexual identity to be at stake. When otherwise benign strangers responded to hearing my name with "I guess your parents really wanted a boy," tears would escape the corners of my eyes no matter how hard I tried to hold them back. But it was when classmates mimicked the cadence of my name by rhyming it with nonsense syllables that I suffered the most.

"Padida, Bamida, Regida, Levida," they would chant mockingly, delivering what to me was the cruelest blow of all as I ran off sobbing: "Davega, Davega, where you goin', Davega?" Davega was a well-known sporting goods chain of the time, and when I was called by that hated name, I felt as if my very soul was being stomped on. I would have given anything at those times to be named Barbara or Margaret. Looking back, I sometimes think that my Uncle Jake had somehow anticipated the indignities I would later be subjected to because of my name, and had tried with his gentle, never hurtful teasing, to toughen me against them.

Uncle Jake was a big man with the demeanor and physical appearance befitting the successful businessman that he was. A printer by trade, he was the only Gottfried brother who made a comfortable living. His face was round, fleshy and red, and his eyes always seemed about to smile. His suits were generally green and vested, worn with starched white shirts garnished with silk ties hand-painted with palm trees and other tropical flora. A heavy watch chain rested on his expansive belly. Even indoors he wore a fedora with a tiny feather in the hatband, perched at a playful angle on his graying hair. The oldest of my grandmother's offspring, he was the only one who didn't share her small stature and sharp features, having inherited the open good looks and ample body of his father. That my Uncle Jake looked nothing at all like his brothers or sister intrigued me greatly. I spent a good deal of time trying to figure out how this could have happened, developing a theory to explain it only after I was exposed to Mendel for the first time in junior high school. It had as its basic tenet the premise that hereditary factors could be consciously controlled by strong-willed individuals of either sex. Since Jake was my grandmother's first child, she hadn't yet learned how to assert her dominant genes in the reproductive process. My theory had her spending the next four years trying to perfect this feature-imprinting technique (by means that I was never able to work out), achieving a greater degree of success with each successive child right through Fanny, the youngest, who could have been a clone.

Uncle Jake kept me and my cousins endlessly dazzled with a wonderful magic trick. He seemed to know only that one, but it provided boundless variety. He'd say he saw a penny hiding in the most unlikely places—behind our ears, in our nostrils, in the cuffs of pants, under a hair ribbon. And sure enough, he'd reach out to wherever he said he saw one, open his hand, and there it would be, lying round and shiny in his cupped palm.

The best coin trick he ever did was on the Sunday after I turned six. My parents had hidden my present—a red purse with a golden clasp—under my bed, just as Uncle Don had predicted. Feeling very grown-up, I took it along that day to show off to those relatives who hadn't been at my party. In the middle of the rhubarb and strawberries, Uncle Jake suddenly put his hand to his forehead and crossed his eyes.

"Vadeeda, go pick up your new purse, close your eyes and count to three. When you open it you'll find a surprise inside."

When I first looked in the purse, it appeared at first to contain only the lace handkerchief I'd placed inside before leaving home. But when I lifted the handkerchief to look under it, a shiny new fifty-cent piece fell out and rolled under Uncle Jake's chair.

"Don't thank me—I didn't do it," Uncle Jake said modestly as I hugged him after retrieving my fortune, almost speechless with the wonder of his newly augmented powers.

"Then who did?" I asked, clutching the huge coin tightly, fearing it might disappear as mysteriously as it arrived.

He wouldn't tell me right away, saying it was a secret. But later he confided that it was a gift from the birthday fairy assigned to all children whose names begin with V.

When I grew old enough to travel by myself I would visit him on occasion, calling out a greeting as I walked into the small front parlor of his house on Coney Island Avenue. There he would sit, wearing his fedora, his legs apart and his arms resting on a cane propped between them. He had lately developed a tremor and a slight shuffle when he walked, and he wore the beginnings of a strange, fixed expression on his face.

"Hello, Vadeeda," he'd say, trying to smile, his face frozen by the disease into a mask, his voice too low to be heard without effort. Even then, if a small child were visiting, he would do his coin trick, taking me back in time to my grandmother's dining room as he extended a shaking hand to reach behind the child's ear. The last time I saw him do this, he dropped the penny and I had to look away.

My personal Merlin, grandmaster of the misnomer, as long as he lived he made magic. He loved me, I think, as much as anyone ever has, but he never once called me by my right name.

Love and Marriage

There was never a time when I didn't want to be married. Even before I was in school, my favorite play activity was to dress up in a torn sheet with a train of toilet paper tucked into the back of my collar and a lace antimacassar bobby-pinned to my hair, pretending to be a bride. In our leanest days, the toilet paper was carefully refolded to be used later for its originally intended purpose. Quite early, I saw the world as being divided into two camps, the married and the single. The latter state was, I realized, something to be avoided at all costs, the ideal of marriage having been baked in with my mother's *challeh*, stirred into the cream of wheat, coddled with the soft-boiled eggs. I don't know why I swallowed it, considering all the unhappy marriages in my father's family, which included his own.

As a child, I never identified my parents' union as a marriage at all—it was simply there, the terrain of my existence. As I got older I became aware of my mother's unarticulated unhappiness, her early gratitude to my father for having chosen her despite her handicap having given way to recognition of their basic incompatibility and her eventual resignation. Never her equal in refinement or intelligence, my father tended to be directive and judgmental even with her. But he treated her with a gentle respect, which he demonstrated toward no one else. It was obvious that he both loved and admired her, and he was aware of the existence, if not the depth, of her disappointment. There was no doubt that this bothered him—he would touch her too often, his look revealing a certain wistfulness, as though there was a part of her he knew he would never reach. Sometimes at night, my brother and I would be startled awake by the sound of my mother and father arguing, or my mother crying alone in the bathroom next to our room, and we would lie there in the dark, trembling and whispering together until it stopped. But those episodes occurred only late at night when she thought we were asleep, and she never knew that we had heard them. I don't ever remember her raising her voice when we were around, and, during those times at least, she submitted to her lot with the quiet grace she brought to everything else.

Despite this and all the other mismatches I saw around me, until my late teens I moved among them like a sleepwalker, continuing to fantasize for my grown self something totally unlike anything I had ever seen—a union of mutual love, unwavering goodness, and unimaginably passionate couplings, while all around me steamed real life, exuding insult, unfulfillment and complaint.

*   *   *

My first information about sex came from my cousin Shirley, when we were both ten. Shirley was a lean, intense child who bore the dark Gottfried look, courtesy of her father, my Uncle Manny. Aunt Rose dressed her in lots of ruffles that were intended to camouflage her thin boyishness, but only accentuated it. Most Sundays, after everyone had finished dinner at Grandma Gottfried's, Shirley would grab my hand and lead me into a closet in an upstairs bedroom where we would sit in the dark and tell each other ghost stories. I liked Shirley's more for their literary than their scare value because they were peopled, if I may used that word, with ghosts who were as colorful and individual as the human beings from whom they sprung. She always finished her stories with a plot twist that called for running her fingers down my back or across my neck, a sure-fire blood-curdler, even if her stories weren't. Mine were nowhere near as good as hers. My ghosts all looked and sounded alike—animated percales wired for moans.

One day Shirley seemed uncharacteristically pensive on the way upstairs. After we settled in, she made a few half-hearted attempts to start a story, but then fell silent. I tried to fill the void with a weak stab at a story about a nine-year-old boy who died and came back as a ghost to tease his older sister—art imitating life with an element of wishful thinking thrown in. All of a sudden she broke in.

"You wanna hear something real dirty?" Visions of unwashed underwear floated momentarily across my mind's eye.

"Sure. What?"

"I know how you start babies."

So far I hadn't given starting babies much thought. I'd only recently learned about where they grew, and that was enough science fiction for me at the time.

"How?" I asked reluctantly.

"Well," she began, "the father sticks his peepee into the mother's peepee and then he makes peepee inside her."

I went into shock. In a couple of minutes I had recovered sufficiently to play briefly with the idea of my parents doing this, which put me back into catatonia.

After a while I said, "I don't believe you."

"Oh yeah, it's true all right. My mother told me. Everybody has to do it to start a baby."

"Everybody?" I choked, rejecting this possibility for anybody in my family, and especially for myself.

"Of course, dummy! Everybody. Your mother and father, Uncle Jake and Aunt Tillie. Everybody." Pause. "Except for my mother."

Aha! Here was an out, a hole in the dike. Either her previous statement was a lie or this one was. I was only ten, but already I had a feel for the universality of natural laws.

"Then if everybody has to do it to make a baby, how come your mother had you?"

Shirley looked hurt at my lack of belief in her veracity.

"Well, she kept saying, 'Not now, Manny, maybe tomorrow.' She kept putting it off and putting it off until finally I was already born and she didn't have to."

For some weeks, the information Shirley had given me in the closet kept flashing into my mind, even when I was trying to think about other things—arithmetic, for instance. I became pale and couldn't eat. The thought of my parents having to do *that*, however disgusting, was no less disturbing to me than my being a product of so sordid a connection. However, Aunt Rose's tactic, which still didn't seem entirely logical, offered some hope. I marveled at her cleverness in holding out until it was no longer necessary.

I waited until I could live with my obsession no longer and told my mother what Shirley had told me about baby-making, hoping she would verify Aunt Rose's subterfuge. My mother was obviously uncomfortable discussing the subject, but she made a valiant stab at it. What she said, speaking more rapidly than usual so as to get it over with as quickly as possible was: "Well, it isn't as bad as it sounds, so don't worry about it. But what Shirley said about Aunt Rose is wrong. Everybody has to do it, even Aunt Rose and Uncle Manny."

I filled in "even me and Daddy". I wanted to cry. I suppose she meant to be reassuring, but she had misunderstood my reason for including the part about Aunt Rose and Uncle Manny. You see, if Shirley had been right about her mother, then there was hope for me. I could start to think up a whole bunch of not-right-now lines and practice saying them so that I'd be ready to use them when the time came for me to start a baby. But I always believed whatever my mother told me. So somehow I'd just have to endure the necessary humiliation and do it like everybody else.

*   *   *

Uncle Manny had married Aunt Rose at twenty, securing the reluctant object of his passion by threatening to throw himself into the Gowanus Canal if she refused him. It astonished me that my Aunt Rose had given in to such a threat, since by the time I heard the story of their courtship she had grown to twice the size of her spidery husband and seemed to possess strength enough to have withstood any kind of pressure. During many a Sunday dinner, as I surreptitiously examined Aunt Rose and Uncle Manny across the table, I asked myself what I would have done in her place. After looking at it from every angle, I was certain that I could never have married Uncle Manny, even to save his life. James Stewart, if he asked me, or Cary Grant, even Clark Gable in an emergency, but never Uncle Manny,

He was just too ugly. His nose curved downward nearly to his chin, his eyes were small and close-set, his ears stood at right angles to his head, and even in photographs of him as a young man, specks of dandruff flecked his thin, greasy hair. His baby pictures herald his later unattractiveness—in them he resembles nothing so much as an infant Punchinello.

It was only when I was thirteen, after I had taken my first dip into my father's not too expertly hidden Krafft-Ebbing, that I was able to come up with a tentative hypothesis. It was just possible, I thought, that Uncle Manny had become Aunt Rose's own personal unspeakable perversion like necrophilia or snakes. This possibility added a touch of the exotic to what had been until then only an enigma, and made my aunt and uncle figures of fascinating, if twisted, sexuality, instead of the unromantic mystery they had been before.

*   *   *

Uncle Dewey, who was at least as homely as Manny, didn't marry until he was in his late forties. He had evidently been less creative in matters of courtship. Notwithstanding these handicaps, he eventually won the hand of Reba Kestenbaum, whose last chance at matrimony he probably represented. Uncle Dewey brought Reba to meet the family on the very Sunday that she accepted him, driving her to his mother's house in the front of his cab with the flag down. That was taking a very big chance—taxi inspectors were everywhere, and for all anyone knew, even worked Sundays—but he was up to taking risks, feeling what must have been an intoxicating mixture of love and pride in his conquest.

I remember well my first sight of Reba. She was a very shy girl in her early forties (any woman still single was called a girl no matter what the year of her birth), who said almost nothing and mostly kept her head down, cringing a little every time Dewey kissed her cheek in bursts of awkward affection and proprietary pride. She was quite plain and had tight, thin lips, but she had one remarkable feature: her ivory skin, which, unblemished by make-up, gleamed exactly like the surface of the pearl ring my Aunt Sophie on my mother's side had given me for my fourteenth birthday. The idea of that cool, exquisite skin ever touching the coarse and swarthy face of my Uncle Dewey seemed unthinkable.

Their wedding was held in the finished basement of a brownstone on Eastern Parkway, which was owned by a kosher butcher who had possessed what was admirably known as the *seichel* to furnish it with a few folding chairs and some bridge tables. By renting it out for weddings and Bar Mitzvahs, he was able to make a little money on the side. Many entrances into Jewish manhood and the holy state of matrimony had been made in this room.

The day of the wedding was the only time I ever saw my Uncle Dewey without the green eyeshade he wore indoors and out, and I remember being surprised that his forehead was just as low without it. Reba was in a heavy white satin dress trimmed with beads, which came to a little above her knees. All of her vulnerability became focused for me in those exposed, slightly knobby knees. I stared at them for a long time, seeing in them miniature faces on which were reflected the loathing and fear I imagined she must be feeling. Because of her knees and her beautiful iridescent skin, the wedding night jokes seemed especially distasteful. By the time the ceremony was over, I felt physically ill. I couldn't imagine those two lying together, except in an act of rape. This vision was so upsetting, so different from my usually romantic sexual fantasies, which at that age seemed to be throbbing behind my eyes even when I was practicing Czerny exercises, that I turned a pale yellow and managed to develop a fever just high enough to warrant my parents taking me home before the end of the festivities. Nightmares in which knees bearing shining faces were being violently forced apart began that night and lasted for weeks. For years after, the word "rape" would summon up images, not of the violation of a woman's dark and secret recesses, but of knees etched with bloodied faces screaming soundlessly, each with the features and the glowing skin of my Aunt Reba.

*   *   *

The most uncongenial marriage of them all was that of my Aunt Fanny and Uncle Moish. Aunt Fanny, my father's only sister, looked a lot like her brother Manny, except that she wore her hair in a bun. Her disposition never rose above surly, and she was distinguished by the fact that she was usually not-talking to almost everybody. While there were times that Uncle Dewey was on the outs with my father and Aunt Rose was not-talking to Uncle Jake, nobody could match Aunt Fanny for length and breadth—she was a marathon non-talker.

The one person she was *always* not-talking to was her husband Moish. I never heard her address a single remark to him, or saw her regard him with anything more neutral than mild contempt, while his behavior toward her remained courteous and attentive through the years. A benign and gentle man, Moish always addressed her with an air of tentative hopefulness, even when he was just asking for more *kugel*. He reminded me of nothing so much as a dog that has just soiled the carpet and is trying to get back in his master's favor.

Uncle Moish would have been difficult to pick out in a crowd, being unremarkable in all things. One looked in vain for some distinguishing mark, an irregularity of feature, a mole—anything that would make him stand out. But so nondescript was he that but for his extraordinary patience with his wife, he would never have been noticed at all.

He made my Aunt Fanny a good wife, doing the laundry, giving her massages when her neck ached, cupping her back with *bonkehs* when she was ill. He even ran her baths for her, checking after she got in the tub to see if her skin was turning red. Aunt Fanny liked very hot baths and would probably have cooked her outer layer several times over if Uncle Moish hadn't kept careful watch over her ablutions. I remember her once telling my mother, the person she spent the least amount of time not-talking to, that that very morning Moish had made her leave the tub a couple of minutes after she'd gotten in, because she was beginning to look like a cooked lobster. I'd seen boiled lobsters on seafood stands in Sheepshead Bay, and the vision of a scarlet Aunt Fanny with lobster claws for hands stepping out of the tub in Uncle Moish's clothed presence created such a hilarious image in my head that I started to giggle, which earned me a look from Aunt Fanny poisonous enough to cause an ear abcess and two whole weeks of not-talking.

Whenever Aunt Fanny said or did something particularly cruel or outrageous, I would try to give her the benefit of the doubt, since my father had taught us as part of our Rosicrucian upbringing that there was, residing in everyone, something he called "Innate Goodness." But to me she seemed quite simply a monster, and no matter how hard I looked, I could see no goodness in her at all. She was the Wicked Witch of the West, the ogre at the top of the beanstalk, Cinderella's stepmother. She could always be counted on to question a motive, come up with a dishonest solution, take advantage of someone's vulnerability.

The day I came to Sunday dinner wearing my new glasses for the first time, she examined me with a disapproving frown, then, after a pause too long to be misinterpreted said, "Isn't it enough that she's got crooked teeth and Augusta's hair? Did she need to be nearsighted, too?"

She even bullied her mother, the only one of my Grandma Gottfried's offspring able to intimidate that formidable lady.

I became fascinated by Aunt Fanny's apparently total lack of humanity. Deciding to put my father's belief in the ubiquity of Innate Goodness to the ultimate test, I accepted for myself the challenge of trying to locate it even in such an unlikely place. I watched her closely every Sunday, hoping to find some evidence of inconsistency in her small-mindedness, some sign of human kindness, especially in regard to my Uncle Moish, for whom, even at my young age, I felt deep sympathy.

Once I sneaked up to their bedroom in my grandmother's house to see if it held any secrets that might help me unravel the mystery of her character. But unless there was a hidden message in the large satin-skirted doll with the skinny stuffed legs and high-heeled shoes that rested impassively against the pillows of their double bed, there was nothing I found that was of any help. Seeking more intimate knowledge, I examined the contents of their dresser drawers, an incredibly daring act for me, but they differed from those in my house only in degree of neatness—Uncle Moish's underwear was as breathtakingly squared off as if they'd been ironed in the drawer. My mother's orientation to laundry was more casual.

This approach having proved unproductive, I cast about for another and soon hit upon a new plan. Together, Aunt Fanny and Uncle Moish ran a luncheonette in the lobby of a building in the ribbon district of Manhattan. All I knew about it was that at 5:00 A.M. every morning they would load up their old Hudson with soups, salads and desserts that they had both prepared in silence the night before, arriving at their place of business before six to set up for their first customers. I decided it was necessary for me to visit the luncheonette and observe them there together.

The opportunity to visit them came sooner than I'd expected. It happened around that time that my brother had to undergo a series of eye tests at a hospital clinic in the East Thirties, and I persuaded my parents to drop me off at the luncheonette on the way there and pick me up when they were finished. They must have been puzzled by the keenness of my desire to spend time with Aunt Fanny, but they were too preoccupied with my brother's eye problems to press me for an explanation. And so it was that I found myself sitting on a high stool at their linoleum-covered counter, watching the object of my intense scrutiny over a chocolate egg cream. It was three-thirty. I had only two hours in which to unearth Aunt Fannie's Innate Goodness, a quality that, if she had it at all, she managed to keep well hidden.

Both she and Uncle Moish wore large butcher's aprons. Hers was stained with what looked like blood, while his was spotless and remained so until closing time. By rights it should have been the opposite: Uncle Moish was the one who handled the food, while Aunt Fanny stood at the counter calling the orders into the air, her back always to her husband. She seemed to enjoy the role of hostess, joking with each customer with a half-smile on her face, even flirting a bit with the truckers as they waited for their take-outs. I was intrigued with this new aspect of my aunt's character. She certainly seemed different here; in Brooklyn she seldom smiled, and had never in my experience joked with anyone. I felt a thrill of anticipation—if ever the other side of her nature was to be revealed, it would be here.

I had been watching her for about an hour and still hadn't seen any evidence of what I was looking for. Except for the calling out of the orders to Moish, which could hardly be called talking to him, her attitude toward him wasn't any different than usual. Until, that is, he put extra mayonnaise on the tuna-on-pumpernickel sandwich. It was then that my Aunt Fanny spoke the only words I ever heard her address directly to my Uncle Moish. "You stupid ox," she shouted, her voice rebounding off the tile walls, "I told you to hold the mayo!"

At the time, this incident caused me no more than a momentary chill and a short-term disappointment. I stored it away with Aunt Rose's capitulation, later to be joined by Aunt Reba's knees, until the time when I could no longer avoid comparing real marriages to the visions of fairy tale romance I'd created for myself.

This merging of fact and fiction was both brought closer and made more confusing by the last transaction to occur between my Aunt Fanny and my Uncle Moish.

Not long after my visit to the luncheonette, Uncle Moish was diagnosed with cancer and wasn't expected to live more than a few months. But even God couldn't resist tormenting him—it was nearly two agonizing years before he finally died. During this time I often heard Aunt Fanny complain to my mother that it was just like that *schlemiel,* who'd never made a penny without her help, to leave her a young widow. I thought it odd that she referred to herself as young, and odder still that she called Moish a *schlemiel*; I had always seen Aunt Fannie as more the *shlemeil* and Uncle Moish as a *schlemazl.* (The difference, according to the old joke, is that the *schlemazl* is the person on whose lap the *schlemiel* clumsily spills the chicken soup).

Not once did Fanny ever acknowledge Moish's suffering in my presence; she treated him no differently than she had before. Toward the end, my mother wondered aloud if Fanny could be counted on to contain her contempt for Moish long enough for him not to be disgraced at his own funeral.

Things were pretty quiet at the service except for some sobs coming from Moish's two sisters and a low keening emanating from his mother. At the graveside my Aunt Fanny stood quietly, her eyes glinting evilly at the coffin. But just after it had begun its slow slide down toward its final resting place, she emitted a strangled moan.

"Moishele, Moishele, my darling, my love, my jewel," she cried. And despite the hands that flew out too late to restrain her, she leapt into her husband's grave. I have never been able to decide if that was an act of hypocrisy, a spectacular change of heart, or the emergence at long last of Aunt Fanny's Innate Goodness. It was almost certainly, I felt, a statement about marriage, if only I could figure it out.

Grandma Gottfried

My father's mother was tight as a drawn wire. She held herself as straight and rigid as her unbending character, her expression much like that of the farm woman in the Grant Wood painting. Her name was Jenny, but none of her grandchildren ever used it, an indication of the distance we felt toward her. As a child I thought it strange that we all called her Grandma Gottfried instead of by her first name (my mother's mother was always called Grandma Becky).

I can't remember her ever holding out her arms for a hug or saying anything that wasn't critical. She ruled her family with the whip of self-righteousness and gall. Besides Aunt Fanny, Uncle Moish and Uncle Dewey, who lived with her until his marriage to the fair-skinned Reba, Grandma Gottfried's household included a Mexican Chihuahua named Trixie. Not a friendly dog, Trixie sulked a lot, the result perhaps of being kicked frequently by my Aunt Fanny to stop her barking. Trixie's sour expression didn't especially distinguish her in that household—in that way, at least, she resembled the rest of the family.

Grandma Gottfried never expressed much of a liking for anyone, but she appeared to have the least amount of ill will toward the Chihuahua. She tolerated Trixie's high-pitched yapping better than she did my cousin Shirley's whining, and when Trixie hopped onto her lap she was usually permitted to stay. Occasionally my grandmother would even invite her to sit there, something she never did with any of us.

Twice a day, rain or shine, she took Trixie for a walk. In bad weather she would tie around the dog's middle a tiny plaid coat she'd sewn for it on the Singer Sewing Machine that sat in the corner of the dining room. Trixie also wore a collar studded with fake diamonds that hung loosely under her pointed snout and hyperthyroid eyes. From the back, her thin, old lady's rump would waggle from side to side as she walked up the street slightly behind my grandmother. None of us paid much attention to Trixie; she didn't pay any attention to us, either. By the time I was eight, Trixie was already a very old dog.

One Sunday, Uncle Dewey announced that Trixie was "terminal". This word immediately elicited somber looks from all of my aunts and uncles. It seems that she'd been throwing up for over a week and appeared to be in some pain. The day before, my Uncle Moish's brother, the family veterinarian, had advised "putting her to sleep". My grandmother was more tight-lipped than usual that day, and she kept looking at Trixie with a stricken expression I hadn't seen on her face even after my grandfather's death.

Whether or not to do away with Trixie became that Sunday's after-dinner topic, replacing the usual family recriminations. Aunt Fanny suggested that it was just another way for her brother-in-law to make a few extra dollars, that *gonif*. My Aunt Rose was in favor of ending the dog's suffering, but my father took the position that it was not up to man to undo God's handiwork (as a Rosicrucian, he tended toward laissez-faire in matters of life and death, even in the case of a dog). My grandmother said nothing at first. She just listened, that odd expression on her face. At the end of the discussion she stood up. Looking around the table with burning eyes she said "Never!" and walked out of the room.

But the next Sunday, Trixie wasn't waiting for us in her usual place, a small wicker basket under the kitchen table. I thought it was strange that nobody mentioned her, but I was afraid to ask any questions, especially of my grandmother, who looked distracted and unhappy. I decided that Trixie must have been "put to sleep" after all.

Death wasn't treated as a secret in our house. On the contrary, it was talked about openly, and always in connection with reincarnation. My father and his Rosicrucian friends called it "moving to a higher plane", which I visualized as a large hovering aircraft where souls just sort of sat around waiting for the next assignment. It wasn't discussed in exactly those terms, but dying was presented as being more like a high school graduation than an ending, with the decision about whether you went to Harvard or a trade school made on the basis of the good you had done during your lifetime. According to my father, rebirth was a recurring event, something that happened to each soul every 144 years. Well then, if everybody continued to be born over and over again, death was no big deal, only a kind of temporary logjam in the continuing stream of life. Although at age eight it was hard for me to think of my body as just a handful of elements (I never thought to ask what those were), the emphasis on the soul's immortality helped me to deal with the fact that after I died, the biodegradable parts of me would most likely be consumed by fire (Rosicrucians opted for the Eastern style of disposal). This was all right with me, since my father had taken great pains to point out the aesthetics of ashes over putrefaction.

When I was five, my Grandpa Gottfried died. One day he was hugging me, and the next day he was gone. He simply disappeared. And what was even stranger, I don't remember any of the Gottfrieds mentioning him once the *shiva* period was over. The fact of his total disappearance obsessed me. This was different from the cozy relationship my father seemed to have with the souls of the few of his friends who had already moved on. He used to speak to them frequently in candlelit sessions in the kitchen whenever he needed advice from someone who could be counted on for objectivity. Because of my growing doubts, I began to do something I knew wasn't allowed—I would peek in at my father when he was communing with the soul of one of his friends, hoping to catch sight of it in the flickering candlelight. Once I thought I saw a wisp of something white curling near the ceiling, but it turned out to be smoke from his cigar. I even lit my own candle once, but Grandpa Gottfried's soul never answered my pleas to visit.

At the time of Trixie's disappearance, I had yet to see my first dead body, or my first soul for that matter, but the question of whether or not souls really existed had begun to preoccupy me. I desperately wanted to believe in their existence, because the idea of my own complete extinction was unacceptable. But despite this and the fact that it made me feel disloyal to my father, I was leaning toward the total disappearance theory, mainly because of lack of evidence to the contrary.

A couple of Sundays after Trixie's unexplained departure, I was wandering through the house after dinner as I often did, looking for something to do. My favorite place to play alone was upstairs where the bedrooms were, each of them crowded with treasures like filigreed picture frames, silver boxes, porcelain animals and what seemed like a hundred dresser drawers stuffed with lacy camisoles and bloomers, embroidered linens, old pictures and letters scented with lavender. I walked quietly to my grandmother's big front bedroom, not wanting my footsteps to be heard downstairs.

What I saw when I entered stopped me dead in my tracks. There was Trixie, jeweled collar and all, standing on a rectangle of marble on the hearth of the ornate fireplace, one ear cocked as if listening for something, her right front leg lifted delicately in front of her. One end of a thin metal rod was set into the marble and the other buried deep in her belly. I stared at her in horror. Trixie might have been "put to sleep" two weeks before, but she certainly looked wide-awake now. She stood in the fireplace, her snout pointing straight ahead. She had been stuffed and mounted so that my grandmother need never lose her again.

I approached slowly and bent down to stare into her beady eyes. They gleamed in death more brilliantly than they ever had in life. The look of misery was gone, and something, a visible nothingness, had taken its place. I hesitantly put out my hand and touched her nose. It was dry, not wet as it had always been. I hesitantly began to stroke her nearly hairless back. It felt much as it had in life, like a baby's skin, but it was unexpectedly cold and unyielding. I lay on the floor mesmerized, my nose nearly touching hers, stroking and staring at her until two hours later when my mother came looking for me to take me home.

I have never forgotten those hours or the thoughts that occupied them. How could death be a complete disappearance when Trixie was still in the house guarding the bedroom? It was obvious to me that although her body was there, some important essence of what she had been was not; that stuffed and rigid hide wasn't really Trixie at all. As I lay there, petting her lifeless body, my dilemma of the past year became resolved. That dead Chihuahua standing immobile on my grandmother's hearth, some invisible but vital part of her missing, convinced me then and forever of the existence of the soul.

My Mother

My mother was not at all a pretty woman. Always too heavy to conform to the popular standard, her body was thick and buxom, forty pounds over the ideal weight posted for her height on the penny weighing machines. Besides that, she had a too-large nose that dominated her wide, angular face. But she had in great amount what used to be called "inner beauty," a term you don't hear much anymore. It made her physical appearance almost irrelevant—her goodness and her loving, gentle nature were all that anybody noticed.

If anyone ever gave my mother a compliment, it was invariably about her legs. They were so perfectly proportioned, in fact, that there were few men who could resist glancing at them as frequently as opportunity allowed. Their graceful, slender shape transcended the unfashionable shoes she chose to wear for comfort; if her feet had been encased in the barest of high-heeled sandals her legs couldn't have received a greater amount of respectful admiration. They were, I felt, far more beautiful than Betty Grable's, whose lower limbs were the inspiration of our troops overseas and were thought to have played a major role in building the morale that helped win the Second World War. Betty Grable's calves were too high and too muscular and met the area above her ankle too abruptly for my taste.

The reason my mother's legs were so important to me was because I knew, having previously spent a great deal of time examining and evaluating every part of my own body, that mine were very much like hers. I felt secure in the knowledge that some part of me would stay near perfect for my whole life despite the other changes that were taking place in my body—almost daily, it seemed to me then—for my mother was nearly forty and her legs were far nicer than those of any younger women I knew.

I suppose I needed to feel that way about her legs because her breasts gave me a great deal of trouble. By the time I was eleven, mine had already begun to sprout, and I rather liked their high roundness. But the difference between my mother's breasts and mine frightened me. Hers were large and flat and were attached, it appeared to my always quickly averted eyes, only at the top. I worried a lot in those days about the time when it would be necessary for me to give up my own firm and upstanding circlets and be operated upon in a kind of initiation rite into adulthood so that my breasts would hang low and loose like my mother's.

It wasn't until a flat-chested friend of hers slept over on a cot in my room one night that I came to realize that adult women were no more shaped alike in their upper front portions than they were in their lower extremities. I had awakened that night, probably to go to the bathroom, and there, illuminated by the intrusive beam from a street lamp, was my mother's friend lying on her back, pajama top up around her neck, with just the suspicion of a swelling on both sides of her chest. I lay awake staring at her breasts, which appeared nipple-less in the dim light, sometimes getting out of bed to take a closer look, much agitated by what I imagined was the result of a surgeon's knife wielded for a purpose worse than I had ever dreamed. In the morning, shaken, I asked my mother why Dorothy's breasts had been cut off. Gently, and without in the least making me feel foolish, she explained about the infinite variety of mammary shapes, but I didn't completely believe her until I went to high school and started to take showers after gym with the other girls in my class.

Throughout the years, my mother's legs remained beautiful. I have a sharply visual memory of looking at them through the clear lower panes of the French doors that separated the dining room from the living room where she gave piano lessons every afternoon from three to six, hours when she was completely inaccessible. Her legs were the only part of her that I could see. I could tell by their position how close it was to dinner, a time when I would no longer have to share her with her students; near the end of the last lesson she would uncross her ankles, stretching out her right leg as if preparing to take her first step back into our lives.

I find it hard to remember too many things about my mother during those early years, because although she may have loved me as much as she did my sad, frightened brother, most of her attention and concern was for him. Coexisting with my love for her was my anger. The anguish I felt as a child when my brother's overwhelming needs robbed me of her was immeasurable. I spent a good part of my childhood feeling jealous and neglected, but never letting any part of my despair show, and I regarded my brother with ever-increasing hatred as my mother continued to give him in excess what I felt cheated of. It would be years before I would forgive her her preoccupation with Bo—not until I had children of my own would I understand how difficult it must have been for her.

The few childhood memories I do have of her have a brightness that must come of the delight with which I welcomed her presence. Most of these have to do with being sick and home from school, the only times I had her completely to myself. I loved those days so much that it's a wonder I didn't deliberately fake illness from time to time. But such duplicity, especially if it required the simulation of weakness, was beyond my capability. Besides, my father, vociferously honest in his dealings with the world (except occasionally) would never have allowed it. I have since learned duplicity, of course, but what I've learned is to hide, not to pretend, weakness—a skill that is, I've always thought, a little less immoral and certainly more useful.

Sometimes when I was home sick, my mother would come into my room with a batch of string beans to prepare for the evening meal. She brought other things to my bedside, too—sharp new crayons and coloring books, construction paper and lumpy flour paste, piles and piles of library books—but what I recall with the greatest clarity are the beans, even to the snapping sound they made when she broke them in half, and the colander, its bottom still moist, filled to the top with fresh, raw beans, half of which found their way into my mouth before they could reach the pot. We would talk about school, about my cold, about my latest poems. I wrote several a day around that time, mostly about love. Once, as she sat down, the bed collapsed under her overweight. As we tried to extricate ourselves, the bedclothes became entangled and the string beans got lost among the folds. My mother had to shake out the sheets and blankets one by one, and I remember laughing helplessly and painfully through my swollen glands to see the beans flying about the room as they shook free. I have never lost my taste for raw string beans. Whenever I've bought them for my own family, I always get half again as many as I need to allow for what I will eat as I clean and halve them, remembering with each snap my mother sitting sideways on my bed with the damp colander resting on her lap.

Through the years, even after I'd become an adult, the perfect lines of my mother's legs defied weight loss and gain, aging, and finally the loss of their greatest admirer, my father, who died when my mother was fifty-eight. She developed diabetes and heart disease after that and began a slow physical decline, during which time her legs remained surprisingly the same and her inner beauty continued to grow, achieving such a brilliance that there were times I found it difficult to look directly at her. Despite her lack of conventional good looks, she attracted the attention of several of the retired gentlemen with whom she shared sunny afternoons in the park. They would walk her home and then sit sipping tea and chatting well into the evening, reluctant to leave. She'd always had so many loving friends of all ages that a decade later over two hundred of them came to mourn at her funeral, crowding into the small chapel we had mistakenly felt would be large enough.

Among the mourners was her lover of the last four years, a widower of eighty-one, who had been a lawyer in the old country and who still worked part-time as a bookkeeper for a small neighborhood store. He was a vigorous, cultured gentleman with the bearing of a Viennese aristocrat, who wrote, my mother confided with equal measure of pride and embarrassment, erotic stories for his, and surprisingly her, amusement. His name was Morris, but he'd asked my mother to call him Marcel for aesthetic reasons; he'd renamed her Gusti, feeling that the name Augusta was unworthy of her graciousness. How they became lovers is something I know about because my mother had asked me for encouragement in the guise of seeking advice. I was startled by the nature of the confidence—we'd always been easy with each other, but never about sexual matters.

It was summer, and she was visiting for the weekend. We were relaxing on the terrace of my suburban house, looking down at a lake dotted with swimming ducks, sitting together silently as we could do pleasurably for long periods. I knew she'd been seeing Marcel and that for her he was everything my father had not been—elegant, intellectual and openly expressive of his love and admiration, feelings that were obviously mutual. She broke the lazy silence abruptly, telling me that Marcel had broached the subject of adding sex to their so far platonic relationship, and that she wasn't at all sure what she should do about it.

I was shocked, not for the usual reason that it's difficult for children of any age to accept parents as sexual beings, but because in one of my father's rare confidences late in his life, he'd revealed that my mother had never enjoyed sex, the only disappointment in their marriage that he'd ever expressed. I had therefore assumed that she would never consider a sexual relationship with another man. As I listened, stunned, my mother went on to explain that although she was very much attracted to Marcel, she didn't know if her health would permit that degree of intimacy, and also (here she hesitated), she feared that her old body would repel him. It took a great deal of effort on my part to regain my composure. After much too long a pause, I managed to suggest that to settle the first question she might ask her doctor, and as for the second, considering his age, she could safely assume that his body wasn't in peak condition either. It was the best I could manage under the circumstances.

To my surprise, and despite her avowed embarrassment, she did summon up the courage to speak to her doctor. He sternly advised her against having sex because of her heart condition. But her feelings for Marcel evidently overcame her fears for her health, because only a short time afterward she revealed that they had indeed become lovers. She had evidently come to terms with her other concern as well.

One night, some four years later, she felt her lungs fill with fluid as they were making love. An ambulance was called, but not until she'd convinced Marcel to help her get dressed so that she would look respectable being carried out of his apartment. He accompanied her to the hospital and stayed with her all during the long night until she permitted him to call me in the morning with the news. She hadn't wanted me to be awakened too early.

I visited her nearly every day after that; Marcel came almost as often. Between visits, he sent her love notes. In one, responding to an uncharacteristically coquettish question she'd asked about whether he would still find her attractive despite her substantial weight loss, he assured her that having loved her at 160 pounds, he would continue to love her at 110. "My love for you," he wrote with his usual formality, "does not depend on fluctuations of the scale."

During most of her first two weeks in the hospital she was hooked up to intravenous tubes, and her legs were wrapped in elastic bandages to prevent the formation of blood clots. On the twelfth day, when I arrived for my visit, I found to my delight that she'd been taken off the IV and was sitting up in bed looking better for the first time since her attack. We kissed, and I asked her if there was anything I could do to make her more comfortable. She told me that the elastic bandages had been removed and that she'd be grateful if I would shave her legs.

But first she asked if I would brush out her hair since she was still too weak to manage it herself. I took out the hairpins that had been holding it in a bun at her neck. Her fine, waist-length hair had become a beautiful color in the past few years, very different from the mousy brown of her youth; the texture was silky, unlike the frizzy bush she'd permanent-waved it into for years at my father's urging. At first, as it grayed, it took on a yellowish cast that hadn't looked well with her strong features and somewhat ruddy complexion. Then, almost overnight it seems, it had reached such a perfect balance of light brown, gray and white, that unless one got close enough to make out the individual colors, the impression was of a mass of pale, shimmering gold. I began to have hope for the future of my own hair—it was the only feature besides my legs that I'd gotten from my mother, and I had always disliked its nondescript color.

For a few moments I brushed her hair slowly from the top of her head to her waist, following the brush downward with my other hand in a kind of caress. I hoped she would understand the gesture for what it was. Having finished, I bent over the night table to find her razor. When I turned around again, she had thrown the covers back. Her legs lay against the sheet, pitifully thin, and worse, completely straight from ankle to thigh. No more swelling calf rising in one lovely arc, curving in behind the knee to broaden out again where the thigh begins. These were sticks, hardly more than skin stretched over bone, white beneath the untidy bristles of hair and looking like the legs of the Auschwitz survivors I'd seen in newsreels of the forties.

My shock must have shown, because she reached for my hand. "Don't worry, Duvie" (this was what she always called me in intimate moments), "They'll come back when I put on some weight." I put a blade into the razor and choking back my tears began to shave her legs. I remember each stroke as the razor followed the flat contours of her calves and the effort it took me not to press my lips to them and weep. Her legs never did flesh out again—there was no time. When she died in her sleep one month later, they had become even thinner.

After her funeral, we went to my daughter's apartment for what turned out to be a cross between a *shiva* and a wake. We reminisced for hours in a curiously joyous celebration of her life. We talked of how she had loved making music, of the many recitals she'd held in her apartment in the past few years at which she and a friend had given sometimes riotous four-handed renditions of the masters, the tempos slowed by arthritis but the spirit still strong and jubilant. I was under control at first, successful in stemming the torrent of tears I knew would come as soon as I was safely home. But the dam broke and grief washed over me in waves so strong I could hardly breathe when my daughter said wistfully, "I hope that wherever she is there's a piano." And I heard my own voice say just as the tears came, "I hope she gets her legs back, those beautiful legs."

That is not the end of the matter of her legs. For they, and not her death, have come to symbolize for me my own mortality. Since that time, whenever I bend to shave my legs, I see, not my own, which remain shapely and show only a few signs of the aging to which the rest of my body has capitulated, but hers as they were near the end, thin and pale, a straight line from ankle to thigh. And each time this happens, I tremble with a sudden chill and I mourn for us both.

Grandma Becky

I have a photograph of my Grandma Becky on the day of her first wedding, her bosom high and rounded like the breast of a pigeon, rising above an incredibly small waist. Her features are small and perfect, her expression serene. She is standing behind her seated husband, a veil of handmade lace atop her dark, puffed out hair; one gloved hand is on his shoulder as she looks confidently into the camera, proud and beautiful.

She was widowed before she was thirty. Her daughter, my mother, was then nine years old. After the funeral, my grandmother and my mother moved back with her parents, stretching family resources thin, since her three younger sisters were still unmarried and also living at home. My mother, perhaps in reaction to the devastating loss of her father, with whom she had been very close, came down shortly after with tuberculosis of the spine, a disease that kept her isolated and immobilized in a body cast for two long years. My grandmother, after a long period of mourning was finally persuaded by her parents to enlist the services of a marriage broker in the hope that a suitable match might be found. It wasn't long before a meeting was arranged with one Israel Wolinsky, a widower in comfortable circumstances, who was immediately captivated by her melancholy beauty and who, after a reasonable period of time, proposed that they join forces.

The advent of my step-grandfather into Grandma Becky's life also marked the advent of six additional children—five girls and a boy. They had been badly spoiled by the aunt who had taken care of them since their mother's death, and it was hard for them to adjust to my grandmother's firm insistence on table manners, cleanliness, and respect. But my mother, lonely for other children, welcomed the noisy clan, and after some difficult months they decided to accept her and my grandmother as family.

The Wolinskys produced one daughter, my Aunt Sophie, born a year after their marriage, when my mother was fourteen. This brought the household to ten—thirteen if you counted my grandmother's three sisters who spent most of their days, even after their own marriages, helping my grandmother prepare the necessarily banquet-sized meals.

Grandpa Wolinsky had started a successful millinery business only a few years after his arrival in America. Portly and taciturn, he always remained somewhat aloof from his grandchildren. He had rheumy eyes and a beard that reached to his watch chain, and always wore a yarmulke that looked like a fez sitting on his bushy hair. He also possessed a magnificent baritone. At the request of some business associates who had some years before established the Millinery Center Synagogue on Thirty-fourth Street, he had, for several years, unofficially performed the duties of Cantor for Saturday services.

One day, when all of his children except Sophie had grown and left home, his secret hope was realized: he was asked to join the synagogue as its full-time Cantor. Delighted, he sold his share of the business to his partner and accepted. He felt that he had been called to the post by God, as is evident in his choice of title for the slim book he wrote about his life, which he published privately and circulated among his family and friends. He called it, *From Shop to Synagogue, or I Yield to Destiny.*

*   *   *

With the familiar ritual, the delectable food, the songs and the games, Passover *seders* would seem to have all the elements necessary to make them joyful and festive occasions. This was not so for me. Because of Grandpa Wolinsky's important position at the Millinery Center, it was his obligation to lead the mass *seders* that were held each year in the synagogue's central room. All of my grandfather's large family and the families of the rest of the members of the congregation would come together to celebrate Passover, some three hundred people sitting at six immensely long tables covered with damask tablecloth after damask tablecloth.

I hated those *seders* because the services were completely in Hebrew and very, very long. I had to endure what seemed like hours of chanting before we could get to the *gefuilte* fish. By the time food was served, my stomach was gurgling—it always made the most outrageous noises when I was hungry—and my step-aunts' children would snigger when the growling got loud enough for them to hear. After the first course, we had to listen to more of the text before the next would be served, and on and on and on until I was ready to scream with the discomfort of sitting on the hard folding chairs.

The only part that was at all pleasurable was near the end when it was time for my grandfather to lead everybody in the singing of the Passover songs—*"Chad Gadya"* was the one I liked best. His rich baritone would soar over our smaller voices, bringing lightness and humor into the room for the first time that evening. Otherwise it was terribly boring. I once fell asleep between the chicken soup and the brisket, knocking over my wine glass with its sip-sized portion as my head hit the table.

* * *

By the time I got to know my Grandma Becky, an ever-present air of anxiety had replaced the confidence that glowed from her first wedding picture. She worried about everything, putting all her energy into supporting the bundle of cares she always carried with her: my father's unemployment, my mother's exhaustion, my brother's eyes, my straight hair, my Aunt Sophie's marital future, her relatives in Poland, my grandfather's health. But despite all this, her love came through. I felt her own warmth to be greater even than that of her soft black sealskin coat, which I used to snuggle into and rub my cheek against whenever we rode together in the back seat of my father's car.

Grandma Becky was an expert seamstress, creating without patterns the latest in feminine fashions. She was always sewing or altering something for me since I couldn't help growing, clucking and shaking her head in mock displeasure as I got taller and taller each year. At every visit she would spend some part of the time on her knees, scores of pins in her mouth, saying "turn" every few seconds as well as she could through her closed lips. Mostly it came out as a grunt. While she pinned the hems or adjusted the fit of a skirt in progress, I would look down at her shining chestnut hair, wanting to pull out the two strategic hairpins that held it in a thick bun, so that it would fall to her waist, but never daring to do so.

The most beautiful dress she ever made for me was on the occasion of my Aunt Sophie's wedding, when I was seven. I was to be the flower girl. Grandma Becky, her three sisters and my mother went one day to a wholesale fabric warehouse owned by a friend of my grandfather's and there bought a remnant of shimmering powder blue crepe de Chine, which my grandmother set about making into a dress. Oh, the fittings, the multitude of pins, the hours of kneeling and turning that went into its production. In the end, my grandmother had created a work of art. It had a sweetheart neck, a wide sash and layers of ruffles cascading from waist to hem. But it wasn't quite complete yet: in a glorious finale, my Aunt Rose, who could paint on fabric, spent two days tracing feathery wisps of silver paint onto every last ruffle with a fine paintbrush.

When it was finished I tried it on for Grandma Becky. She stood looking at me, her thumb and index finger pushing her lips into a worried circle, frowning slightly at the sight of her plain, plump granddaughter with the crooked teeth and the limp hair modeling that magnificent creation. I remember hearing her sigh and say in a voice she thought too soft for me to hear: "Well, maybe we can curl it for the wedding".

I wasn't exactly sure what the duties of a flower girl were, and I waited in feverish anticipation to find out. At the rehearsal, I learned that I'd be walking down the long aisle all by myself, strewing rose petals from a little basket that would hang from my wrist. I practiced walking the length of the aisle only pretending to scatter petals, since the basket wouldn't be delivered until the morning of the wedding.

That Sunday I was up before daybreak, pestering my parents to let me get dressed. I bothered them so effectively that they let me put on the dress two hours before we were to leave, with a promise to do nothing more active than read a book. I felt like a princess in that blue and silver masterpiece, and I stood before a mirror admiring myself until it was almost time to leave. Shortly before we left, my mother took her curling iron and crimped my hair for the first time. I was thrilled, but my father didn't like the effect and kept on brushing it until only a slight wave remained. By the time we got to the synagogue it was as straight as ever.

My nervousness increased as my big moment approached. Trembling, I started down the aisle in response to a shove from someone behind me, taking the little measured steps I had rehearsed. But with the added responsibility of reaching repeatedly with my right hand into the basket that hung from my left wrist, I found myself veering toward the left, making it necessary to adjust my direction every few feet. I began to hear an undercurrent of laughter as I made my way drunkenly down the aisle. When I reached the altar, I was to turn right, walk three steps and turn around to wait until the bride, who had started down the aisle behind me, reached the front of the synagogue. As I turned, the buckle of one of my black patent leather Mary Janes caught in the fringes of the wine-colored rope that lined the aisle and I fell sideways, sending a shower of rose petals all over the front row guests. I think the humiliation I felt at that moment and which plagued my dreams for years, was the reason for the almost pathological nervousness I would experience years later whenever I sang in public. I was never able to walk out on stage without expecting to fall on my face, marveling each time that I had reached the piano without disaster.

*   *   *

As much as I disliked the *seders* of my childhood, I found myself celebrating Passover with my children when they were young, trying, I suppose, to create for them what I felt I had missed. Not even sure they were the right symbols, I'd cover some *matzohs* with a napkin and set in the middle of the table a lamb shank, a roasted egg and some parsley in salted water. This was in an effort to set that particular meal apart from the chicken dinners I made the rest of the year. Aside from these, I haven't been to a real *seder* since my grandfather died. I am reminded of him only when I do my once a year spring-cleaning and come upon his book stuck away in the back of one of the dresser drawers. But not so my grandmother. Whenever I'm having slacks shortened or a hem taken up, I look down at the tailor kneeling at my feet and see instead my Grandma Becky, straight pins between her lips, asking me to turn.

Aunt Sophie and
Uncle Harvey

At the age of eighteen, my Aunt Sophie, at whose wedding I'd made my memorable pratfall, became the bride of Harvey Berlin, a young man with opal eyes, a widow's peak and a hand-carved jaw. As far as I was concerned, my new uncle was blessed many times over: by his almost excessive good looks, by his having acquired my Aunt Sophie, who possessed an absolutely luminous smile and a beauty almost Christian in its perfection, and by his having been born heir to a large and successful wholesale carpet business, which made him very rich without trying. It also made him subject to my father's disfavor. In fact, it wasn't long before my father now found a conversion from mysticism to socialism to be an emotional necessity. His socialism was not so much a matter of political ideology as a manifestation of the ancient envy of the have-nots for the have-a-lots. But I knew nothing of the immorality of inherited wealth; to me my Aunt Sophie and Uncle Harvey were a fairy princess and her prince come alive.

The newlyweds spent their honeymoon in Bermuda, an island that has forever remained the quintessence of romance in my imagination, making it impossible for me to visit it lest I suffer a severe attack of the disillusions. I used to imagine them on their honeymoon, floating down rivers of lily pads with no visible means of support, covered with white hibiscus blossoms, with soft tropical breezes gently rustling my aunt's taffeta wedding dress.

Aunt Sophie and Uncle Harvey were very generous to us. Aunt Sophie supplied me with expensive hand-me-downs outgrown by Uncle Harvey's sister's children, and gave my mother her own hardly worn clothing (I often suspected that my aunt wore things once or twice to ease my mother's suspicion that they'd really been purchased for her). During our leanest times, Uncle Harvey lent my father money to carry us through. They seldom visited us, but would often invite us to their house on Long Island, a marvel of wall-to-wall carpeting, elaborately draped and curtained windows, and exquisitely furnished bedrooms, which grew in number with each new daughter. Every time we visited them there was a new piece of furniture, a change of drapery, a different, always thicker, plush velvet carpet. It seemed to my delighted eyes that they were constantly achieving new heights of perfection. I could hardly wait for each visit to see what exciting and unpredictable changes had been made in the décor. Their extravagances only made my father angrier. When it came time to leave, we'd make our way past their shiny Chrysler to our old Ford, our stomachs stuffed with incomparable brisket, delicate parsleyed potatoes and high, flaky-crusted fruit pies made by my aunt's Dominican housekeeper. Before we got into the car my father would say in a voice loud enough to be heard by all of my aunt's neighbors, "What did they need a new carpet (sofa, bedroom set) for? Just think how many families in Harlem could live for a year on what they spent!"

Every fall, my Aunt Sophie took me to S. Klein on the Square to buy me a winter coat and hat. Powder blue was the color my father always instructed her to buy—he was fixated on powder blue, determined that everything I wear reflect the color of my eyes, (It was he, in fact, who had dictated that color for my flower girl dress.) Aunt Sophie deferred to his request only once. The resulting lack of contrast with my sallow skin and mousy hair created an effect so glaringly innocuous in her eyes that she decided to use her own judgment ever after.

To my gratitude and amazement (how did she dare counter my father's wishes?), she purchased instead coats and hats of electric reds and royal purples. Every year, my father and Aunt Sophie locked horns over the color of my coat on the day she took me shopping, her hazel eyes flashing with anger when he insisted that it was time she did it his way. And each fall, secretly delighted by the color those bright hues lent to my cheeks, I'd come home to show my new acquisition to my father, only to have him berate my Aunt

Sophie roundly for subverting my best feature. Needless to say, everything he bought me, when finances allowed, was powder blue, a color that to this day I will not have around me even in toilet paper.

Until I was thirteen, my aunt continued to outfit me in winter coats. Going to S. Klein with her was a rare treat—it was the only time I wasn't made conscious of what things cost. This was a welcome change from shopping for price tags instead of clothing, something that occurred every time my father took me out to buy the rest of my wardrobe. I still fight an internal battle to keep from buying two cheaper items in place of the more expensive one that I prefer, hearing, every time I lose, my father's voice saying "Good girl! That's some shopper you're turning out to be!"

The October before my father finally went back to work, making it possible at last for him to buy my winter coats himself, Aunt Sophie took me to a wholesale fur house instead of S. Klein on the Square. A few weeks before, she had taken her oldest daughter, then six, to the same place and had custom-ordered for her a beaver coat with matching hat and muff. My father had labeled this just another example of capitalistic excess and fumed loudly about the long overdue revolution. I didn't say so, but I thought the coat was absolutely beautiful. My cousin Debbie looked a little like a small beaver herself when she modeled it for us in her newly furnished bedroom with its white coverlet and new powder blue carpet. ("Wouldn't you know it," grumbled my father. "Powder blue on the floor! Just to spite me"). Besides, Debbie had two younger sisters who could wear the coat when she outgrew it, so it didn't seem as much of an extravagance to me as it did to my father.

The next day, when my mother told him where Aunt Sophie was taking me shopping, he perked up; while he resented the rich treating themselves to luxuries, he was very much in favor of their supplying them to the poor. "It's about time," he said to my mother, who had given up trying to defend the generosity of her sister against my father's attacks. "The kid's almost fourteen already and all she ever got from your rich sister is wool."

The day of the big purchase dawned. I fixed my hair with special care in preparation for the trying on of dozens of fur hats in the search for the Perfect One. The warehouse was a menagerie of tailored pelts. We were led to a rack of mouton coats, smooth, dark-brown furs so dense they felt as heavy as coats of mail when I tried them on. I had never been happier. Plagued with thin skin and low blood pressure, it pleased me to know that fur, not cloth, would stand between me and the winter. I talked my aunt into letting me get a coat that was a size too big, so in case I put on a couple of inches I could still wear it the following year. The backing was so stiff that when I bent over to scratch my leg the coat wouldn't bend with my body. To me this was only another sign of its impenetrability against winter winds. I threw my arms around Aunt Sophie's neck and kissed her, my unexpected tears smudging her face powder. She smiled her beautiful smile and bought me a hat to match.

I couldn't wait to get my prize home to show my parents. My father stood waiting impatiently as I struggled with the cord on the enormous box. At last I raised the coat free of the box and held it full length against me, awaiting their words of admiration. My mother had just begun to speak when my father reached out and touched the fur. An expression of disappointment overtook his look of expectancy.

"God damned capitalist," he said disgustedly. "She bought her *own* daughter beaver."

* * *

One of the last times I saw my Aunt Sophie was on a day that she came to visit my mother in the hospital during her last illness. Afterward she gave me a lift downtown in her pearl gray Lincoln. I thought she was as striking at fifty-eight as she had been as a bride, but looking a little worn around the eyes. They had a haunted look, and there was a downward cast to her mouth. We talked about old times, about her children. Two of her daughters had recently been divorced. I could see that she felt bewildered and betrayed by what she saw as her failure as well as theirs. She had been thrust into a reality she hadn't anticipated; bitterness and loss had intruded into her cared-for, beautifully decorated life. Fairy princesses weren't supposed to have to cope with separation, by death or otherwise—everyone was expected to live happily ever after.

I looked hard at my aunt as she spoke of her disappointments, remembering her as she was, generous and good of heart, as serene as her own mother had been in her wedding photograph and confidently expecting from life only the good, and getting nothing less. I wanted to say something comforting, but what can one say to a woman who'd been overtaken by the events of a time she didn't understand? I recalled how at my wedding she had casually reached into her handbag for two crumpled hundred-dollar bills, a fortune in those days, and how she had stuffed them into my new husband's pocket, walking away quickly before he could overcome his incredulity and thank her. She'd been generous, too, with her daughters, wanting not thanks, only an adherence to the old ways: the orderly progression of life's milestones, the taking of counsel from those who had passed that way before, marriages that endured. Her life had been comfortable and protected, made busy and full with nothing more competitive than canasta, nothing more demanding than managing her beautiful home, nothing more threatening than the hint of a drizzle on the morning of her middle daughter's wedding, planned to take place outdoors.

So she anguished over her children's marital problems, doubted the wisdom of their decisions, fretted about the extent of her responsibility for their unhappiness. They tried to get her to fill her time with work instead of worry, to interest her in the design end of the carpet business, even to learn needlepoint or take up painting. But she told me that she felt too great a sense of failure over her children's marriages to be able to put her mind to anything that serious. When the pressures would begin to build, she and Uncle Harvey, tall, smiling and handsome as ever, would go on a trip. Since the second divorce, they had traveled all over Europe and South America, once even to Bermuda where it all began.

"I thought things would turn out differently," she said wistfully as she brought the car to a stop. "What happened? What went wrong?"

We sat in silence for a moment or two, then I leaned over to kiss her goodbye. As she turned her head to watch me get out of the car, I saw her eyes suddenly glaze over with memory. For an instant, a trace of her old smile played on her lips, the corners lifting slightly.

"Stay away from powder blue," she said, and drove off.

Cousin Leslie

If it hadn't been for the Gelfinds, distant relatives of my mother's through one of her married aunts, we would never have gotten out of Brooklyn the summer I was twelve. The Gelfinds owned a *kochelayn* (a resort with a community kitchen) near Monticello, New York. Behind the main house, which contained the enormous kitchen where as many as ten *balabustas* could make noodle pudding and *tsimmes* at the same time, were clustered several small cabins, which the Gelfinds rented out every year from July first until Labor Day. Set away from the cabins was a small shed about to fall apart—a converted chicken coop—in which a sleeping platform had been erected four feet under the flat wooden roof. It was necessary to climb a ladder and keep one's head down in order to get into bed. Every year the shed rented only after the season began. Some canny family would wait until the first week of July had come and gone and then get it at a cut-rate price after the Gelfinds had just about given up any hope of finding tenants for it. But this particular summer it was still empty in the middle of July, and we were offered its use for nothing in recognition of my father's long-time unemployment.

The shed was unbearably hot during the day and cold and drafty at night. Lying in bed, I could see the stars through the spaces between the rotted slats and feel the sharp night air piercing the worn army blankets the Gelfinds had provided. Although my mother didn't have to use the common kitchen as there was an old two-burner stove in what passed for our living room, I think she would have liked to, because not cooking with the other women kept her fairly isolated. But my father, who considered us far superior to everyone else, welcomed and reinforced our apartness and discouraged us from having anything to do with what he called "the cabin yentas". A yenta, according to my father, was a woman who wasn't smart enough to do anything but gossip.

Even though my father left every Sunday night to drive into the city to look for work, not returning until late Friday, we felt his unseen presence; none of us wanted to be the object of his scorn, and so we kept more or less to ourselves as he desired. We entertained ourselves by reading the library books we had brought from the city, took long walks in the woods and dunks in the brook that widened beyond the Gelfinds' property, and sang rounds and played word games in the evenings. My brother and I were making a not too successful effort to get along, since we had no one but each other to play with. This state of affairs continued until the day my cousin Leslie came up for the month of August.

My mother had written to my Aunt Rose about a cabin that would be available for August at the Gelfinds' that year, hoping that Aunt Rose would take it and provide my mother with company that my father might find less objectionable. But Aunt Rose, unable to afford the cost since Uncle Manny had had a bad year, told her sister-in-law Bernice about it. Bernice was a teacher and might be able to manage it, even though she had recently been deserted by her husband, Aunt Rose's brother Jack. Aunt Bernice was English. She had met and married Uncle Jack when he was in England making the world safe for democracy.

Her daughter Leslie was thirteen that summer to my twelve. I had seen her occasionally over the years at Aunt Rose's house, but not for the last year or so. During that time she had turned into something magical. She was slender, a head taller than me, and her skin was golden without benefit of sun. Her eyes were green, the pupils flecked with mauve, and were shaped like fat almonds, tilted exotically and set wide apart in her pixyish, open face. I was enchanted by her beauty and adored her instantly. She responded, to my amazement and joy, by becoming my best friend.

We would meet immediately after breakfast and not separate except for meals until bedtime. Our delight in each other grew to the point where soon we were holding hands all the time, leaning over every few seconds to give each other light kisses on the lips. My memories of those weeks are filled with Leslie, gazing in dizzy wonder at her fully developed, perfect breasts when we changed into our bathing suits, the sweet torment of having to leave her for the night and the rapturous lift of my heart when I ran to her cabin each morning. And I remember especially the feeling that my life would never hold greater pleasure than those times when we lay in our secret place, pine needles in our hair, fingers touching, looking for animals in the shifting clouds. I was aware of my lonely brother watching us enviously from a distance and turning away when he saw us looking at him, but I was too caught up with these new feelings to give him much thought.

One morning near the end of the month, my mother took me aside and told me that everyone in the *kochelayn* was talking about Leslie and me, especially the way we were always kissing each other. She understood it was because we were such good friends, but other people might interpret it differently.

"How?" I asked, beginning to feel sick in that special spot in my stomach reserved for darker feelings of guilt and shame.

And then my mother told me that there were women called lesbians who loved other women the way men and women loved each other, and the other ladies at the *kochelayn* were beginning to think that Leslie and I were behaving like those women. I hadn't yet made connections between physical contact, sexual desire, and what every one called love, and so I didn't really grasp exactly what she meant. But I did know that something that had been beautiful was now soiled and made to seem ugly, and mixed with my shame I felt anger toward those who had spoiled it.

I ran to Leslie's cabin determined not to let it matter, my heart pounding with this unfamiliar combination of emotions. We had planned to spend the morning at a nearby lake catching turtles. To my surprise, she wasn't out front waiting for me as she usually was. I knocked on the wooden screen door and called her name. After a moment she appeared, her lovely face red and swollen, an unaccustomed downward turn to her mouth. Her eyes wouldn't meet mine as she told me through the locked screen door that she wasn't feeling well and didn't think she wanted to catch turtles.

I knew immediately that her mother had spoken to her about the kissing, too, though I suspected not as gently as mine had. But I persisted, feeling sick and desperate.

"Maybe after lunch?"

"No, I can't," she said softly, her eyes still downcast. Without another word she turned and walked back into the cabin.

We hardly spoke for the remaining two weeks. Miserable, I went back to my reading and the long walks with my mother and Bo. I would sometimes catch Leslie looking at me despairingly, but she would lower her eyes as soon as she was aware that I had seen her.

Leslie and her mother went back to Brooklyn a few days before we did, and I never saw her again. Since Uncle Jack seemed to have dropped out of sight permanently, Aunt Bernice decided to go back to England and left several months later, taking with her what I realized only much later was my first love.

Cousin Millie

By the time I was six, I had already begun to pick out tunes on the piano, using only the white keys. My mother had a fairly intractable philosophy against starting formal training until age eight, but when I moved on from "Happy Birthday" and "Yankee Doodle" to the opening bars of Beethoven's Fifth Symphony, she knew she had an exception on her hands. She capitulated by giving me a few minutes of instruction every day, starting with the use of the black keys to save her sanity. I was soon playing some easy pieces by Bach and Beethoven (my mother was a purist and disapproved of transcriptions like "Humoresque", which I would have preferred). I actually bit my tongue one day trying to play the B-flat major scale with the same fingering that works for C, a task not even Van Cliburn would attempt.

After three or four years of my mother's informal and undemanding tutelage, I began to cut down on my practicing. This caused my father great alarm as he daily watched his dream of famous fatherhood slip away. After much discussion, it was decided to approach my mother's Cousin Millie for help, hoping she would become another link in my father's now long chain of swaps. In exchange for my brother's cello lessons, for our dental work and tonsillectomies, he would sell large life insurance policies to the professionals involved and give them his yearly commission in perpetuity. Considering the minuscule size of the commissions, I don't believe there was parity in this arrangement, but because of everyone's affection for my mother, we never suffered untreated pain, lost our permanent teeth or held on to our adenoids past the appointed time. This time, however, the ultimate deal was not a complete victory for my father—Cousin Millie was as shrewd as he. She consented to give me piano lessons only after he agreed, in addition to his yearly commission, to throw in two hours of my mother on Saturday mornings to teach Beginning Theory to Millie's nine o'clock class.

Cousin Millie was a monolith of a woman. Nearly six feet tall and large boned, she had thick, almost black hair plaited into a tight braid that she wrapped around her head and secured behind her left ear with a large silver hairpin. She wore a pince-nez, the only person I ever saw use one. The glasses caused two vertical lines to appear between her eyes from the effort of keeping them on, and when she took them off, there were angry red welts on both sides of the bridge of her nose. She was a loud, hearty woman, tactless to the point of drawing blood, who ran a large and successful piano-teaching practice out of the parlor floor of her Carroll Street brownstone. Every day she gave a score of half-hour piano lessons in the front room, which held her two magnificent Steinways, and taught group theory lessons all day Saturday in the back. Upstairs was her apartment, furnished exquisitely with fine antiques and oriental rugs, quite unlike our own Salvation-Army-fire-sale collection.

Although she was uncompromisingly strict and discouraged familiarity, I adored her. It took me some years to understand the reasons for my strong feelings of admiration. Cousin Millie was not only an original and inspiring teacher, she had established her own music school and made it into a successful business, a rare thing for a woman in those days. Her air of independence and autonomy made her stand out among the other women in my family, none of whom questioned their traditional roles. Cousin Millie had not only remained single until she was past forty, a source of great discomfort to her family, but had moved out to live independently at the age of twenty-two. Even men older than she didn't leave their parent's home if they were still single. It was her independence more than her spinsterhood that had upset them.

Cousin Millie's husband, Sam, was an orthodontist with whom my father later swapped the commission on one hundred thousand dollars' of insurance in exchange for a complete four-year rerouting of every tooth in my mouth. Years later, Sam told me that a less comprehensive protocol would have served the purpose just as well, but my father had researched the matter by asking the advice of those of his customers whose children wore braces, and had insisted on a treatment plan that Sam, a meek man, was not able to talk him out of.

When they stood together, Sam appeared to be about half Cousin Millie's size. He was certainly half her presence. When she entered the room, it seemed to get larger to accommodate her. Sam, as quiet as she was stentorian, was as good as invisible. Where she stood tall in Oxfords with double lifts, he slumped to a shortness far greater than his height called for. After their marriage, he moved into her brownstone, making not the slightest mark on its décor. He didn't want to be noticed; his wish was usually granted.

Cousin Millie put me on a strict practice regimen, which, because I worshipped her, I adhered to rigidly. She required that all of her pupils learn at least one piece from each of the musical periods, and that one of them be a solo with an Add-a-Part record. These had just come on the market and consisted of an orchestral arrangement of a well-known musical composition, minus the solo part. All of her students were expected to play their Add-a-Parts at the final recital of the season. In the only democratic aspect of her otherwise autocratic rule, we were permitted to choose whichever one we wished to study.

At one recital, seven of her students, myself among them, selected the same one—a piano and orchestra arrangement of Tchaikovsky's Nutcracker Suite. The audience of parents and other relatives seemed to be having a hilarious time. They were only partly able to contain their mirth as each of us fought a losing battle to keep up with the record's furious tempo. No one ended with the orchestra, although I'm proud to say that I came closest, finishing only a couple of beats behind. We all received wild and enthusiastic applause accompanied by stomps and whistles from the younger members of the audience when we got to the final chord, sweating and breathing hard with the effort to keep up.

We also had to play a solo, and I remember how year after year I would try to perfect the piece Cousin Millie had chosen, so as to merit her rare praise. During the actual performance, I was oblivious to the rest of the audience. It was Cousin Millie alone that I was playing for, watching her out of the corner of my eye and trying to guess her reaction from her expression.

There is a poem I read in high school that has a line that makes me think of how I felt about my Cousin Millie. It goes something like:

"*. . . we wept with delight when she gave us a smile and
trembled with fear at her frown.*"

* * *

There was a boy named Stanley in my Saturday theory class. He was short and round and what is thought of even among Jews as very Jewish-looking. Nonetheless, he struck me as sexy, and I wasn't alone—the other girls in the class were always trying to catch his eye. Stanley's appeal was that he made us all laugh; his wisecracks, delivered with an intimate leer, had the effect on our pubescent imaginations of a rough caress. From the day he first joined the class when I was fourteen, I was in love. I dreamed about him every Friday night in anticipation of seeing him the next day. But he did not, alas, feel the same way about me; after looking me over once or twice, he ignored me completely, thereby causing my heart to break anew every Saturday at eleven. The other girls would whisper about Stanley before he arrived and hang around with him after class. One by one he used them up, spending about a month of Sundays with each of them in turn at the Prospect Park Zoo, the Botanical Gardens and the Brooklyn Museum, never beyond walking distance from his house. Nickels for the subway were hard to come by.

Near the end of the season, Cousin Millie assigned the Bach Arioso to Stanley and me as a two-piano duet for the coming recital. I had never spoken to her about my infatuation, but I often caught her looking at me as I hung back after class, watching him as he stood in the center of a group of admiring, giggling girls.

A week before the recital, he invited me to his house to rehearse our two-piano piece. I didn't see how we could manage it, because I knew that all he had was one truncated upright, but I kept my mouth shut, opening it only to accept. I didn't sleep at all the night before, especially since he'd told me that his parents would be visiting an aunt all afternoon. Needless to say, I didn't reveal this information to my parents when I told them where I was going. Good girls would never find themselves alone in an apartment with a boy they weren't related to, but I was getting tired of being a good girl.

I rang the doorbell in the dark hallway and stood shaking with fear and desire as I waited for Stanley to answer. To my disappointment, the first thing he did as I walked in was to offer me a glass of milk and a cookie, something more like my Aunt Rose would have done. I didn't really want any, but I was eager to make a good impression, so I said yes. He sat opposite me at the kitchen table, his chin in his hand, silently watching me drink my milk. I, too, was silent, struck dumb by the knowledge that I was alone with the boy I secretly loved, and deliciously apprehensive about what I both feared and hoped would follow. I wondered if we would neck or pet, not exactly sure what the difference was, but wanting desperately to find out.

We went into the living room, where we tried unsuccessfully to rehearse the Bach on his miniscule piano, but too many of the notes required us to cross hands. So we agreed to do something else instead, and get together at Cousin Millie's later that week to rehearse. He led me down a long hallway toward what I suspected must be the bedroom area. My moment of truth was about to arrive. I can't remember before or after anticipating any event with such delectable dread. At the end of the corridor, he opened a door and we entered a small room furnished as a library. The walls were covered from floor to ceiling with books, except for an alcove set into the bookcases where a small loveseat stood. I shivered slightly, wondering what would happen there. Stanley went directly to an oversized book on the top shelf, took it down and sat on the love seat where he motioned to me to join him. My heart, which had been palpitating wildly until that moment, seemed to stop beating. To my great confusion, Stanley opened the book and began to read with exaggerated expression a scene from Clifford Odets' thirties drama, *WAITING FOR LEFTY.* As I sat down, he asked me to read the next lines, and there we sat for several hours acting out with ever-increasing fervor scenes from that and other Depression plays of the era. Never has that genre seethed with so much sexuality.

Before I left that afternoon, Stanley asked me for a date. We made arrangements to spend the following Sunday in Central Park. I went home ecstatic, hardly noticing the long lecture my father delivered after he had wormed out of me in my weakened state the information that Stanley's parents hadn't been home. Central Park! I floated on an ocean of euphoria—Stanley must really like me if he was willing to spend twenty cents in subway fare, five cents each, there and back. I spent the week in a trance, counting the minutes, each of which assumed the dimensions of half an hour. My thoughts about the unimaginably delicious things in store for me on Sunday ran so wild that I looked up the word "nymphomaniac" in the dictionary to see if I could possibly be one.

At my lesson that week, Cousin Millie twice had to tell me sharply that I seemed to be elsewhere, and would I please come back to Brooklyn. I didn't resent her for scolding me. Actually I was feeling sorry for her—she could never have known such passion as I was feeling, having missed Stanley by about forty years. My exultation undiminished, I apologized and tried hard to pay closer attention.

Sunday morning arrived at last. I met Stanley at ten o'clock at the Nostrand Avenue subway station of the IRT and took the express train to New York, gazing into each other's eyes for the entire trip. I remember that day as one of the few perfect days of my life. The sun was shining, a warm June breeze was blowing, and we walked through the park, talking about all of the important things in our world: our parents, our schoolwork, our music, our hopes. My Friday night dreams had come true. There are no words jubilant enough to describe my feelings during those hours—"orange" probably comes closest, since I felt like a sunrise.

It was beginning to get dark, time to start home. As we slowly walked toward the nearest park exit, Stanley asked me if I had ever been kissed. My heart gave evidence of stopping for good. I answered truthfully that I had not. Stanley said that was too bad, because he never kissed a girl who didn't already have some experience. This statement shattered me. Was it, I thought, because he didn't want to have to teach me how? Or was it because he didn't want to be responsible for starting me on a path that might lead to nymphomania and eventual disgrace? His refusal to kiss me only strengthened my resolve that he should. I argued with such passion against his reluctance that he finally reconsidered. Just a few yards short of the exit, he led me abruptly into a clump of bushes, put one arm around my waist, the other on my right breast, and touched his lips to mine. I was acutely aware of the parts of our bodies that touched—the track of fire his arm made as it circled my waist, his left hand touching the small of my back, his right hand cupping and lightly pressing my breast, which suddenly seemed to swell to twice its size—and his lips, feeling warm and fleshy against mine, his tongue running gently along the length of my upper lip.

Then he let me go. I stood there, eyes closed, feeling dizzy, becoming aware of a strange, sweetish sensation beginning to grow in the pit of my stomach. I think he was a little frightened by my reaction, because he put his hands on my shoulders and shook me roughly. When I opened my eyes, he was looking at me apprehensively, uneasy about my sudden catatonia. I walked with him dreamily out of the park unable to speak, hardly noticing where we were walking, playing that kiss over and over again like a record with the needle stuck in a groove. I don't remember the ride home or even saying good night to him. I was in a state of shining grace.

A few days later, we played the Bach at the recital. I'm not sure if we played it well or badly because I was still in thrall to that Central Park kiss. I even forgot to look at Cousin Millie for her approval; it just didn't seem important. She seemed a bit distant during the cookies and punch, so I suspected that we hadn't done too well. But I told myself that I would make it up to her next season—after all, I'd be able to see Stanley every Sunday for the rest of my life, and wasn't love supposed to nurture Art? According to the movie *LUST FOR LIFE*, I remembered, only one night of love had been enough to inspire Vincent van Gogh to a veritable orgy of painting. Standing with Stanley and sipping grape punch, I was suddenly infused with love for everyone in the room, especially Cousin Millie, whose theory class had been responsible for my having met him in the first place. Next season it would be different, I told myself. I would practice, between Sunday kisses, four, five, eight hours a day.

A few days after the recital, Stanley and I left for different summer camps. We corresponded—or rather I did—writing him long, passionate letters every night. Stanley sent me only one post card, noncommittal and offhand, ending with a joke. Not a word about our lovely day in the park. I solaced myself by imagining that he was just being cautious—everybody knew how counselors sometimes open their campers' mail.

When I arrived back in Brooklyn that fall, I waited for his phone call. It didn't come. As the days passed, I became more and more heartsick. I could barely contain myself until the first theory class, when I knew we would meet. I invented elaborate scenarios to explain his silence: his mother was dying and he had to stay with her in the hospital, leaving him no time to call; *he* was dying and his mother, knowing nothing about our Sunday in Central Park, didn't think to call me; he had burned the tips of all of his fingers and couldn't dial.

I walked up the steps of Cousin Millie's brownstone that first Saturday in a near panic. Suppose he wasn't there? Suppose he was—what would I say to him? When I entered, he was leaning against one of the Steinways, bantering with a girl new to the class. He saw me come in, waved nonchalantly, and resumed his conversation. He made no move to talk to me then or later. I spent the next hour in dumb misery, staring at the back of Stanley's head, half-blinded by tears.

Just before I left, Cousin Millie came over to me and put her arm around my shoulders, the first time she had ever touched me. She bent down, her lips close to my ear.

"I know it hurts," she whispered, "but don't take it seriously. He just doesn't know who you are. Someday, somebody will. So grieve not."

Such sweet, archaic words, such an unexpected kindness. Made speechless by the startling new intimacy that had suddenly arisen between us, I stared at her open-mouthed, threw my arms around her and kissed her hard on her cheek, knocking off her pince-nez in the process. Then I ran home, a jumble of incredulity and abject misery, and spent the rest of the day under the covers trying to sort myself out.

Whenever I think back to that time, it is only with difficulty that I can conjure up a clear image of Stanley, except for his disembodied lips, hovering some five feet above the ground, meeting mine in bright, erotic purity. But Cousin Millie appears to me often in my dreams, exactly as she was in every detail, causing me each time to experience anew the sharp, joyous shock of the unexpected gift.

Aunt Evelyn

I was admitted to the High School of Music and Art after a botched piano audition and an ear test. I never understood how I made it. My father said it was probably my musicianship, a mysterious something he insisted I had in abundance. Whatever got me in was OK with me, as I'd wanted to go to that prestigious institution ever since I learned of its existence.

At the time, every entering pianist was assigned a second instrument, so that he or she could participate in ensemble playing. My assignment was bassoon. It was a bit of a misfit: at the age of twelve, I was just under five feet in height, and the instrument was only a little shorter. For the next month, I plumbed its mysteries and was soon able to get an occasional sound out of it that vaguely resembled music. I liked the contrast we presented: besides our relative sizes, my own voice was light and high, while its was deep and mellow, lending me an air of authority I did not otherwise possess.

The following week, my father's bartering efforts launched me on four years of orthodontia. This unfortunate timing scotched my future as a bassoonist; braces, which in those days included wires threaded between each tooth and twisted around the bar that ran across the front of the teeth, made it impossible to avoid shredding the reed. So it was goodbye to the bassoon, and hello to the freshman chorus, the default setting for anyone who, for whatever reason, was unable to stay with their second instrument. This was the first time I noticed that my singing voice was fairly pleasant.

It took my father only a year to decide that I had as much of a future as an opera star as I had as a concert pianist, at which time he contacted my Great-Aunt Evelyn, a sister-in-law of my Grandma Gottfried. She auditioned me shortly thereafter and advised him to come back in three years when my voice was more mature. Though he was disappointed, he followed her advice. When he resubmitted me a couple of years later, she agreed to take me on.

Aunt Evelyn gave singing lessons in a little studio apartment on the sixth floor of a residential hotel on the west side of Manhattan that catered to European émigrés; White Russians, Hungarian aristocrats and German Jews who had fled the Holocaust made up most of its tenancy. She had been widowed in her forties by a husband who was subject to fits of violence and had, it was whispered in the family, beaten her severely on several occasions. It was no doubt his Magyar temper that involved him in a feud with a blacksmith in a neighboring village, who finally settled their differences by bludgeoning him to death. Aunt Evelyn never spoke of her husband, nor did she ever remarry, retreating into a cold silence if the subject ever came up.

She was one of the most cultured women I knew, and certainly the most beautiful, remaining so even into her seventies. Short and slim with an erect carriage, her face was a study in planes and curves. When she smiled, her skin stretched taut across her sharply etched cheekbones, making exotic oval hollows beneath them. As she aged, her skin became delicately lined, the wrinkles fine as the strands of a spider's web. I would wait for opportunities to look into her eyes—they were the color of emeralds, clear as a tropical sea, with an extra fold of skin over the lids, giving her a slightly Asian look. She spoke in a lightly accented literary English, her voice bearing evidence of her vocal training in its melodic lilt. She smelled, always, of lavender.

As she had never remarried, Aunt Evelyn was not a candidate for insurance, so my father's arrangement with her was different. He became her chauffeur at specified hours during the week, driving her to visit those of her friends who lived in the less accessible areas of the city and once a month on a weekend to see her sister, who had inexplicably settled in a little town upstate called Tillie Foster.

Aunt Evelyn had missed fame and fortune by an accident of fate. When she was twenty, she had somehow wangled an audition with Victor Herbert, the acknowledged king of operetta, who, struck by her petite beauty and spirited performance, offered her the leading role in his next production. But he died only days later, before he could make good on his promise, and she'd had to remain in the relative obscurity of the chorus. Embittered, she had married soon after.

Following her husband's death, she came to the United States. Here, she was forced to teach voice to support herself. Her own near miss years before had imbued her with the desire to find a young singer who would achieve the success that had eluded her. She took me on as her protégé when I was sixteen, hoping I might be the one to fulfill her frustrated ambition.

Her passion and mine, although I'm not sure if it resulted from her influence or not, was German Art Songs, known as *lieder*. At the beginning of every lesson, another one of her students would join me in singing Mozart duets. But afterwards, Aunt Evelyn and I would spend a joyful hour digging out the subtle meanings buried in the poetry of Heine and Goethe in the songs we both loved, so that I might interpret them with the fullest understanding.

Each time I entered her cluttered studio, she would search my face to gauge my readiness to work. Aunt Evelyn was quick to catch any wavering of purpose, and although she never asked me any questions about my life away from her, she had an uncanny knack of knowing when I was unsettled or distracted. If she doubted my dedication on certain days, she would capture my attention with dazzling predictions about my future. It always worked.

With Aunt Evelyn, singing was as much a muscular as an artistic act. I left each lesson flushed with the physical effort she demanded of me during my vocalizations, but exhilarated by my deft turning of a difficult phrase and the heady possibilities of divadom she held out for me. Then, during the third year of her tutelage, I fell in love.

Joe was the much younger brother of my mother's best friend. She and my mother had schemed to get us together as soon as he returned from overseas after the war. I loved him on sight. He possessed every quality I found attractive in a man, including unattainability, having, unbeknownst to his sister, fallen in love with an English girl he'd met while serving in World War II. He was torn about their becoming engaged at the time, but planned to bring her to this country so that they could make a decision based on real life instead of on the heightened emotions of a war-time romance. He told me about Peggy early on, hiding none of his intentions toward her, insisting that he had not made a commitment. He had revealed all this to me, but not to his sister. Although I had little confidence in myself, I decided to try to win him over by being as wonderful as my father and Aunt Evelyn kept telling me I was.

Joe was cautious about spending money, as he was saving up for Peggy's ship passage, a project that would ultimately take him two years. This resulted in our spending a considerable amount of time alone in his garret room on the top floor of a small limestone building around the corner from Aunt Evelyn's studio. There, partly due to our raging hormones and, I suppose, for lack of other entertainment, we became lovers.

It was my first affair, and it opened up to me a world of emotional intensity and delicious sensation that eclipsed my interest in all other things, including my lessons with Aunt Evelyn and her dizzying predictions about my future. I increased the number of my voice lessons from two to three a week so that I would have an excuse to go even more often into Manhattan from my home in Brooklyn. I would spend a couple of delectable hours with Joe on his narrow bed, then go to Aunt Evelyn's studio, barely able to contain my impatience for the hour-long lesson to end, because Joe would pick me up afterwards and walk me back to the subway. The hours between our meetings were filled with thoughts of Joe and of our lovemaking. My schoolwork plummeted to a C, and my practicing of both piano and voice became mechanical exercises, my mind on Joe's and my most recent encounter instead of the Schubert Fantasia or Mozart aria I was working on. In 1946, the year I was nineteen, a love affair was not a subject one discussed even with a close friend unless she was also having one. So I was forced to keep it to myself, guiltily turning it over and over in my mind until it crowded everything else out.

This state of affairs did not escape the notice of my Aunt Evelyn. Her perceptions were too sharp to miss the aura of sexuality and guilt that covered me like a burnoose. She began to regale me with little homilies like these:

"Art to an artist is like love to an ordinary man or woman."

and

"Music will nurture your soul more than anything
else, so do not waste your time on passing fancies."

And oddly, revealing her uncertainty about the gender of my distraction:

"Never sleep with a woman. If you do, you will give up
all other forms of love, and possibly even your music."

I wondered how she'd found out.

One day, unable to contain herself any longer, she asked me point blank if I was having an affair. I felt an enormous sense of relief at being given this unexpected opportunity to share my secret, especially with someone I so admired, and who, I felt, would love me despite my transgression. So I joyfully told her about Joe and my newly awakened feelings, marveling aloud at what wonderful things love and sex were. She listened, one finger pressing into the hollow beneath her cheekbone, the other tapping on the closed piano lid. There were lines in her forehead that I had never seen before.

"And he, what does he feel for you?" she asked.

I did not welcome this question. Could I admit to her that it was only during our lovemaking that he seemed to love me, that the most positive comment he'd ever made to me about myself was that I reminded him of his sister—intense, bright-eyed, busy, and always with a Schirmer's music folder under my arm? No, I could not. So I composed what was probably an unconvincing tale of ways he demonstrated his love. I don't know if Aunt Evelyn believed me or was even listening, because it became obvious that she was already preparing her response. Still frowning, her expression became one of extreme distaste, and she began to speak.

"Now listen here, child. This sex business, it is disgusting. It takes only a few minutes out of every day. How can you think even for a moment of letting it replace your devotion to music? What do you think makes Elizabeth Schwartzkopf a shining star? Is it that she is debauched by some clumsy man in the middle of the night, or is it how much joy she gives to the world with her God-given talent? If you neglect your music for a few moments in bed with someone who is using your body for his own filthy purposes, then you are a fool and you should never have been given the gift of your voice!"

Her lips clamped shut in a thin line and she glared at me with flaming eyes.

Her words left me dumbfounded. I couldn't believe that my beloved teacher had actually spoken them. With those few sentences, she severed the bond that had existed between us for more than three years. Feeling sick, I left without taking my lesson and didn't return for a week.

My liaison with Joe lasted for the better part of two years, until he finally accumulated enough money to send for Peggy. Their wartime romance was re-ignited and they married soon after her arrival. I had resumed my lessons with Aunt Evelyn, but we never recaptured the exhilaration of the shared sense of purpose we'd had in earlier days. A part of me, an angry part, had closed to her. When I married a year later and gave up music altogether, I felt equal parts relief, regret and a cold malice toward Aunt Evelyn.

Ironically, she died of throat cancer not long after. My mother told me that in pain and almost voiceless, Aunt Evelyn had once asked wistfully why I never came to see her. It was many years before I could understand her speech to me for what it really was—an expression of her own lost opportunities and the tragic emptiness of her emotional life—and acknowledge for the first time my own capacity to inflict cruelty. For in my anger and disappointment at what I had interpreted as her callousness, I had matched hers, in far greater measure, with my own.

Ralph

From the time I started to date, a man had to have three qualifications in order to interest me: humor (not too broad), intelligence (not too narrow) and talent (for anything but sports). But there was a fourth, which, if he lacked, nothing could make up for: he had to be less attracted to me than I was to him. Looks had nothing to do with it—I went for the head. I could have fallen in love with Quasimodo if the first time I saw him he was chipping away at a piece of marble and didn't give me more than a passing glance. My romantic history bears this out.

Two years before my affair with Joe, I had a dreamy, long-distance relationship with Sasha, the son of our piano tuner. He was being trained in the art by his father, and was turning out to be one hell of a piano tuner. The Mason Hamlin would sing like a coloratura after he had finished voicing it. Handsome he wasn't—he had a lantern jaw—but that didn't make any difference. I had a mild crush on him before he was drafted, but he became infinitely more desirable to me when he was sent to Texas and fell in love with a Dallas girl, who, his mother told me, had never seen a Jew before. We had been corresponding, and I continued to write to him even after he told me about his fiancee, my letters filled with the pain of unrequited love. Then he got married and his wife asked me to stop.

After Joe there was Jerry, who had discovered war when he was inducted into the army in 1943, spending the war years as a paratrooper who dropped every so often inside enemy lines. He liked the unpredictability of it, and the danger. For a couple of years after the war ended, something he very much regretted, he would periodically scoot over to the nearest international conflict, eventually collecting a good number of "Dear John" letters from disaffected girlfriends who couldn't take the competition.

At the time I met him he was a philosophy major at Princeton, thereby meeting one of my requirements. He also had a dry sense of humor, meeting another. My talent requirement was also met: he made nice little watercolors of bodies of water. What was missing was the fourth: unavailability. But a short time after we started going together, he volunteered to go to Israel to fight for a Jewish homeland. He first spent two months training secretly in a kibbutz in New Jersey, working up quite an appetite for the coming battle. He wasn't even Jewish. He would write me amorous letters from somewhere in New Jersey and later from Jerusalem, but they didn't fool me—I knew when I was being rejected. As my husband would later say: "If somebody says he loves you, but he's walking in the other direction, believe the feet." I spent a lot of time looking at the back of Jerry's shoes, and loving it.

Following Jerry, the son of another one of my mother's friends crossed my orbit briefly. Ted and I had only a couple of desultory dates, but I dreamed about him for a long time. He was dark and intense, and a poet. He had no sense of humor to speak of, but he made up for that by being so intelligent that I could understand very little of what he said. Every sentence he spoke was elliptical, abstruse, or studded with obscure references. It's too bad it didn't work out because he was also a depressive, which, in addition to his lack of interest in me, would have made him my ideal lover.

Then I had a brief interlude with the brother of one of my friends. Charlie was a cellist, a professional—he played with the New York Philharmonic most of the week and with me on Saturday afternoons. At first it was platonic. I waited impatiently for him to finish an affair he was concluding with an accompanist he had worked with in Boston. When that was over, he began to concentrate on me. The trouble was that as soon as this happened he lost his appeal. Even his cello playing, which I had found almost unbearably erotic, failed to move me once he turned his feet in my direction. I suddenly became aware that he was shorter than I was and fat, and that beads of sweat would form on his upper lip whenever he kissed me. When I refused to go to bed with him, he gave up on me in disgust. Poor Charlie—how could he know that now that he'd become available, it was time for me to move on to less green pastures.

* * *

My friend Blanche had been trying to get Ralph and me together for several months. She had met him through her fiancé and wanted to introduce us, but Ralph had steadfastly refused to participate in anything so contrived as a blind date. He wouldn't accept invitations to her parties because he knew I'd be there, nor would he take my phone number to call me on his own. I think part of his reluctance had to do with the fact that I was twenty-one and Jewish. He preferred to terrorize his mother with *shiksas* in their thirties. In reality, they were just friends from the film business, but how was his mother to know that?

One evening around dinnertime, the phone rang. It was Blanche telling me excitedly that Ralph had finally agreed to meet me. It was a week before her wedding, and she and her fiancé were visiting her grandmother, who was too old and frail to attend. By coincidence, her grandmother lived in Bensonhurst, only two blocks from Ralph's apartment. He would walk over that evening if he got home in time.

My first reaction was annoyance. It meant an hour on the subway—Bensonhurst was a world away from Crown Heights in more ways than one—and I'd intended to wash my hair, a weekly ritual that was overdue by two days. Anyhow, what kind of *chutzpah* was it of him to give me such short notice and to be tentative about it to boot? Then I began to feel faint stirrings of interest. Blanche had already described him as having a great sense of humor (wry), intelligent (no college, but a prodigious reader), talented (currently working as an assistant editor on a Robert Flaherty documentary) and good-looking (irrelevant, but a nice bonus). And now the piece de resistance—he had rejected me before we'd even met! It augured well, So, I asked for directions, quickly dry-shampooed my hair, put on a dress that showed some breast, and took the train to Bensonhurst to meet what I didn't know then was the next forty-seven years of my life.

I needed my glasses to see the number on the house, but just before I rang the bell I slipped them into my purse, leaving me for all intents and purposes half-blind. Without my glasses, the world was one big pointillist painting, but I could manage all right if there wasn't too much walking involved. I groped my way into the kitchen, met Blanche's grandmother, and made conversation until Ralph arrived a few minutes later.

Even with my dim vision, I could tell that he was as Blanche had described him: tall and very good-looking. But he greeted me stiffly and took a chair as far from where I was sitting as he could get, making it difficult for me to examine him further. His obvious disinclination to be there made me angry, and after a strained half-hour I decided I never wanted to see him again. I preferred my rejections a little less overt.

But I hadn't counted on Blanche's grandmother, a tiny, wizened gnome of a woman in her nineties, who had some ideas of her own. Just as the visit was coming to an end, she made the motion 'wait' with her hands. She disappeared into her pantry, came out with a small jar containing a translucent pink liquid, and filled two delicately etched wine glasses to the top. She handed one to Ralph and one to me.

"Drink!" she said imperiously in Yiddish.

"What is it," I asked Blanche, who translated my question and came back with the answer.

"She said that it's rose wine, and that you should drink it."

Amused, we drank as Blanche's grandmother watched us intently. She then motioned that we should exchange glasses and take another sip. We did, and her face broke into a wide smile. She told us that she had known the minute she saw us together that we were a match made in heaven. Rose wine was a love potion, she said, with Blanche translating, and once having drunk it, we would fall in love and never love anyone else. Basically, she was right, with one or two detours. Powerful stuff, that rose wine. It broke the ice. We all walked over to Ralph's place, and before we left, he asked me for a date. I accepted.

Three weeks later on the Staten Island ferry, Ralph turned to me in the damp spray, put his hands on my shoulders and said, completely out of context, "If I can get over my hang-up about responsibility, will you marry me?"

This was totally unexpected. We had seen each other several times with enjoyment and a promising exchange of feelings and philosophies of life, but marriage? After so short a time?

I reviewed our relationship so far. We had spent one afternoon at the beach with his mother and his Aunt Leah; I had debated with myself beforehand whether to wear my modest bathing suit for them, or the skimpy one for him. Skimpy had won, but he hadn't seemed especially impressed. I had played and sung for him once, my ace-in-the-hole, but although he listened intently, he hadn't asked me for an encore. We had gone to the theater one night and he'd been unnaturally quiet on the way home; later he told me that he had been disgusted at the way I was swept right onto the stage by a very bad play, this deplorable lack of discrimination on my part causing him to question my suitability as a prospect. (He didn't know it was my first play.) He had kissed me only a couple of times, but I was already developing a taste for his mouth. I'd already seen his depressed side and what seemed to be an over-concern about financial security; he was working in a freelance field. But I blamed his depression on what he had told me of his father's recent death after five years of taking care of him at home and having to drop out of college at the age of sixteen to support his parents. His insecurity, like his depression, struck me as just another romantic manifestation of sensitivity, a trait I greatly admired. And we had never been to bed together, his never having raised the subject satisfying my ever-present appetite for rejection.

I ruminated further. He was far more interesting than anyone I'd ever gone out with. Funny, bright, attractive and still uncommitted, he met all of my requirements and more. I stood there weighing Ralph's pros and cons as the lights of the ferry terminal drew near. It was true that he met my darker needs, but he also met my healthier ones. Five minutes after his proposal, I had made my decision.

"Sure," I said. "Let's go home and tell everybody."

This seemed to dampen his enthusiasm for a moment; I think he wanted me to mull it over until he himself was comfortable with the idea, but he agreed. That night, my mother and father called all our relatives to tell them the good news. Marrying off a daughter in those days was tantamount to winning the Irish sweepstakes. It was worth about the same amount of money in savings over the years.

The next evening, Ralph came over for dinner. Aunt Sophie and Uncle Harvey, who lived miles away across the East River, were first—they said they were just passing by. Then Grandma Gottfried, and my father's brothers and sisters-in-laws, dropped in with Aunt Fannie—just out for a walk, they said. My Grandma Becky even took the train down from Thirty-fourth Street on the pretext of delivering some altered dresses, and one by one, my mother's aunts arrived, happy for my mother, but in some pain over the fact that their daughters, all of them older than I was, were still single.

Everyone approved of Ralph. They liked his overgrown *bar mitzvah* boy looks and the fact that he was employed in motion pictures, though none of them quite understood what it was he did. I wasn't exactly sure then either. We celebrated our engagement that weekend by making love for the first time in a little motel in Tanglewood, having gone there with Blanche and her new husband as chaperones to satisfy my father and Ralph's mother.

Ralph's family wasn't quite as happy about me as mine was about him. His Aunt Leah felt he deserved someone better, someone from a moneyed, or at least a professional, family. She wanted to know what the rush was, getting engaged after only three weeks and planning to be married only a couple of months later. She was sure that I was either pregnant, a divorcee, or in the terminal stages of some dread, preferably social, disease. Only the passage of time and a check she ran at the marriage license bureau eased her suspicions.

Where to get married became the next problem. We were both contemptuous of organized religion, as was fashionable among young people of that time, trying to escape their origins. Still, the prospect of a civil wedding seemed too impersonal to both of us. One of my friends had recently been married in the study of the assistant rabbi of Temple Emanuel, an imposing synagogue on Manhattan's Fifth Avenue. I had liked the relative informality of the setting—a small, wood-paneled room with just enough space for a few close friends and relatives—and suggested it to Ralph as a good compromise. He agreed, and we set up an appointment to meet with the rabbi.

Rabbi Perelman, a bland, mild-mannered man who nearly faded into the wallpaper behind his large mahogany desk, did his best to put us at ease, as we were obviously intimidated by the situation and the enormity of our decision to marry. After a few minutes of small talk, he asked if we had any special requests for the ceremony. I hadn't thought about it because I didn't know we had any choices, but no one would have known that from the alacrity with which I answered.

"Yes," I said to the man who was next in line for the chief rabbinate of one of the most prestigious synagogues in the country. "Make it as short as possible, and please don't mention God." To his credit, he didn't even blink.

The ceremony went off without a hitch. Although the rabbi did find it necessary to mention God once near the end, I'm sure that the deity had never made so brief an appearance in Temple Emanuel. And short it certainly was. Ralph's Aunt Leah, who arrived just before the rabbi spoke the first words of the ceremony, was still removing her hat when it ended.

Before we could leave on our honeymoon, Ralph had to finish an editing job that would take a couple of weeks. So we moved directly into our new apartment on the second floor of my parents' brownstone, and I set about learning to do the things that wives commonly did. There was one problem: I had never made even a cup of tea. In my father's house, my mother did all the cooking. It had never occurred to me that someday I might need to do my own. My father, having expected me to have servants when I married, hadn't thought of it either.

It was expected that from the day after the wedding, I would be doing the cooking. The prospect filled me with dread. What should I make? How does one go about making a meal and having everything ready at the same time? I was too proud to ask my mother, and anyway, she was giving piano lessons that afternoon. I sat with my head in my hands, a married woman planning her first dinner with a heart full of dread.

When Ralph returned home from work that evening, I greeted him at the door, a new apron wrapped around my waist. Excitedly, I led him into the kitchen. Dinner was already on the table.

"Look," I said proudly. "Our first meal."

There, in a large bowl, I had placed two sliced bananas. In a smaller bowl next to it, was a half-pint of sour cream, and as a decorator touch I had carefully stood a tablespoon upright in the middle of the sour cream bowl. It was beginning to list. Two slices of buttered toast, no longer hot, lay hardening on a plate next to the bananas; I had toasted the bread too early.

I was too pleased with myself to pay much attention to Ralph's look of dismay. His sense of humor has never operated in situations where his comfort is at stake. He had never thought to ask me if I could cook. Even he could cook. He thought everybody could. We sat at the table and ate in silence, me feeling mature and nurturing for the first time in my life, and Ralph wearing an expression bordering on panic, fearing that marriage to me might mean the permanent loss of hot meals.

Eventually, I learned the secrets of the kitchen. But there are few things I've made that have tasted as good to me as that dinner of bananas and sour cream on the first day of my new life.

My Daughter

Emily was conceived by thermometer and expelled by laxative—not a very romantic genesis. Reluctant to begin, she was also reluctant to emerge. The birth pains were at first indistinguishable from the contractions of my upper bowel, which had been subjected to a large dose of castor oil. But soon the one separated itself from the other and Ralph and I hurried off to the hospital. We arrived close to midnight and she wasn't born until nearly seven the next morning, the intervening hours filled with an intensity of pain I had never imagined possible. The birth, at my insistence, was to be without the help of any drugs. Many times during that night I came close to asking for something that would relieve the terrible pressure on my back and the contractions that seemed always at their peak. But I had been trained in the virtue of seeing things through, and besides, I was an unshakeable believer in Grant Dick Read, the doctor who had pushed for a rebirth of natural childbirth (no pun intended) and had written a bestseller to that effect.

An eternity later, it became time to move me to the delivery room. A loud rushing sound filled my head. Around me there seemed to be wild gyrations of movement and activity. My glasses had been taken from me, which only added to the sensory unreality. Everything was gray and swirly and out of focus. I was chaos itself. Although conscious, I was not aware of anything but the pain, which was total and eclipsed all other sensations.

The activity around me seemed to become more frantic. The sound of rushing water was getting louder and louder. It seemed there was no end to the pain—my entire life had been spent in agony on this table, my arms strapped down, people bending down to peer between my legs, exhorting me to "Push harder, HARDER!" There was one last enormous contraction. For a moment my whole being was a clanging, a tearing, a screaming.

Then silence. Brightness. Bodies in pale green moving slowly about the room. And an unfamiliar weight on my stomach. My head was swimming, but I felt a deep, deep calm. Someone said, "You have a little girl." I raised my head to see what was pressing on my belly. It was my daughter, lying on her back with her tiny arms waving, a nurse steadying her with one hand. My head fell back against the delivery table and I looked up at the ceiling, seeing it only dimly through the haze of my nearsightedness. And then I felt something begin to build in me. It started in the spot where my baby was lying and slowly infused every inch of my body. I felt as if someone was blowing me up. I was getting as big as a Thankgiving Day parade balloon. I would soon float off the table, grow too large for the room, burst through the ceiling. What I was feeling was joy—pure, exquisite joy, more intense than any sensation I'd had before.

Other women have described this sensation as orgasmic. I am very fond of orgasms myself, but they don't begin to match what I felt at that moment. Looking back from the final years of a life that has contained its share of splendid moments, there is nothing I have ever experienced that comes close to the wild, cosmic rapture I felt when, fully awake and free of pain, I first looked upon my daughter and felt the weight of her body on mine.

Emily, as children do, was growing, changing, learning. I was not. After a second child, a move to the suburbs had granted us the boon of fresh air, greenery and good schools. But it also meant for Ralph new responsibilities, a tedious commute, and the start of a new kind of irritability. He had only reluctantly agreed to have children, and had not, as I'd expected him to, fallen in love with fatherhood. For me, children and full time housewifery meant the acquisition of a whole new set of skills of otherwise limited usefulness: how to judge the fastest moving line at the supermarket, how to gracefully turn down requests to contribute to the temple or join Hadassah, avoid subscribing to The Watchtower or buy an oversupply of Girl Scout cookies, how to dodge invitations to local dinner parties where the most interesting topic of conversation was on the level of how to separate different kinds of garbage for the twice-a-week pickups, how to say no graciously to my next door neighbor when she invited me for coffee at ten, martinis at three, an orgy at nine.

I was restless. I might have gone back to music, but that was my father's ambition, not mine, and I was glad to be rid of it. My days were filled with household chores and the care of my two children—my son, Paul, had been born the year before—but my mind was on idle. I felt as if I were living in a Thurber house that with its occupants had totally enveloped me. It seemed to me that I had no identity but those of wife and mother, and that on my shoulders I was carrying a shrunken head. The responsibility for the growth and well-being of my family was something I had accepted willingly and had no wish to give up, but my own growth was at a standstill, my own well-being unattended to. I was still too steeped in the social system of my time to understand that that aspect of my life, fair or not, was my responsibility and mine alone to change.

Emily started kindergarten. I would watch her go off each morning holding her Mickey Mouse lunch box with a mixture of love, sadness and dissatisfaction. When she got to the top of the hill, she would turn and wave one last time, and I would go back into the house to my son and my housework, dulling my vague feelings of unhappiness with immaculate dishwashing, creaseless bed-making, the impeccable ironing of Ralph's socks and the creation of nightly gourmet dinners far beyond our ability to digest. My situation was certainly not unique in 1956, but I chaffed at it, it seemed to me, more keenly than any of the other women I knew. Then I began to have a recurrent dream about taking tests.

I had finished college twelve years before, grateful that I would never have to take another written examination. For years I hadn't thought about those days: the anxiety, the sleepless nights, the tense time spent in limbo waiting for the grades. That I always did well made no difference—I suffered each time with the same intensity. Now, all at once, I found myself taking an examination every night in my sleep.

It was always the same dream. After walking up an endless staircase, naked among clothed strangers, I enter a large hall and take a seat at a desk chair with a thick stack of test papers on its arm. The proctor, always my father, gives the signal to start. Everyone begins to write. Panicked, I realize I don't have anything to write with. The clock maddeningly ticks away the time. After an interminable search, a pen miraculously appears in front of me. With relief, I pick it up. At that moment the bell rings, signaling the end of the test. With fresh panic rising in my throat, I awaken, choking.

I can take a hint. Other interpretations aside, and I know there are many, I took this to mean that I had to go back to school. Not only was I feeling the need more and more to fill the growing hole in my head, but I knew it was imperative that I prepare for the time when both my children would be occupied all day and I would not. Our digestive systems wouldn't have been able to take the effects of further sublimation. For a while, I cast about aimlessly for a direction. I might have taught piano again, but that life was behind me. A career in education seemed a reasonable choice, mainly because of the hours. The problem was that nursery school teaching was out—I couldn't face the thought of having to buckle all those galoshes—and so was classroom teaching, because I had patience for children only in small groups.

Around this time, Paul was showing evidence of a delay in his speech development and I'd begun to do some reading to calm my growing anxiety. It wasn't long before I'd become interested enough in speech pathology to think about making it my profession. So I set about getting Ralph's permission (*of course* he and the children wouldn't be inconvenienced—I would do everything I had done before, only faster), enrolled part time at Columbia, and kept my promise to be Wonder Woman, finishing my degree exhausted but triumphant in less than three years. As before, dinner was always on time and the house kept pristinely clean. Within weeks of my graduation, I began working as a speech pathologist in the local public school.

When the same dream returned some ten years later, I didn't waste any time. I knew I had no choice. I left my job, which by virtue of its routine was becoming less and less rewarding, and started to work on a Ph.D., this time without asking for permission. I had embarked on still another of the series of changes that has marked my adult life, and continues to do so to this day.

But what of Emily? It was inevitable that she get less than her full share of my company and my attention, especially with the extra measure of both that my son required. I often worried if, because of this and my work, she missed anything important of me, or if, perhaps, I missed anything important of her. But I convinced myself that she would survive because she seemed so together. I was busy all the time, and something, I suppose, had to be lost, but there are still a few things I can remember . . . .

Emily and Paul are taking a bath together. She has just started kindergarten; he is about two. I am busy folding towels in the bathroom, careful to keep one eye on the bathtub to prevent drowning. I am especially enjoying the scene because the only time they play together is during bath time—the age difference is too great for them to share any interests, and anyway, Emily has lots of friends her own age to play with. I am careful not to give her too much responsibility for Paul, and I try to share my time equitably between them. This isn't always possible, because Paul requires a great deal of care: he is not developing as he should and is cranky and demanding a good part of the time. But Emily doesn't seem to mind; her generous nature gives her an aura of maturity and understanding beyond her years.

Emily is soaping herself, the ends of her braids trailing in the water, foamy with suds. Suddenly, Paul stands up in the tub and begins to urinate, the stream emerging from his penis in a high arc, making a hole in the soap bubbles. Emily watches in fascination. He finishes and sits down. She claps her hands delightedly. "What a thing for tomorrow's show and tell," she says. "Do it again!"

It is hot. Emily is fourteen. She is sitting back to back with her friend Bonnie on the steep slope of our lawn. My daughter is beautiful, slim and serene. Her waist-length hair is caught in a silver barrette, shorter tendrils curl damply on her forehead. Bonnie is her antithesis: plump and impish, cropped curly hair framing her pretty, round face. They are bending over their guitars, their hands moving silently across the strings. I sit a short distance away, holding a book I'm about to read. I am drowsy from the heat.

One of them idly begins to strum a few chords. In a moment they're singing *Where Have All the Flowers Gone*, their young voices drifting down the hill to where I'm reading. Bonnie's sweet, high voice carries the melody; Emily's darker alto stays a few tones below, following the melodic line in simple harmony. I place the book down on the grass and turn to look at them. My heart begins to swell with the beauty of the scene. I try to commit it to memory: the smell of the grass, the heat of the sun, the purity of their voices.

That was more than forty years ago. Where have all the flowers gone, indeed? We sold the house on the hill; it got too big when the children left. But often, when the grass is a certain shade of summer green and the air a certain texture, I close my eyes and live it again, that perfect moment. It is my sweetest memory: the two girls sitting on the hill, singing their song into the still air.

*　　*　　*

One sultry May afternoon, the year before Emily entered high school, I opened the front door to find standing there a tall young warrior in sneakers, his bare chest glistening with sweat and his shirt thrown over his shoulder.

He had obviously been running for a long distance and was breathing hard. He was about Emily's age, very black, and awesomely beautiful. Em had run to the door radiant when she heard his voice, and they went out to sit in the back. I could see them through the kitchen window as they sat on the lawn holding hands, sometimes moving their heads together to look more closely at a clover or a dandelion that one of them had plucked from the ground.

Every day for weeks, Olonzo, who was the junior high school track star, ran some two miles to spend an hour with Emily after school. He was almost the color of ebony, with a close, perfectly shaped Afro on his splendid head. Emily was fair-skinned, her dark hair long and silky. She usually wore it in a ponytail, but when Olonzo came, she would let it fall loose to her waist. They would sit together after his track practice, his hands idly playing with the ends of her hair as they talked, she reaching up once in a while to feel the rough roundness of his Afro. They made a charming chiaroscuro on the lawn.

One day, a few weeks after Olonzo had begun to make his daily appearances, Emily came home from school crying uncontrollably and threw herself on her bed. It was a while before she was able to tell me what had happened. Her gym teacher, a woman I'd often seen at faculty meetings, had taken Emily aside after class and advised her to stop seeing Olonzo. They'd been spending their lunch hours together walking on the school grounds and holding hands. Interracial friendships were uncommon in New Rochelle at that time, even between two people of the same sex, and the sight of those two joining hands from the opposite ends of the color spectrum aroused emotions in some members of the faculty that would have done justice to a Kentucky colonel during the Civil War.

The teacher had told Emily that her friendship with Olonzo would cost her the respect of all the Jewish boys she would want to date the following year when she got to high school, and that if she didn't give him up, her reputation would be ruined forever; she would be known as that loose white girl who dated a Negro. Olonzo's track coach had given him the same speech.

I was furious. I can't deny that when Olonzo first made his appearance at our door, I'd felt some discomfort. But it was soothed by my recognition that here was a chance to put my liberalism to the test. So far, I'd passed it admirably. I was outraged.

I raced to the school, hoping to catch Emily's gym teacher before she left for the day. Pulling the car to a screeching halt, I ran to the gym. She was on her knees helping a very fat girl do sit-ups by holding her down by the ankles. I strode up to her, grabbed her by the arm and pulled her to her feet. The fat girl fell heavily back to the floor.

"Now listen here, Helen," I said angrily, "How dare you make those racist remarks to my daughter! Tomorrow you will talk to her and retract everything you said. And it had better be convincing or I'll file a complaint with the principal, the school board, and the ACLU!"

Then I stormed out, leaving her standing with her mouth open: she'd expected me to feel the same way she did. The next day, Emily told me that her teacher had apologized, but gave me no details, though I pressed her to do so.

Emily and Olonzo continued to meet, but less and less regularly. The following year they entered high school, made new friends and drifted apart. I basked in self-congratulation over the stand I had taken when the chips were down—putting my money where my mouth is, so to speak. But something continued to nag at me. I found myself thinking often about that day, looking at the incident again and again for the part of it that didn't ring true. Why that strong surge of anger, the immediate involvement on my part? That kind of intervention wasn't at all my usual style. Was it simply a matter of the lioness rushing to protect her cub? If so, what was I protecting her from? Olonzo, not Emily, had received the deeper cut. I finally figured it out, and I didn't like what I learned.

What I had felt at that moment was not indignation but fear, and the fear was that any opposition placed in their paths might draw them closer, cement their relationship and increase the odds of their remaining together to an age where it might become serious. That episode taught me not always to be sure of the strength of my commitment to principles I supposedly espouse. For the fact is that despite what I thought then, I didn't pass the test. The Kentucky Colonel was me.

*   *   *

It was with mixed feelings, mostly positive, that I watched my daughter begin to emerge as a sexual being. I loved the new way she looked at boys, the dressing up, and the unaccustomed attention to her hair. Once, she even ironed it. Ralph was furious, but I understood that it was her generation's version of the permanent wave. We had never had any difficulty talking about sex; the only time I worried a little was when she told me at age fifteen that she intended to be a virgin until she got married. I had nothing against virginity per se, but I felt that it should be something that exists by default, not by intent. I expected her to take the next logical step and ask me about my own premarital history, but I was glad when she didn't. I wouldn't have enjoyed finding myself in the uncomfortable position of playing the wanton to my daughter's prude.

When she was seventeen, things began to change. She fell in love with Steve, a college sophomore, a status that added immensely to his appeal, and she was soon struggling with the decision of whether or not to go to bed with him. It was around the same time that my mother was asking my advice about Marcel. It made me feel more than a little hypocritical to be encouraging my mother's autumnal sex life and at the same time trying to hold my daughter back from the springtime of hers. For just as Emily had undergone a change of heart, so had I. I feared that she might get hurt, get pregnant, get married. These were real concerns, of course, but what I was also feeling was a kind of envy.

My marriage was going through a bad time. Ralph and I were barely talking to each other—the depression and dissatisfaction I had dismissed as unimportant when I'd first met him had grown more pervasive, as had his anger. I was feeling old, undesirable and discarded. Part of me dreaded Emily's entrance into the sexual arena as my equal; the way things were going, it would verify my obsolescence.

The combination of her awakening and my own deteriorating marriage led me into an odd relationship that might not have occurred otherwise. I don't suppose it could be called a love affair, but surely it was some kind of love.

I was working at the high school by then and had developed a reputation among my students for knowing how to listen without being judgmental. Some would come to my office after school hours to talk about concerns unrelated to their communication skills. One afternoon one of those students, John, came in very upset: a friend of his had made a suicide attempt the night before. His friend had been unhappy for a long time. Would I see him, to see if I could help?

The next day after school there was a tentative tap at the door. "Come in," I said, and when there was no response I walked across the room and opened the door. There stood a very thin, long-legged blond boy wearing wire-rimmed glasses and a look of such pain that I had to stifle an impulse to put my arms around him. He had a thick bandage wrapped around each wrist and his hands hung loosely at his side. He walked in and dropped listlessly into a chair. "I'm Mike, John's friend," he said.

We began to talk. It wasn't long before I realized that in addition to being depressed, he was unusually bright, with interests not typical of any of the other eighteen-year-olds I knew. He spoke of Korzybski, Hayakawa and Chinese ideographs, ancient civilizations and Greek myths. But when we talked about why he'd tried to kill himself (it wasn't a serious attempt—the razor cuts were fairly shallow) an air of detachment came over him. He said he never got close to anyone because he wanted to erase all feelings from his life. He had no intimate friends, not even John. Feelings were his enemy, he told me. They hurt. When I pointed out that he must have felt something pretty strong when he decided to cut his wrists, he shrugged.

"The only feeling I had about that was 'why not'?"

Mike began coming to see me every day after school He would talk to me in his strange monotone about something he was currently reading in philosophy, explain some obscure theory in general semantics, but through this intellectual smokescreen an unspoken message came through: Care about me. Love me. And so I did.

Sometimes, when his misery was so deep that he couldn't speak, I would hold him, feeling, despite his age and his superior height, as if I were comforting a very young child. Once in a while it crossed my mind that I could lose my job if we were ever found in my office with my arms around him, his head bending to rest on my shoulder, but I ignored my own concerns because he was so needy, and I very much needed to be needed.

I took him for long walks in the local park after school, strolling along the edge of Long Island Sound and watching the water form little pools of froth as it met the rocks along the shore. Sometimes we talked, and sometimes we walked in silence. Once in a while, he would ask something about me. But mostly, he talked about his despair.

Spring became summer and my children went to camp, Emily as a counselor in the same camp where Steve would be working, Paul as a camper. Ralph was seldom home, leaving my evenings as well as my days free. One summer evening I was sitting in my car with Mike. As we talked, darkness fell. Suddenly, a policeman drove up and beamed his flashlight into the car. He told us roughly to move on, as if we were a couple of lovers. I suppose that in some way, we were.

One evening I began to see us from an outsider's point of view and it struck me as ridiculous as well as dangerous: this tall, skinny, now nineteen-year-old hanging around with a somewhat overweight, forty-year-old lady who had children almost his age. I realized then that I must end it.

Over the next weeks, I watched him gain confidence and begin to be interested in the things and people around him. His passivity began to recede and he was smiling more often. He had lost that distant, distracted look that reminded me so much of my brother. Soon, he had fallen in love with Emily's friend, Bonnie, the singer on the hill, and embarked on his first affair. Part of me rejoiced in his metamorphosis, the other part ached for those summer afternoons when we would walk for hours along the Sound.

Summer was nearing its end. My children returned from camp. I wondered whether or not Emily had gone to bed with Steve. A year later she moved into his apartment, and I didn't have to wonder anymore.

*   *   *

The telephone rang while I was lying on the beach a few steps from our rented beach house. I heard it through the sound of the surf, the almost audible beating of the torrid heat and my own musings. Having leased the house for only a month, I would ignore the phone if I was outside when it rang, something I could never do in the city. But this time I found myself attributing to its ring more insistence than usual, and was running toward the house before I was conscious of having decided to answer it. As its ring had shattered the quiet air, so its message shattered my sandy tranquility. It was Emily, trying to hold herself together as she told me her news. The telephone has brought me many terrible messages—news of my father's death and my mother's, the loss of a friend—but never had one brought with it such terror.

When I became pregnant with Emily, a small amount of bleeding around the time of my second missed period suggested that her hold on my interior might not be sufficiently strong. It was feared that I might miscarry. In those years, there was a simple treatment routinely given in such cases: bed rest and a little white pill taken daily. These latter were diethylstilbesterol, or DES. The bed rest gave me no more than a mild case of boredom, which became an unexpectedly pleasant lassitude before my three-month bedroom exile came to an end. The other resulted twenty-three years later in this telephone call.

An "irregularity" had been found on her cervix. There was no way of knowing if it was benign or malignant until it could be excised and biopsied. The doctor, not knowing which, had carefully prepared—more accurately over-prepared—her for the possibility of a malignancy and a subsequent hysterectomy with a chance, while admittedly a small one, of it being a form of rapidly developing cancer that would take her life within months. The doctor's extreme response was perhaps understandable. He had delivered her nearly a quarter of a century earlier, It was he who had prescribed the medication that now was suspected of being the cause of cancer in many young women whose mothers had taken it during their pregnancies. His feelings must have been extremely complicated: a mixture of compassion, guilt and the need for self-protection.

My sun-baked brain didn't fully absorb the message and its implications until after she had agreed to stay here with us at the beach until the day two weeks hence, when she would enter St. Vincent's Hospital for surgery. I would pick her up at the train station that evening at seven.

That phone call stopped time. I had barely placed the phone back in its cradle when the shaking started. It was as if a finger of ice had touched my center. I walked into the bedroom and got into my warmest robe. I couldn't stop shaking. Gasping for air, I was suffocating in the terror of impending loss. I couldn't imagine losing her. My reaction was at first completely self-involved; it took a while before I could imagine what she must be feeling. I must have lived her death a thousand times in those first few hours, experienced a bereavement much greater than that which I'd felt after losing my mother.

I lay in bed shivering despite the warmth of the terrycloth robe, feeling alternate waves of love and loss and shaken by bouts of spasmodic sobbing that left me totally spent. After a couple of hours, I wondered how there could possibly be any tears left, but there were. In those hours, I had mourned my daughter as surely as if she had already died. But I was determined not to let her know how frightened I was. By the time she arrived, I had pulled myself into a semblance of calm by the force of a will I didn't know I had. She told me later that my false air of equanimity had reassured, but also infuriated her. She'd expected me to be more emotional.

Somehow we got through the waiting. Two agonizing weeks later, a benign tumor was removed and we were given an optimistic prognosis. But despite this, my life, as well as Emily's had been irrevocably changed. I'd been made aware of possibilities that I had never had to consider before. If I ever merit celestial retribution, I pray the sentence is not the taking of one of my children during my lifetime. In a very real way, I had already experienced the loss of a child. No one should have to suffer it twice.

*   *   *

As a child, she was elfin, good-natured and charming. I saw her as a gift. There was no situation that wasn't enhanced by her sweetness and quickness of mind. She lent an air of brightness to our often overcast household. Ralph's anger was like a tornado—charging the air, picking up nearby objects and leaving them broken and useless after it passed. He had never hurt the children or me, but the threat of danger was palpable every time a tempest hit. Emily always seemed able to find the eye of those storms and wait them out, emerging from them apparently undamaged. She was the only one of us that Ralph could tolerate in their aftermath, and so she became the one who negotiated a truce. I learned only much later how much she feared those destructive upheavals and resented her role as a conciliator.

As Emily grew older, she and I shared what I saw as an uncommon comradeship. Although we never lost sight of the fact that we were mother and daughter, we forged a friendship of a rare kind. In an effort to be as unlike my father as possible, I tried never to be needlessly directive, judgmental or arbitrary, preferring reason to demand, discussion to dictum. I was grateful every day for her presence in my life and believed that unlike me, she would remember her childhood years without rancor and come to maturity unscathed. But I had underestimated her resentment about the role Ralph and I had forced her to play.

The summer after her surgery, something changed: she was often sullen and depressed. We talked about it one day, and I remarked how sad it was that she had become so unhappy, especially when she had been such a cheerful child. It was then that she told me bitterly that her childhood hadn't been at all what I believed it to be, that instead of the self-assured, secure and happy child I had thought her, she had spent her early years in terror of Ralph's unpredictable eruptions and felt that instead of shielding her from them, I had used her as a buffer to protect myself. She told me, too, that she'd been extremely jealous of the extra time and attention I gave her brother.

I was astonished to learn about these feelings, never having guessed the depth of her fear or sense of neglect, so absorbed had I been in my own. It wasn't easy for me to integrate her truth into mine. Still, there was no doubt that for some time now she had seemed angry and unhappy. Notwithstanding the events of the summer before and the effect they might have had on her peace of mind, some of that change had to be due to the surfacing of those early, hidden resentments. But how could I have been so undiscerning? Could I really have known so little about my beloved child, I, who had always prided myself on my sensitivity to others' feelings? Was it possible for me to have so misread her state of mind? I agonized about it for a long time, unable to understand how insensitive I had been, failing to notice her pain. And then around the anniversary of my mother's death, I had a dream.

In it, my mother is standing over my brother, her back to me, grooming his hair in the manner of primates with their young, gently parting the strands and running her fingers along each one. I stand close by, watching them. She is young, in her thirties; I'm about ten, wearing my silvered flower girl dress. Wanting to attract her attention, I open my mouth to call her, but no sound comes. I try again, but again I hear nothing. I continue trying to call to her, feeling the air rush past my dry throat, jagged as a torn fingernail, as I desperately try to make myself heard. I begin to run toward them, only to find a wall of clear plastic between us. As I pound the thick sheet with my fists, it gives and stretches around me, enveloping my body in its folds. I am screaming soundlessly as I awaken.

I am thinking about that dream the next morning when all at once, I understand about Emily. I am amazed and ashamed at not having noticed the parallels before.

Just as my mother had been preoccupied with my brother, I had been preoccupied with hers. Worried about Paul and fearful of Ralph's anger myself, I hadn't noticed her terror or her feelings of abandonment. I had blithely accepted her façade as the reality. Like me, she had assumed the form but not the feelings of strength, and she'd pretended, as I had as a child, not to need what she desperately craved: protection and a fair share of my attention. She had learned to dissemble, knowing that they were beyond her grasp. Always perceptive, she had seen that my eyes, like my mother's before me, were turned in another direction.

My Son

In a way, birth is the first of many alienations we suffer during our lifetimes. In Paul's case, this was true in an especially poignant way. When I went into labor on March 20, 1955, I was suffering from bronchitis. Although I had planned to have a natural birth, as Emily's had been, my doctor was concerned about my lungs—in those days, only an inhalation anesthetic could be used if an emergency arose, and it might have caused me serious respiratory complications. So at his urging, I agreed to be put under completely before my labor got to an advanced stage. As a result, I saw Paul for the first time when I was already back in my hospital bed, still groggy and a little nauseous from the anesthesia, with no memory of his exit from my body. When I looked down at that tiny, red-faced stranger rooting blindly for my breast, there was no sense of recognition, attachment or accomplishment, nor was there any of the exhilaration I'd experienced with Emily. Instead, I felt cheated and depressed. Besides, I'd expected another girl. Since there was no logical reason for this expectation, I suppose "hoped for" are more appropriate words. I remember feeling surprised and disappointed when I was told his sex. Perhaps it was for this reason that my milk dried up within days of his birth and Paul was forced to go onto a bottle.

Considering my history with men, it seems almost predictable that I wouldn't do well with a boy child. Until Paul's birth, the only males with whom I'd had close contact were my brother, who with his incipient illness had tormented and later frightened me, my father, who in different ways had done the same, and later, the young men I'd become involved with, who, like Joe the Anglophile and Jerry the war lover, had ended by rejecting me. And my ordinarily troubled husband, who had only reluctantly given in to my desire to have children, was feeling increasingly more resentful for my having forced the issue, so to speak. This only reinforced my belief that men were difficult, dangerous, and unreliable. Now, at twenty-nine, still feeling very much like a child myself, I was expected to raise one of those fearsome and unpredictable creatures. I was terrified by the responsibility and set about it as surely as if I were acting by design to prove that I could only do it badly. Nature gave me all the help I needed.

Paul was in a lot of trouble as an infant. He had a digestive problem called celiac disease that gave him a great deal of pain, crossed eyes and a low tolerance for frustration. He cried for the first two years of his life, Ralph and I spelling each other every night to rock him over a door sill in his carriage so that we could each separately get some sleep. He would continue to cry even when I held him. I held him so much that I think he must have come to associate me with his pain.

As he got older, slow to reach the developmental landmarks immortalized by Gesell, we began to think he might be retarded. When he was just barely beginning to walk and was not yet talking by the age of two and a half, we were nearly certain that this was the case. We felt none of the special kind of love we're told most parents of handicapped children feel. We just became more and more tense, self-pitying and in Ralph's case, angry. I couldn't blame him—Paul was my idea. So to all my anguish was added a portion of guilt. The doctors were not encouraging.

Then, to our relief, but too late to give us any real sense of celebration, the words began to come, and it soon became evident that Paul was not retarded at all. His sentences were a bit eccentric, perhaps, but they made sense. Nevertheless, he pronounced words oddly and was often difficult to understand, unlike most of his contemporaries, who by this time were sounding like little adults. By the time he was ready for school, he was talking the proverbial blue streak, though most of it was unintelligible to everyone but me. He had by then abandoned walking for his tricycle, which he could maneuver as skillfully as an experienced parking lot attendant.

School was a difficult and frustrating experience for Paul. He learned to read, but didn't understand most of what he read. He could do simple arithmetic, but not the 'new math' that required complex mental operations. In second grade, when all the other children were learning abstract vocabulary words like 'security' and 'happiness', Paul, insecure and unhappy, was left feeling confused and inadequate.

It was around this time that Paul first expressed the wish to play the violin. I don't know where the desire came from, any more than I understand the time when, at the age of four on a trip to Jamestown, he suddenly announced in his strange syntax, "Me smell goat". As far as I knew, he had never seen, much less smelled, a goat. Then, with complete confidence, he led us across a field and behind a barn, where two goats stood quietly grazing. His attraction to the violin struck us as being comparable. We had no violinists in the family, and although we listened to a great deal of classical music, we had never singled out any one of the instruments. We tried to convince Paul to wait a while, since he was having difficulty in school and needed to spend a lot of time on homework. But he was so insistent that we finally gave in. We found him a teacher, and to his delight, a half-size violin that looked almost like a cello next to his small frame and delicate fingers.

He practiced four hours a day for the first month, two hours for the second, and hardly ever after that. But by the time he was eight, he had been accepted into the school orchestra and developed enough technique to reveal a sensitive and engaging musical spirit. He was made concertmaster shortly thereafter.

He loved to play at school concerts. And since he was enchanting to listen to and even more delightful to watch, he was often asked to be the soloist. Paul was short for his age, very thin and wore large round glasses on his as yet bridgeless nose. His hair was always uncombed, with a cowlick standing straight up on the back of his head. After a careful tuning, which often lasted long enough to cause repressed giggles in his audience, he would take his stance, as tense as a fencer preparing to lunge, and begin to play a Bach air or a Handel sonata, pulling from that tiny instrument sounds as sublime as birdsong. Listening to him play or accompanying him on the piano were among my most exquisite pleasures. But by the time he was nine, he was practicing no more than a few minutes a day, and those under protest. This situation created a great deal of friction between us, and colored much of our relationship for years.

The summer Paul was ten, we enrolled him in a music camp in Maine. I hoped the association with other musical children and his participation in the camp orchestra would help him socially—he had few friends—rekindle his ambition and motivate him to practice. We didn't discover until near the end of that summer that his experience there was a musical and personal disaster.

On the second day of camp, all the children were asked to audition in order to determine their place in the orchestra. Paul, hoping to make concertmaster, chose a Vivaldi concerto that had a flashy first movement, which had recently earned him kisses and compliments from visiting relatives. The camp director was so taken by the sight of that skinny little kid with the big glasses who stood so proudly with his back arched and his elbow held high and played with such sweetness and gusto, that he not only gave Paul the position of concertmaster, but also of unofficial camp mascot, which might have been good for his ego if it hadn't also earned him the undying hatred of his fellow players. The orchestra embarked on their rehearsal schedule, but to the children's increasing chagrin, they mostly rehearsed the Vivaldi.

There was a reason for this single-mindedness. The director, in an effort to publicize his camp throughout New England, had arranged to visit several local television stations with the orchestra and deliver a pitch for the next season. He did this by enlisting the help of the world's only classical commercial jingle, the Vivaldi Violin Concerto in A minor, with my son the star playing the solo part. Every weekend they would pack up their instruments, board the camp bus, and travel to one or another of the stations to perform the only piece they'd rehearsed all summer.

We heard its final performance at the farewell concert on the last day of camp. The parents, having come to collect their children, were an enthusiastic, if captive, audience. Paul stood alone in front of the podium, one sock hanging over his sneaker, a streak of dirt on his left cheek. The baton descended and the music began. He had never played so badly—it was obvious that he had simply worn the Vivaldi out. At the end, in the space between the last note and the beginning of the applause that was accompanied by the boos of more than one orchestra member, he heaved a great and clearly audible sigh of relief.

After several deep bows, he came toward us with an embarrassed smile, knowing how badly he had played, but hoping we'd be kind. He searched my face and evidently read it correctly, because his expression changed. Battered by his summer-long exploitation and the dislike and envy of the other children, he stood before me and fearfully awaited my verdict.

"You've disappointed me, Paul," I said. "If you'd bothered to practice, you'd have played it better."

Shades of my father! No, that's too easy. My words were hateful and without compassion, as his had been all those years before. But these were my own words, not his, and I cannot think of them now without shame.

*　　*　　*

There was a house at the end of our block that had stood empty for nearly a year. One spring morning, a huge moving van pulled into the driveway. By the time evening came, all of the furniture had been unloaded, but the new family was nowhere to be seen. The last people to own the house had been a trial to the neighborhood. So had their oversized sheep dog, who would run free, leaving great, steaming mounds of feces on all the lawns except his own. Wally, a boy in his late teens and the oldest of three sons, had been in the habit of making obscene phone calls to the neighboring women. He called our house once and got Paul, thinking it was me. Paul later told me that a high-pitched male voice had giggled some scatological words, the most memorable of which, as far as Paul was concerned, was "kaka". He got a big kick out of it.

We had to drive past their house to go almost anywhere. On a summer's day, all five of them would be bending over, gardening, their thighs billowing out from under their Bermuda shorts, their oversized buttocks shaped exactly alike. This wouldn't have been a factor had they not also been argumentative and abusive, but their obesity became just something else on which to peg our general outrage. So it was for esthetic as well as personal reasons that everyone was relieved when it became known that they had lost their house to foreclosure.

The morning after the moving van's appearance, Roz, the unchallenged block yenta, came out of her house and saw me sitting outside.

"I'm going to say hello," she called, gesturing in the direction of the newly occupied house. She turned and walked up the hill.

Three minutes later, she was on my front lawn in a state of extreme agitation, her face flushed and her arms waving in alarm.

"They're *Negroes*!!" she wailed. "They'll turn the neighborhood into a slum! They'll bring all their relatives to live with them! What will happen to my sixty thousand dollar investment?"

This last was news to me—her house, an exact duplicate of mine, had been valued at less than thirty thousand earlier that year. Wringing her hands, she ran off. By the time her mahjong group arrived an hour later, everyone in the neighborhood had been apprised that Mohegan Place, that old Indian enclave, now populated almost exclusively by Jews, had been invaded by the black hordes.

I was thought of as antisocial on the block. I never asked the other women in for coffee or participated in the usual welcoming ceremonies whenever someone new moved in, guarding my privacy with a fervor bordering on paranoia. But I did go to the emergency meeting that Roz called the next day, because my sense of fair play was being violated. After listening awhile to my neighbors' supposedly fiscal panic, I'd had enough. In the middle of one tirade, I announced that I was going over to welcome our new neighbors, and invited them to join me. No one moved.

As I walked up the hill, everyone came out and stood on Roz's lawn to watch. I looked back once and saw them standing together on the manicured grass, their hands on their hips, eyes hard, watching me. It was more than two years before any of them spoke to me again.

The new neighbor welcomed me warily and introduced me to her two daughters, one only a year older than Paul. She apologized for the mess and offered me a cup of coffee. We sat and spoke about how nice it was that Paul and her younger daughter were around the same age and could play together, then about the neighborhood school, their previous location—Michigan—and our husbands. As I was leaving, she looked me squarely in the eye and thanked me for coming. Her meaning was unmistakable. She could hardly help but know the consternation her arrival in the neighborhood had caused—the day before, Roz had stood open-mouthed at her door, unable to say anything at all before recovering sufficiently to mumble something about having the wrong address, and running off.

That evening, I told Ralph and the children about the new family. I described the neighborhood meeting and my defection. This was my children's fist exposure to bigotry, and they were fascinated. Emily, in the middle of reading a children's book on black history, was indignant; Paul, then eight, sat wide-eyed and silent, listening intently as I spoke.

After we finished, the children went out to play in the fading August light. A few minutes later, I received a phone call from my new neighbor. She was half-laughing and half-crying as she told me her story. She'd heard someone tapping at her door a few minutes before and opened it to find a small boy standing there, his fly open and his shirttail out, looking up at her over glasses that were hooked over only one ear. In his hand he held a bunch of buttercups and daisies that he'd picked on his way up the hill. He thrust them into Margaret's hands.

"Hi," he said "I'm Paul Rosenblum. Is there anybody in your house that needs a friend?"

I hung up choked with feelings of love and guilt. Because he was different, Paul was himself the victim of injustice, not only at the hands of other children, but, I must sadly admit, at mine. Perhaps it was this that even at that tender age had instilled in him the strong sense of justice that persists in him to this day, and which was never so sweetly evidenced as the time he sought to redress a wrong with the offer of his friendship and a fistful of wildflowers.

*   *   *

I love my son no less than I do my daughter, but because that love has always been overlaid with other less positive emotions, it was many years before he came to believe it. As a child, Paul drained all of my energy. On any given day, there were at least two or three places he needed to be driven to, waited for at, and driven back from. These included the dentist, the orthodontist, the ophthalmologist, the optometrist, the psychologist, the allergist, the reading and math tutors and the speech therapist. Later, added to these, were violin lessons and his orchestra rehearsals and performances. These were only the demands on my time. There were other demands—on my anxiety pool and psychic reserves. These I found to be the most difficult.

I was always receiving notes from his teacher complaining that Paul hadn't done his homework or had been daydreaming in class instead of filling in his workbook pages, or from the gym teacher complaining that he hadn't brought his sneakers to school for a month, or from his violin teacher complaining that he hadn't practiced enough, or from the orthodontist complaining that he wasn't wearing his rubber bands, or from the dentist complaining that he wasn't brushing his teeth properly, or from the school nurse complaining that he wasn't wearing his glasses in class.

When I wasn't driving him to and from all of these complainers, I was reminding him to do all the things he was reported not to be doing, and spending hours trying to help him understand what he hadn't grasped in class. I was often in a rage at having to listen to all the complaints about him. There were times I would weep from exhaustion and resentment over his excessive need for my time and involvement, which prevented me from giving either of these in great enough measure to Emily, my husband or myself: I had just started to work in the New Rochelle school system as a speech pathologist and was trying to give some attention to my own work as well. I was always worried about what the next complaint about Paul would be and how I would find the time and energy to handle it. I was always tired, and while I felt deep sympathy for his suffering, my inability to make any difference in his life despite the endless amount of help and extra time I was giving him made me want to scream in frustration. And I did, and often, turning my exhaustion and my feelings of helplessness into anger against the small creature who needed instead my love and support. His music, which had originally provided him with his only real source of enjoyment and sense of accomplishment, I made into an unpleasant duty by constantly nagging him to practice.

Too late I realized that I had played both my mother and my father with Paul. I had punished him for his fragility and for his talent with something very much like my mother's anxiety and my father's ambition. I gave him the kind of attention he would have been better off without, and obscured my love for him with impatience and anger. Paul and I have both suffered as a result. I wish it had been otherwise. But it is only because my son was so vulnerable that I've learned to weep for my brother. It is only because of my own unrealized ambitions for Paul that I have come to understand my father. And it is only because of the fears I've had for Paul that I am able at last to forgive my mother for Bo.

*　　*　　*

Ralph and I have spent the day with Paul in Hartford, where he is a freshman at Hartt Music School. It is a few weeks after he has begun hosting a jazz program on the college station. We say our goodbyes and set out for New York; he leaves for the studio to do his show. It is due to start in half an hour. We promised to listen to him on the way back, but as we drive on, his station begins to fade and static replaces the voice of the announcer. A little further on, we lose it entirely. We stop and debate whether or not to turn around and go back a few miles so that we can pick it up again. We're tired, it's late, rain is threatening, and we have a long drive ahead of us. But we have never heard Paul's show, and with his future in college tentative because of his poor grades, there is little enough for him to feel good about just now. We decide to turn back.

As we drive toward Hartford, the station begins to come in clearly. We stop on the side of the road, impatient for Paul's show to begin so that we can resume our trip. We are also a little apprehensive about what we're about to hear: Paul stutters when he's under pressure and gets very upset when he does. We want to be able to say truthfully that he was wonderful, but he won't believe us if his speech fails him. His having pursued this show in the first place had been a surprise to us because of his concern about his stutter, but he'd gone after it with a tenacity he hadn't shown since he first insisted on studying the violin.

The five o'clock program is ending. The station identifies itself. And then the voice of our son, rich and uncommonly fluent, makes the following announcement for all of the greater Hartford area to hear:

"I'd like to dedicate this program to my parents, who are on their way home somewhere on the Connecticut turnpike. My father taught me everything I know about jazz. Without his help I could never have done this show. Dad, this is for you." And then he plays "Ice Cream," a George Lewis recording and one of Ralph's favorites. It's a damp ride home—it is raining heavily and our cheeks are wet.

I sit there thinking of friends who are suffering through family problems and ask wearily, "Children—are they worth the hassle?" Then I remember Emily's birth, the two girls singing on the hill, Paul, nose running, playing his fiddle, this unexpected tribute, the sweet fullness of the sense of family.

"Yes, I whisper to myself, the car racing homeward. "Yes."

My Brother

I haven't seen my brother for many years. He would be eighty now, but I'm not even sure he's alive. Despite this, he remains a significant presence in my life. His image thrusts itself above the threshold of my consciousness like the sudden, sick throb of a dying tooth, emerging to the particular timbre of a voice, a similar profile. At such times I reluctantly, painfully, fearfully—though he was never really a threat—remember Bo.

I wasn't aware of his advent into my life, as I was fourteen months old when he was born. My parents named him Omar Cobb, the first name for its vibrations to please my father, and the second after Irvin S. Cobb, an author whose humorous account of his operation had caused my mother to laugh so hard that she opened her stitches two days after an appendectomy. As far as I can remember, he was never called anything besides Brother, later Bo, by anyone in the family until in his twenties when, in an effort to exorcise the Gottfried in him, he changed his last name to Henderson and his first name to John.

Until his middle teens, at which time the imprint of my mother's least attractive features began to emerge, he was a beautiful child with dark, curly hair. He had been born two months prematurely, and we grew up with tales of his fragility as an infant, an identity that overtook and finally eclipsed everything else about him. We were often told how, as an incubator baby, he was brought home during the fourth week of his life to lie in a bassinet lined with sterile cotton and be fed diluted formula every two hours with an eyedropper. He was so tiny that there was some doubt he would survive his first months. He did, though, eventually growing plump and healthy. But my mother never lost the uncertainty about his survival that she carried home with him from the hospital.

Her preoccupation with Bo's physical health left me feeling ignored. When I grew older, I came to understand that what seemed to be her preference was rather an obsession, but as a child, it hurt. For instance, when, at the age of ten I complained that I was having trouble seeing the blackboard, my father took me by subway to Laufer's Cut-Rate Optometrists on Rivington Street on the Lower East Side, where he got them to knock two dollars off the cost of the frame (the cheapest one in the store), assuring me that it was the only one that brought out the vivid blue of my eyes and didn't obscure my long lashes. A year later, when my brother showed similar symptoms, it was to a Park Avenue specialist we went at my mother's insistence, all of us, including my grandmother and her sister Esther, squeezed into the old Ford with high anxiety riding as an extra passenger in the rumble seat.

After the eye examination, we drove downtown to the same optometrist I had been taken, where the selection of frames took an hour as the women fretted over which ones would give my brother the greatest peripheral vision. And from the time he began to wear his glasses, a new item was added to the morning ritual. After washing, brushing our teeth and dressing for school, we would eat breakfast while my mother held up the cereal box at various distances from my brother's eyes to see if he could read the small print. This, my mother's homemade version of a Snellen test, was sandwiched between the cod liver oil and the Rice Krispies.

At the age of eleven, when only his right but not his left testicle had descended, she added to the vision test a weekly palpation of his left genital region to see if the recalcitrant globule had decided to join its fellow. I can still see my mother seated on the piano bench, my brother standing before her with his pajama bottoms dropped to the floor, her eyes closed or turned up to the ceiling the better to concentrate, feeling gingerly for the missing part. It did eventually show up. But the image of my brother as an undernourished, sickly child with damaged or missing parts was indelibly etched on my mother's mind. For her, he would always be the two-and-a half-pound, seven-month-preemie, who might not live through his first year, even when at a height of six feet and weighing close to two hundred pounds, his pectorals threatened to burst through his shirt front.

As a young adult, he possessed a kind of otherworldliness and demonstrated a complete unconcern about the impression he was making on others. I didn't spend too much time thinking about either of these characteristics until one winter night when I was standing in the hallway of our Brooklyn house at around two A.M. with Ralph, then my fiance. We'd been nibbling at one another for about two hours, breaking every so often to walk to the Kingston Avenue subway station with the intention of Ralph boarding the train toward home. But each time, unwilling to part, we would walk back to the house, where we would resume our leave-taking. We always tried to be as quiet as possible to avoid rousing my father, who never went to sleep before he heard me close the door to my room and who invariably asked me in the morning what we were doing in the hallway until all hours. I couldn't understand why he kept asking a question to which he already knew the answer.

This particular night, we were on our third or fourth round of saying goodbye. The house was dark and completely still. Just as we'd settled back again against the banister, my brother's strong baritone came wafting down the stairs as he sang in full voice a chorus of "Onward Christian Soldiers". If I was astonished at this vocal demonstration of religiousity, I was even more surprised by the selection: *Hatikvah* it wasn't. Since sexual tension is hard to sustain around someone else's religious fervor, Ralph suggested that we walk to the station again. This time he got on the train with more alacrity than our activities of the past two hours would have predicted.

But my memory is playing tricks, adding humor where there was none. I didn't find my brother amusing then, nor did I later. His presence, which as a child filled me with irritation and dislike, later came to inspire in me something very much like terror. I can't explain why. In all the years of trying to know myself, I have never attempted to deal with my feelings about my brother, or investigated why they exist in such intensity. I find it frightening even to contemplate the subject and have therefore chosen not to.

When my brother was twenty-one and only one semester short of earning his B.A from City College, he went off with an early female version of the Reverend Moon whose name was Renata Massey, and who collected a group of loyal and devoted schizophrenics, fed them saltpeter and faith-healing (my father had planted his mysticism in fertile soil) and took them all to Puerto Rico, where they made a clearing in the forest and devoted the next five years to building her a temple. At the time of Bo's leaving New York, symptoms of his mental illness had already begun to surface. By the time he returned, he had become very, very sick.

His only friend, a young man he had recruited into Massey's service, had cut off his penis in an attempt to supplement the effects of the saltpeter. This incident had jolted my brother to the realization that he was living among very disturbed people in an exploitive and dangerous situation, and with great effort, he wrenched himself out of that life and come back to New York. This move, although in itself healthy, had little effect on the course of his illness. Before this, Bo had been schizophrenic and loving (love being one of the bases of Massey's and my father's brand of mysticism, and also one of the virtues my father had tried to beat into him along with courage). Now he was schizophrenic and angry. He moved, much to my father's dismay, into my parents' small apartment and began to look for work. But every time an agency sent him out for an interview, he couldn't get his hand to extend as far as the doorknob of the office he was about to enter. He soon ran out of agencies.

My parents then appealed to any relative in a position to give him a job, but all of them, including my usually soft-hearted Uncle Harvey, were frightened of this peculiar stranger who talked so intensely and incessantly about himself, and who seemed so loosely connected to his surroundings. But Ralph, who was then going through an altruistic stage during which he populated his cutting room with such a diversity of disadvantaged souls as would have done credit to the casting director of a picture about a B-29 crew in World War II, added (to the paraplegic, the angry black, the non-English speaking Puerto Rican and the poorly trained woman who had appealed to his sense of justice regarding equal opportunity for females) my now officially certified paranoid schizophrenic brother, who would answer the phone, ask who was calling, say, "Ralph, it's for you," replying when asked who it was, "I forgot".

I was upset when Ralph told me he intended to put Bo on salary and teach him editing. I knew how difficult it was even for ordinary people to deal with Bo, and Ralph was no ordinary person. Caring for a paralyzed father and supporting his family for five years between the ages of sixteen and twenty-one had left him with a horror of responsibility and a low threshold of irritability that had already created serious problems in our marriage and with our children. I knew that taking on my brother would only add to our difficulties. But like the junkie who continues daily to shoot into his veins the very substance that is destroying him, Ralph couldn't resist adding my brother to his growing list of dependents, despite my strongly voiced objections.

Ralph kept Bo on as an assistant editor for eight long years, tolerating his eccentricities with a patience I've never seen him show toward anyone else and shaping him finally into a competent film editor, while my brother, the worst symptoms of his illness temporarily dormant, continued to alienate clients and coworkers alike with his suspicious and argumentative nature. Finally, even my husband's closet masochism reached its limits, and he began to think about ways to ease Bo out of his employment. The problem was that while Ralph was reluctant to leave my brother without a job, he also didn't want to saddle any of his professional colleagues with him. So he kept him on in pity and frustration until an unexpected opportunity presented itself.

At that time, Ralph was supervising the editing of a weekly network television show, which he was about to give up in order to concentrate on feature editing. The producer of the show, who had spent very little time in the cutting room and therefore hadn't gotten to know my brother very well, thought it would be a good idea to take him along so as to ease the transition period for the new staff. After an initial period of panic, Bo agreed, and so the changeover was made. Ralph considered the several thousand dollars in severance pay due Bo by union rule a small price for ridding the cutting room of the tension his presence brought with it. So he figured up the amount due, handed him a check, and with a great sense of relief wished him luck in his new position. My brother, ever suspicious, decided to do his own figuring and came up with a different total, some thirty-five dollars more than the amount of the check. When he phoned to call the discrepancy to Ralph's attention, Ralph, about to leave on vacation, told him he would take care of it when he got back, and promptly forgot all about it.

Two weeks after our return, an ominously official-looking letter was delivered to our door registered, return receipt requested. It was from the union to which they both belonged, stating that Bo, by that time John Henderson, had filed a formal complaint against Ralph, charging that Ralph had shortchanged him thirty-three dollars and forty-two cents, and threatening to bring him up on charges if said amount was not paid by certified check within five days.

* * *

At some point during his employment at Ralph's cutting room, Bo had moved out of my parents' apartment. He was lonely at first, and at my mother's suggestion he joined a social group at the Y. It was there he met Ruth, an open, outgoing, maternal young woman in her early thirties who had fallen deeply in love with my brother's sickness. They were together for more than six years before it finally defeated her efforts to marry him.

Ruth took the role of a benevolent drill sergeant, talking him through his episodes of delusion into a semblance of normalcy during the times between, protecting him from the impatience and dislike he inevitably aroused in people and urging him toward mental health with the fervor of a nineteenth century missionary. At their engagement party, he looked mildly confused, like a stranger who had wandered in by mistake, while Ruth stood radiant among her grateful relatives, who had given up on her ever getting married. But eventually, he broke their five-year engagement, during which he had postponed their wedding date twice, feeling, he told her, that their impending marriage was a vise that threatened to crush him in its grip.

Nevertheless, Ruth continued to stay in touch with Bo, hoping that someday his therapy would 'take' and she would be invited to move back officially into his life. But in a burst of the self-destructiveness that he'd refined into an art, my brother finally told Ruth that he didn't want to continue their relationship and stopped seeing her altogether.

A couple of years later, I ran into a friend of hers, who swore me to secrecy and told me that Ruth was currently making her living as a call girl, having given up stenography for something more lucrative. She had been in that line of work for over a year now, and had a regular clientele of older men who liked zaftig Jewish women. She was doing very well, he said. I was less shocked than surprised: I hadn't know that such an esoteric specialty existed in that business, and I still find it difficult to connect her particular qualities with paid sex. So much for stereotypes.

*   *   *

In 1951, shortly after Bo began to work for Ralph, my father died. The fact that Bo felt no grief, only an ever-increasing sense of alienation, was what launched him on a search for his feelings that would eventually escalate to daily therapy sessions and several sojourns in mental hospitals. This was financed in part by money from my father's insurance, which Bo demanded from my mother as his due. During the long period of his decline, he began to feel deep anger toward my mother, which caused him to break completely with her, except when he needed money to pay his ever-increasing therapy bills. At those times, he would write her long, accusatory letters demanding reparation for the damage she and my father had done him. She never failed to give him what he asked, soon depleting the small insurance settlement she had received at my father's death. I was unable to forgive her for the foolish and unending generosity she extended to him, and she was hurt and bewildered by my failure to understand.

For a number of years after Bo had left Ralph's office, Ralph deliberately failed to maintain contact with him, his tolerance for self-punishment having at last reached its limit. So, when four years later the telephone rang just a few minutes after we had returned home from a late evening out, he was totally unprepared for what he would hear from the voice at the other end. It was one of my brother's therapists telling him that Bo had been having what she called an 'episode' for the past several hours in her office and that she couldn't send him home to be alone because he was too agitated. Would we please come and get him so that she could get some sleep. Ralph said that he'd call her right back and turned to me to give me the news. I had collapsed into a chair as soon as I understood the gist of the conversation, and was sitting there shaking.

Even though it was after one in the morning, Ralph was prepared to get into the car and drive back to the city, pick Bo up and bring him to our home where he could stay until we could decide what to do about him. This suggestion had an even more extreme effect on me. Now in a panic, I sat there repeating, "He will not come here, he will not come here," over and over again until Ralph, at first upset by my callousness, realized that I'd lost control and that now he had not one hysteric on his hands but two. In the spirit of compromise, he called the therapist back and explained the situation, suggesting that she hire a nurse at our expense to keep Bo company through the night and promising that we would be there at nine the next morning. I spent most of the night walking the length of my living room muttering "He will not come here" like a mantra, until its repetitive sound and the reassurance of its message calmed me somewhat, and I was able to get a couple of hours of restless sleep.

Early the next morning we rang the bell of the psychologist's West End Avenue apartment. The door was opened by a sleepy Hispanic woman in a white uniform.

"I glad you come now," she said. "He no sleep, poor man, he just talk and talk and talk." She shook her head in pity as we walked into the living room. It was dark, the blinds closed against the sun. Bo was standing in the center of the room, his arms outstretched, the remains of a sentence emerging from his mouth. His eyes were wild and unfocused—they didn't seem able to rest on any one thing for more than a second. His face was unshaven and he was much thinner than I remembered him. He told us that he'd been hallucinating all night, convinced that he was Christ, that he'd been talking nonstop for the past week, that he'd lost close to thirty pounds in just a few days and that he didn't know what in God's name he was going to do. All my desire to flee left me, and for the first time I felt to my marrow the full horror of his life.

We took him out for breakfast. He couldn't eat more than a few bites, each momentarily interrupting the torrent of words, coherent but frantic, that poured forth from his mouth. I cannot recreate that day in its particulars, but I do know that we went to see two of the doctors who had treated him. The second one came up with the only practical suggestion we'd heard that day. He told us of a place in Connecticut where Bo could stay for a while and "try to work out some of his problems". Since it was less expensive than many similar institutions, he expected that the cost would be covered by his insurance. Before we left his office he had called to prepare them for Bo's arrival. Feeling a little less desperate, we took Bo to his apartment so that he could pick up a few clothes. Bo had always been compulsively neat, and so we were shocked at what we found when we walked in.

Bedding and soiled clothing were strewn about the room. In the cluttered kitchenette, open cans and dirty dishes were piled together in the sink. A half-empty container of sour milk rested on the drainboard, and several encrusted pots stood on the stove. The bathroom was filthy. In it were several stuffed laundry bags, their contents spilling out onto the floor. But what gave the apartment its most horrifying aspect were the windows. The window shades, black and of double thickness, had been pulled tight against the wooden frames and nailed down. Not a crack of daylight could enter.

As we sat in the darkened room, Bo told us about the strategy he'd devised a couple of years before. He had put together a portfolio of health insurance policies that were designed to enable him to quit his job and claim a mental disability. He had lived on a combination of insurance, Medicaid and my mother's help during the three-year, seven-day-a-week course of therapy that he hoped would finally solve the emotional problems that had plagued him since childhood. He had conceived this plan with the knowledge and tacit approval of the therapist in whose apartment he had spent the night. She had been treating his gaping psychic wounds with the Band-Aid of conventional talk therapy five days a week for the past three years, the last of which he had spent hiding in a virtual cave from which he emerged only to buy food, pick up his mail, and visit his therapists (he had a second one for weekends, as well as a psychiatrist). She had watched him withdraw from his job and all contact with people and had encouraged him to air endlessly his lifetime of grievances, knowing nothing about the dark, cluttered room to which he would return from their sessions. Ralph drove him to Connecticut that evening and spent the night holding his hand from a cot next to his bed, because, terrified by the new surroundings, Bo had pleaded with him to stay.

He stayed at the home six weeks, unwilling to participate in the group sessions that constituted the only type of therapy offered there, and refusing the medication prescribed by his doctor. We visited him there once. He spent the afternoon in a rambling diatribe, insisting that the couple who ran the home were Fascists, that they hated him, and that there were two patients in a room down the hall from his who wanted to kill him. As we drove off that day, I looked back and saw him standing on the lawn watching us leave, wearing the dejected expression of a child in summer camp who wants to go home with his parents at the end of visiting day. It was one week after his forty-third birthday.

A few weeks later, we were asked by the directors to make other arrangements for him. Most of the other patients were very much younger and had more gentle manifestations of illness. My brother's raging tirades had terrified them. A mental hospital was now his only alternative. To our surprise it took only a few days to arrange his admittance to Hillside Hospital, an institution that we were assured by his psychiatrist had an excellent reputation. Patients were kept there a maximum of three months, during which time they were established on a drug regimen.

He wasn't permitted any visitors or phone calls for the first few weeks. But after that, Ralph, my mother and I, occasionally accompanied by one or the other of my teen-aged children, would drive out to visit him, never knowing how we would find him because of the unpredictable effect of the many drugs that were being tried. One time he was completely rigid, as if there were a steel rod running up his legs, up his spine and into his head. That day, even his eyes seemed unable to move; he had to turn his entire body to address whomever was standing by his side. Another time he refused to see any of us. As soon as we appeared, he ran into his room and began shouting at us through the closed door to go away. Once, we found him cowering in a corner, where, sounding completely coherent, he told us in a voice totally devoid of emotion that every nerve in his body was screaming in pain and that he couldn't stand it another minute. In all the time he remained there, no drug was found that didn't carry with it intolerable side effects.

As the weeks went on, he started to regain his lost weight and was remaining rational for more and more of the time. But as the three-month limit approached, he began to express panic at the thought of leaving the protection of the hospital, relaxing only when his doctor spoke of the possibility of sending him to a state hospital when his time at Hillside came to an end.

One morning, my mother phoned me crying. She had just spoken to Bo's social worker, who told her that since Bo wasn't considered a danger to himself or others, he wasn't eligible for the state hospital. Instead, he would be released to her custody the following Friday. It was the only time I've ever seen my mother come close to denying my brother anything. Until his breakdown, her last couple of years had been good ones. She had responsibility to no one but herself, she and Marcel were spending most of their time together, she had dozens of friends and a two-piano partner, and she was able to make each day into exactly what she wanted it to be. For a few hours, her desire to continue her life as it was almost overcame the customary sublimation of her own needs to Bo's. But in the end, resigned and depressed, she gave in to a lifetime of guilt and took Bo in to live with her for the last six months of her life.

When my mother had her heart attack, Bo smothered his panic under a blanket of frenetic activity. Apparently in control and surprisingly lucid, he kept in touch with the cardiologist, arranged for consultants, called a Canadian foundation that was investigating the efficacy of vitamin E therapy then in vogue, brought my mother nightgowns and toiletries from home, saw to it that the relatives were kept up to date, paid the rent and utilities, arranged for Medicare, and took care of himself and the apartment in her absence. Consumed with worry about her condition, my own family problems and my recent entrance into graduate school, I was glad to be relieved of those chores, and marveled at what looked like Bo's recovery under fire. I remember saying to Ralph in some wonder that maybe all Bo required to stay sane was a stream of emergencies to cope with.

Bo was so efficient and seemed to be managing so well that I failed to notice that all was not going as well as it appeared: the fact that the cardiologist would no longer take my brother's calls, the fact that he had taken to wearing a cone-shaped filter over his nose and mouth, not only in the hospital, but everywhere else as well, and the fact that his excessive talkativeness was gradually creeping back. I was not aware at the time that my mother had given him power of attorney after the most acute stage of her illness had passed in order to enable him to pay the bills while she was hospitalized. While he did keep up with the bills, he had also begun to spend her remaining few thousand dollars in a manic buying spree that would, a few weeks after her death, leave him living without enough money for rent in an apartment full of freshly purchased, expensive merchandise. These included two Sony tape recorders, an adding machine, three Polaroid cameras, an expensive stereo set, a Barca lounger, a Mixmaster, an Oriental rug bigger than any of the rooms, twenty-seven old photographs that he had found in her album and had restored and tinted, a fourteen carat gold pin and a hundred dollar silk tie from Countess Mara that he'd planned to wear on my mother's first day home, but wore instead to her funeral.

I had been to her apartment only once since she'd been hospitalized. So when I forced myself to go there to dispose of her clothing a few days after her death, I was unprepared for the changes Bo had wrought. During my mother's absence, he had reupholstered the couch in a garish pseudo-Persian print, bought dozens of appliquéd and hand-embroidered pillows in every conceivable color, replaced the semi-sheer white curtains with striped damask, and altogether transformed the erstwhile conservatively furnished living room into something that looked as if it had been thrown together by a drunken pasha. He was very broke and very scared. When I'd recovered enough to speak, I suggested that he return some of his recent purchases, including the hundred-dollar tie. His answer left me more than a bit puzzled.

"I can't return the tie," he said. "It's in the jewelers".

"The jewelers," I repeated mindlessly. "What is a tie doing at a jewelers?"

"I ordered a sapphire to be set into the center of the design," he said calmly. "I'll need a hundred and a quarter to redeem it."

I somehow got through the next hour, but the old feeling of panic that I'd been able to suppress throughout his last crisis and my mother's illness reasserted itself. Leaving before I'd finished sorting her clothes, I went home with my stomach in knots and cried for the next two days.

Bo remained in the apartment for a couple of years, selling off his purchases and pieces of my mother's furniture—even Toney, the piano of my childhood—to pay the rent. Once in a while, he would call Ralph for a loan or for help writing a resumé—he spent a lot of time writing resumés—but he never found a job. If I picked up the phone and heard his voice, I would immediately be overtaken by the same old terror, and it would be days before I'd feel calm again.

* * *

He used to send me birthday cards, but I haven't received one from him in twenty years. Occasionally, someone would ask me how he is. When I said I didn't know, I'm sure they thought me cruel and unfeeling. Cruel I may be, but unfeeling, no. If anything, the thought of him drowns me in feeling. I once dreamt what I think of as a very literal dream after one of his last phone calls. In it, a giant leech was attached to my breast, and I was leaping around, screaming in terror, trying to shake it off.

Before moving to Massachusetts three years ago, I lived on the Upper West Side of Manhattan, which at one time was the dumping ground of hundreds of the mentally ill. Many didn't take their medication regularly and could be seen walking along Broadway ragged, crazed or talking to themselves. Once in a while I would see someone from the back who might have been my brother. Feeling the old dread and wanting to fall even further behind, I would instead quicken my steps so that I could look back and assure myself that it wasn't Bo. It never was, and each time I would tell myself that I was glad it wasn't, thankful for another day's reprieve. But if this was so, why did I search those dark faces so carefully? And why, in the center of my relief, was there always a small, bitter core of disappointment?

My Husband

We are walking down Broadway, almost casually discussing the possibility of a separation. We can't seem to talk about much else these days. My stomach is lead, as it always is when we discuss this subject.

"We could start by taking separate vacations," he says.

"I thought our whole marriage was a separate vacation," I say bitterly, the flippancy of my words denying the pain his have evoked.

For a few minutes neither of us speaks.

Suddenly I ask, "What kind of woman would you look for if we ended it?"

"Well, she'd have to be young," (a dig—I'm in my mid-forties). "Her breast size isn't important," (another dig—mine are large; he's always liked large breasts). "She'd have to be in show business," (yet another—by this time I'm a teacher; he often speaks disparagingly of 'educators').

He pauses. "What about you?" he asks. "What would you look for?"

It comes out without my expecting it.

"You," I answer, "With your head on straight."

He stops and turns toward me, startled by my reply. Then he looks away and we walk on.

One day, crying, Ralph said he was leaving. He packed a bag, told me he wasn't sure why he needed to go, and walked out of the house. After he left, I began to notice changes in and around me. Suddenly I became sensitive to the absence of sound—the jazz records he played, ordinary household noises. The silence was an almost tangible presence. My footsteps, the ticking of the antique silver clock, even the small movements of my head, hands and feet, caused a wave in the silence as though I were breaking calm water with a breast stroke. I had to stop the clock's pendulum—its beat was a reminder of the time I would have to endure alone; it was sending ripples in the air that struck my ear with a vibration so deep it felt like pain. I sat down inside the silence and let it cover me. I remember hoping that if I sat very still, it would fill my eyes, ears, nose and mouth with its substance, which was like cotton candy but white, and snuff me out. It felt thick, soft and spongy. When it began to feel like self-pity, I stepped outside of it and began to walk the length of the house.

I became acutely aware of every part of my body and how they fit together. The articulation of each finger joint seemed an exquisitely significant detail. I felt as though I were learning myself after years of rote living: until this moment my body had simply come along on my errands; now it was asserting its partness and apartness. I listened for the message—the silence, having been broken by my footsteps could no longer drown it out—and it came.

"You're on your own now. Time to learn how." It seemed terribly meaningful for all its banality.

All at once the pendulum of the silver clock started up again (time is inexorable after all), and the clock struck some half-hour or another. Tears began to run down through my closed eyelids. After a few minutes they stopped. I went to the telephone and watched my newly discovered finger dial a friend. It was Friday night, and she had plans. Regrets were spoken. But I really preferred to stay home that night and alternate between the silences and the new, not completely unpleasant awareness of my solitary being. I am complete in myself, I thought. This seemed a very important piece of knowledge, something I hadn't known until now. I wondered if our separation would be permanent. I wondered if I might want it to be. Strangely, I was feeling stronger and had stopped being afraid. Whatever happened, I knew I'd be all right.

When Ralph came back, he told me it was because of a butter dish. He had been out with the young woman he'd been seeing, something I had known nothing about. They had entered a craft shop and were browsing, when he suddenly noticed an earthenware butter dish that fit the description of one he knew I'd been searching for. He turned to show it to the woman at his side, forgetting for the moment that it wasn't me. When he saw her face and not mine, he was momentarily disoriented. He stood there for a long moment. Then he mumbled an apology, turned, and came home.

Our next separation came about when I decided I could no longer tolerate the months of angry silence he had imposed on me, broken only by harsh criticisms of things he'd never complained of before. Since he wouldn't or couldn't explain his behavior, I met with his therapist (with Ralph's grudging permission) to ask him a question, the answer to which might help me decide what to do.

Was it really our marriage that was at the root of Ralph's unhappiness? The answer seemed obvious to me, but Henry's unequivocal denial surprised me.

No, he said. The marriage wasn't the problem. It had simply become the scapegoat for Ralph's inability to move away from film editing, where he was subordinate to often talent-less or inexperienced directors, and become a director himself. Economic insecurity and recurring self-doubt were holding him back. I knew he had hungered to do this for years, but was immobilized by fear. My recent entrance into a doctoral program had only pointed up his inability to move on.

Henry had given me a new perspective. I thought a great deal about my options. The situation was becoming intolerable, but I couldn't get Ralph to talk about it. Since I had no way of knowing if he would ever solve the problem of his work, something I was coming more and more to believe must happen if our marriage was to survive, I asked him to leave. I felt both relieved and frightened. Although my request had made him even angrier, he moved without protest before the end of the week.

I spent the first few days talking to myself and playing the Bach Unaccompanied Violin Sonatas very loudly on the record player. I, too, was unaccompanied, and they were just tense enough to match my mood. After a few days, I was getting used to being alone. For two peaceful, but very long, weeks I didn't hear from him. Then one night he called. Would I drive into New York and have dinner with him? His tone was unusually warm. I agreed, with some trepidation.

It took me two hours to dress that night. By the time I'd finished, the bed was strewn with pieces of discarded clothing that I had decided against for various reasons. This one showed too much breast and that one was too tight around the behind (I didn't want to be provocative). This one made my skin look sallow (I didn't want to appear bereft) and that one was too conventional (I didn't want to look too old, either).

At last I was ready, chastely attired in a tailored slack suit and a red silk blouse (no jewelry for added dignity). I put on some eye make-up (a little less than usual so he wouldn't think he was being vamped), slipped on my raincoat (especially fashionable because it wasn't raining), tied the belt instead of buckling it (to look more contemporary), and drove to Manhattan from my empty house in New Rochelle to an old-fashioned date with the man I had lived with for nearly twenty-five years.

I hadn't had such a marvelous time with him in all our years together. He kept telling me that he loved me. He kept touching me. Since he wasn't ordinarily much of a toucher, I was delighted. But suspicious of this unaccustomed warmth, I kept warning myself not to let him come back for the price of a meal and some sweet talk. That evening I felt like a medieval maiden standing on a balcony, wearing a pointed hat with a veil hanging off the tip, being wooed by a romantic stranger in pantaloons and a saber. My periods were mixed, but I wasn't thinking very clearly.

We then proceeded to play a scene from a 1930's Clark Gable-Claudette Colbert movie. He asked me up to see the place where he was staying. At first I demurred, saying it was getting late. He said I needn't stay long, and anyway, it was just a couple of blocks away, a residential hotel on Central Park West. We went to his room; he had a great view of Central Park. Once there, he asked if I wanted a drink. Again I demurred, reminding him that I had to drive home. He suggested I stay over since it was already midnight. I said I never had sex on a first date. He said who said anything about sex? He just wanted to save me a long drive at night. I gave it a moment's thought, then agreed to stay if he promised to observe the rules; it was late and I had to be in town the next morning anyhow. He regretted that there was only one bed. I said that it didn't matter if he promised to stay on his side. We got into bed. We lay there tensely for a few minutes, each of us hugging an edge. Then he yawned and stretched, gently brushing my shoulder. I asked him to stay over on his side if he didn't mind. He promised that if he could only hold my hand, he would ask for nothing more.

By this time, we were both at a high pitch of sexual excitement, my feelings heightened by that sneaky aphrodisiac, guilt. There was something deliciously immoral about sleeping with the man from whom I was separated; I had started that evening committed to chastity. But the script called for our getting together, and so we did, going on to share the sweetest and most passionate lovemaking we had enjoyed in years.

We dated every night for a month. It was quite wonderful—it was the courtship we'd never had, the reassurance I needed and the fun that hadn't been a part of our marriage for too many years. It was also a turning point for Ralph. He started to move his life off dead center, preparing a proposal for a course, submitting a portfolio of his photographs to The City Museum and being granted an exhibition there, and beginning to write the book he'd been ruminating about for years. He put his directing urge on ice for the moment, but just immersing himself in these new projects took the onus off editing. He would begin directing several years later.

It wasn't long before we resumed our life together. Ralph moved back home on the day of our twenty-fifth anniversary. We celebrated with borscht and Moscow Mules at the Russian Tea Room. Coming through the tangy flavor of the ginger beer and lime, I could just discern the faint taste of rose wine.

*   *   *

It is a hot June afternoon, two hours before I'm to leave for the City University Graduate Center to defend my dissertation. I have worked five years toward this moment, enduring the death of my mother, my children going off to college, my own doubts, and despite years of relative marital peace, the subtle sabotage of a husband who has admitted to being envious of my ability to change the direction of my life. He has not yet worked up the courage to direct, and sees my Ph.D. as a painful reminder of his inertia. Ralph is distant and irritated—I have been closeted and inaccessible for a month, preparing for this day. I am also angry. The week before, in a fit of frustration, he had smashed my favorite hippopotamus. I'd been collecting hippos for some years, and by now had a sizeable collection, each item of which had a special association for me. But the one made of porcelain—William, from the Metropolitan Museum of Art, given to me, ironically, by Ralph himself, was the one I prized most. I idly wonder which of his plants I might kill in revenge, but they're living things and I could never go through with it.

The hours pass, the inquisition comes, and then it is over. I have just been called "Dr. Rosenblum" by the members of my committee, my damp hand solemnly shaken by each of the men, cheeks touched and kisses blown past my ear by each of the women. I'm incredulous that it was so easy, a little disappointed that they didn't challenge me more on those points for which I'd prepared especially ingenious rationalizations. I get into the elevator, my spirits soaring as it descends.

Outside, I sit on a concrete ledge in front of the building, oblivious to the heat, waiting for Ralph to pick me up. We had planned to have dinner out, win or lose. A young man, obviously a street person, sits down beside me and begins to tell me his story. He is thin and unshaven. He reminds me of my brother. I talk to him with a kindness I cannot muster for Bo and commiserate with him on his ill fortune. I tell him that things will get better, and encourage him to take certain steps that might help. He asks me to join him for a cup of coffee. At that moment, Ralph drives up. I slip off the ledge and prepare to leave my sad companion. Instead of "Goodbye," he says, "You're beautiful". I'm almost fifty, ten pounds overweight, slightly battered from the evening's main event, and sweaty from the humidity and excitement, but I smile at him, beginning, in fact, to feel beautiful. I'm not, of course, never have been. But at that moment, I feel a glow that could pass for beauty. I thank him warmly and get into the car, victorious and yes, why not—beautiful. Ralph reads my expression correctly. He is washed of all negative feelings. He grins and leans over to kiss me.

"Congratulations, Doc," he says.

We go to a jazz spot that we both love, and I can't stop smiling. I tell him about the defense. When I am finished, he takes a small box out of his pocket and hands it to me. I unwrap it slowly, trying, as I always do, to preserve the paper, even though I know I'll throw it away a few minutes later: it prolongs the moment. Finally, I open the box. Nested in cotton is a massive silver ring. I am touched. Ralph gives presents reluctantly when they're obligatory (he is very generous at other times), but he really seems to care about my reaction to this one. He searches my face. I begin to slip it on my finger.

"Look at it more carefully," he says. It is hard to make out in the dim light. He strikes a match and then I see it—the head of a hippopotamus, its open mouth providing entrance for a finger, flat square teeth rimming the inner circle.

*   *   *

We are on a trip to Mexico with friends. It is evening and the four of us are sitting in the town square, sipping aperitifs and planning the next day's activities. I am musing about the afternoon. We've been shopping for gifts for the children. For Emily, a bright poster and a carved wooden comb; for Paul, a hand-tooled belt in the smallest size to fit his narrow waistline.

It has been a lovely day, much talking and laughter among us. Ralph is often restless on vacations, but there is something about the dry heat and the sun-baked look of the countryside that pleases him. I am feeling happy and relaxed. Moving among the tourists are some country people, seeking to sell their brightly colored serapes. Idly, I glance across the square, where several vendors have set down their large, basketlike carrying cases and are holding up serapes one after another, hoping to catch the eye of a gringo with money to spend. One serape in particular attracts my attention. It is striped, and the colors: brilliant oranges, blues and yellows, are unlike the duller earth tones of the others. I lean over to point it out to Ralph and tell him I'd like to have it. I ask him to handle the negotiations, as the thought of doing the bargaining myself makes me uncomfortable. As an adult, I'm as reluctant to bargain a price down as I was as a child to finger-paint. I guess I equate them both with dirty hands. Intellectually I understand that it's expected in the poorer countries like Mexico, it having become an integral part of the buying and selling process. But emotionally, I'm not convinced. My sympathy is always with the seller, his obviously less-favored state nagging at my conscience.

We have been watching the dealing in the square for some time. It's all very businesslike. A price is stated, a counter-offer made, and in a rapid stepwise progression, a figure about halfway between them is agreed upon. This is a ritual, as predictable and stylized as a bullfight, and if done well, just as dramatic.

I look again across the square. My serape is several feet closer. Its upper edge is being held in both hands by its ancient owner and is being shifted gently from left to right and back again. Even from that distance, he has noticed my interest. My friends warn me to look away: if he thinks I want it too much, the price will rise. So I turn back to my drink. Each time I sneak a look, there it is, a little closer, being waved in a tantalizing ballet as the vendor moves almost imperceptibly across the square. Suddenly he is at our table. He bows to me and then to Ralph. My husband, who loves to bargain and is anticipating with pleasure what is to come, bows back.

"Cuanto?" Ralph asks, using the only Spanish word he is sure of.

"Solamente ciento cincuenta pesos, senor."

In a combination of pidgin English and high school Spanish, Ralph manages to communicate that we like the serape very much, but that since we are among the poorer American tourists, we can regrettably offer only ten pesos. I wince at what I imagine is an insulting offer. I really want that serape.

The old man smiles. "No, no, senor. Is no enough for this beautiful serape. See the colors, the weave." He pauses. "Ciento treinta pesos."

"We admire the serape muy mucho, senor," my husband says, "So we will raise our offer to twenty pesos." For emphasis, he raises both hands twice.

They keep bowing to each other in mutual respect, the old man coming down a few pesos, Ralph coming up as many. There is such a spirit of suspense at our table that people sitting nearby fall quiet and begin to listen. The bargaining continues, the excitement rising as the gap between them gets narrower. In what has the grandeur of the last triumphant chords of a Beethoven symphony, they arrive at a final price of sixty-three pesos. The serape, which by this time has taken on the desirability of the Holy Grail, is now mine. There is applause from the surrounding tables. The old man grins, the furrows in his bronzed face deepening as he turns and bows to us all. He folds the serape carefully, wraps it in green tissue paper that he has pulled from underneath the rest of his wares, and hands it to me with a salute.

At this point, Ralph reaches into a bag that has been lying on the table and takes from it a small object wrapped in newspaper. It is the leather belt we bought for ten pesos that afternoon for Paul. He unfolds the newspaper and holds up the belt for the old man to examine.

"Look at this beautiful belt," he says. "See the fine workmanship. It is yours for twelve pesos."

At first the old man is startled. Then an expression of delighted complicity passes over his face, and he begins to smile. Eyes twinkling, he makes a counter-offer. He opens at two pesos, bargains Ralph down to six and walks off with the belt tied around the handle of his carrying case.

I think then: this is my husband at his best. These are the things I've come to value most about him: his playfulness and his humanity. I can overlook his fears and his moods for these and the other admirable qualities he possesses. That night, I turn to him and we make love. Afterward, we wrap ourselves in the new serape and reminisce about the day.

*   *   *

The sun slants through the living room window and strikes the black slate table, where we sit drinking our breakfast coffee. From the radio comes music of the forties and earlier. We have recently discovered this new station, which plays old popular music. We find the music wonderful, but the artists are not identified, a maddening omission. We make a game out of trying to guess who they are. I recognize most of the songs, but it is Ralph who usually names the singers or the instrumentalists—he's been listening to popular music and jazz since he was fourteen, and I know them only through him. Once in a while he's stumped, and I'll be the one who comes up with the performer's name. At those moments, I feel the delicious superiority of the trivia expert. Whichever of us knows who the performer is teases the other with hints in a kind of musical foreplay before revealing the name.

This particular morning, Ralph has already identified Helen Forrest, Bunny Berrigan and Lee Wiley. I'm beginning to feel stupid; my ego is drooping. Then I score, first with Peggy Lee, then with Hildegarde. It is now three to two and I'm hoping for at least a tie. The next number begins. The slick male voice is tantalizingly familiar, but I can't place it. Ralph already knows who it is. He gives me a hint.

"He's Jewish."

"Jewish!" I exclaim. "A Jewish popular singer?"

The record is nearing its end. Once it stops I know I won't have a chance, that at the last note the thin thread to my memory bank will snap. I begin hurriedly to guess.

"Steve Lawrence?" Ralph shakes his head.

"Eddie Fisher?"

"Nope."

"Is Frankie Laine Jewish?"

"Maybe, but that's not who it is."

I'm getting desperate, almost shouting now.

"Al Jolson, Eddie Cantor, George Jessel."

I know they're not right, but they're the only Jewish singers I can think of. Too late, the record is over. He has won. I'm dejected.

"OK. Tell me. Who was it?"

His answer is triumphant, and not without a hint of gloat.

"Sammy Davis Junior."

I decide that he has earned summary execution. But I can't bring myself to do it. I could never kill a man who makes me laugh.

*   *   *

My husband was very attractive to women. He was genuinely puzzled by this, which only added to his appeal. There was something monumental about his presence; he wore an air of authority that covered him like a toga. Whatever his private insecurities, he exuded a quiet strength that acted as a gravitational pull at cocktail parties. Tall, his body was substantial but not fat, his head large, leonine and bearded. He wore over all of this a thin veil of depression, something that, when it wasn't in its acute stages, acts as a sexual stimulant for many women. Jewish angst is powerful musk. I understand this, because although long ago I stopped finding that aspect of his character the least bit interesting, it was a large component of my initial attraction to him at twenty-one. When he walked into a roomful of people, the combination of his appearance, his wit and his reputation in the film business got him instant attention. I used to hurt a lot at the difference in our reception. I'll even admit to having had the fear that one of those tight-breasted, denim-clad, mascara-lidded beauties would stand out from the crowd around him and capture his interest. This did happen from time to time, but for reasons I still don't completely understand, our union managed to withstand those episodes until his death.

Unlike Ralph, I attracted little attention, especially at parties. Within the first minutes of our arrival, he would be surrounded by adoring young people in contemporary dress, while I, in my Kimberly knit and sensible shoes, would find myself chatting on the fringes of the action with someone who looked as if he or she would prefer to be anywhere else. Inevitably would come a time when I'd be asked what I do. When I said, "I teach," the words would drop heavily to the floor and lie there, my conversational partner not quite knowing how to pick them up. The response I most cherish was that of a young actress who first looked stricken, then smiled lamely and said, "Well, at least it gets you out of the house."

Editing was Ralph's profession and his art. Although film was his medium, his desk was always stacked with the manuscripts of colleagues and friends awaiting his attention. Writers in all media came to him for advice—his suggestions often turned something that appeared at first glance to be lusterless into a shining achievement. I don't know how he did this, what particular mixture of intelligence and skill gave him this ability, but he was extraordinarily gifted at it.

One evening, we were visiting at the home of friends. One of the guests was an unhappy-looking young woman, who, she told us in no time at all, had just produced her first badly received off-Broadway play, ended a love relationship, tried unsuccessfully to lose twenty pounds, and was evidently holding herself together with safety pins. As she and Ralph talked, I could see her interest increasing. It rose further when it emerged that he was in films. And by the time she discovered that he was an editor, her excitement had reached fever pitch, and a light of recognition began to shine in her eyes. Her adulation was so evident that I expected her to break into a scene from that Anouilh play in which a young girl says practically her only line of dialogue: "How wonnnnnnderful you are!" over and over again to her aging lover, much to the disgust of his wife, who is looking on. What she actually said was: "Oh, my God, you're the Ralph Rosenblum who edited the PAWNBROKER and MINSKY'S and ANNIE HALL?? Would you do me a favor? Would you edit my life?"

Actually, that wasn't an altogether outlandish request. Ralph edited everything: films, books, screenplays, the refrigerator, the drawers, the closets. When the soufflé was about to fall and he was standing between me and the oven trying to decide whether to put the basil behind or next to the marjoram, I didn't ask him to get the hell out of my way and stop playing Craig's wife to my Julia Child. No, I would wait for him to finish editing the spice cabinet and *then* I'd save the soufflé. After all those years, I knew better than to interrupt the creative process.

Our marriage wasn't easy, but it certainly wasn't dull. Like my father, I prize talent and consider it a fair trade for the difficult temperament that often accompanies it. I figure I'll have time to marry a good-natured accountant in my next life, but for this one, I liked the excitement. Ralph's tendency toward detachment, while often hurtful, was good for me, even though I sometimes missed the attention. In one respect, it has allowed me to grow freely and in my own direction, unstunted by the kind of over-involvement I was forced to endure from my father when I was young.

Because we were so different, it always surprised me that our odd combination worked as well as it did. He was a star; I generally go unnoticed. He attended to the design, I to the details. He was mercurial, often depressed; I am more stable, mostly content. He expected the worst, I the best. I have come to the conclusion that it isn't how different two people are as long as it adds up to 100 percent. But I think our marriage worked, especially in the years following our separation, for yet another reason. It took me a long time, but I finally came to like and respect who I am. And that is a woman of independent thought and some talent. Ralph was a man of similar attributes. We were, in short, each other's match.

*   *   *

We are walking along Eighty-fourth Street on a late spring day. I am looking at the sky, which is a brilliant blue interrupted by puffy, cumulus clouds. Ralph is looking at the pavement. Every so often, he nudges me a little to the right or left so that I won't step in a puddle or a pile of dog droppings, or trip on a garbage can cover lying on its back like a dead crab in the sand. Once in a while, I point out to him an odd shaft of light on a building or an interesting cloud formation. He usually looked down, the eternal pragmatist. I looked up, my father's daughter. If only for this reason we needed each other. He kept me out of the dog shit, I reminded him about the sky.

Myself

It is years since I've seen any of my relatives. Those few who are still alive must think of me unkindly if they think of me at all. I have not even made an effort to keep up with news about them. Maybe it's because, as Oscar Wilde put it, "We can't stand other people having the same fault as ourselves." But I think it's more because I've always been a private person, preferring to spend my time alone except for immediate family. I don't enjoy or do well making small talk. I don't often call friends, even those I count as close. This isn't arrogance or uninterest—the impulse to see people, even now that I am a widow, has never been strong in me. But those who care about me understand this and make the effort to keep in touch. Even my children, whom I love inordinately, complain that they don't hear from me often enough.

Once in a while, I'll take out a tape I made forty years ago, long after I'd sung my last concert. I listen to my light soprano singing "Lord Rendall" or "Greensleeves", my voice already less pure than it was at is best, and I say to myself "How lovely," as if it were someone else, as indeed it is. I have never felt the slightest regret for having given up music. I may have done it for the wrong reasons, but I've lived several lives since then, all of them rich.

As much of a struggle as it was, I am glad to have lived during a time of change, which required that I play the traditional roles as well as permitting me those I chose for myself. Because of this, I feel that I have done it all, marrying at a time when society decreed that I marry, having children at the time it decreed that I have children, then moving in more self-serving directions when I realized that I could decree for myself. Although being a wife and mother has required a great measure of selflessness, I have always been careful to save some part of me for myself. I have my father to thank for this, I suppose, even though a lot of what he taught me was confusing at the time. His message to me, mixed as always, boiled down to:

1. Marry for love, but not if he's poor.
2. Don't ever stop educating yourself. You're as smart as any man, but don't let any of them find out.
3. Follow your muse wherever it leads you, but don't let it interfere with the housework.

These gave me some trouble until I realized that they could be split down the middle and everything to the right of the commas thrown out. But by far the best thing I ever learned from him, and it has almost made up for Uncle Don, was: Everything is possible, so never stop dreaming. It doesn't cost a penny more than giving up.

*   *   *

Summer is ending. I have started to have dreams that contain fragments of family scenes I haven't thought of for years. At first the dreams are short and infrequent. Most are of my mother playing Scarlotti sonatas, listening to my childish poems with her eyes closed, pulling up coarse lisle stockings over her lovely legs. The dreams occur every couple of weeks at first, becoming more frequent as the months go by. Winter settles in, and others of my relatives begin to appear: Uncle Dewey in his green eyeshade, Grandma Becky with her full high bosom as she appears in my only photograph of her, my father packing moving barrels, my brother crying. Before long, the nights are crowded with family events: dinners at Grandma Gottfried's, seders at the Millinery Center synagogue, Uncle Moishe's funeral. I get up in the morning drained by the feelings these intrusive phantoms arouse—ghosts from my childhood, who have remained dormant for so long. Their resurrection fills me with a new sense of connection, even congruence.

I begin to write. As I commit my relatives to paper, I see in myself traces of those I disliked and search, often in vain, for traits of those I admired. I find that those I loved most have had the least influence on my character, while the ones I loved least have provided me with what I've needed to survive.

Ironically, the very things I devalued in my father I now most prize in myself: ambition, optimism, a sense of justice, the spirit of adventure. The qualities I most esteemed in my mother are ones I seem to have in shortest supply: gentleness, sociability and patience. I've also learned that I am as much a result of what I've refused to become as what I've chosen to be: as much a product of my Aunt Fanny by rejection as I am of my Cousin Millie by embrace. Even where I made myself an observer in their lives, they were participants in mine, shaping me in their image so subtly that for a time I believed that I'd escaped their imprint.

But I have learned better. I've come to know the deep personal truth that lies at the heart of the truism: At once my past, present and future, my relatives are the sum and substance of my self.

The Mourning After

The End

Sometime during the early morning hours of September 4th, 1995, my complex, charismatic, funny, iconoclastic, cynical, volatile, uncompromising, adored husband died. Even weeks later, when I had finally assimilated the reality of that unbelievable fact, I awakened to it each morning convinced that I was still asleep and in the grip of a nightmare. Now, more than twelve years later, I can think of that night only in the present tense, something that despite all that has happened since, will never truly recede into the past; it lies just below my level of consciousness ready to be triggered into instant replay by a stray thought, a sight, a sound.

Ralph and I hadn't done very much that Sunday beyond finishing the New York Times crossword puzzle and taking a short walk in Riverside Park. We were still exhausted after the long drive back to New York from Maine three days earlier, the rigors of unpacking and resettling into our apartment after a summer away, and a cousin's wedding the day before. A friend had joined us for dinner that evening, leaving around eleven. Ralph went straight to bed, but as much as I longed to do the same, I took advantage of his absence to steal into the kitchen to address invitations for his surprise seventieth birthday party, secretly arranged to be held at a friend's apartment in October. He wouldn't start his classes at Columbia University until after Labor Day—he had been made a Full Professor there seven years before, after having given up editing and made a short-lived foray into directing. Since he would be home most of the time until then, it was necessary to sneak in the preparations whenever the opportunity presented itself.

He appeared in the kitchen just as I began addressing the envelopes. I tried to conceal the invitations as best I could by draping the sleeves of my dressing gown over the evidence. I needn't have worried; he made straight for the fridge.

"Still hungry," he said.

I tried to look nonchalant while he prepared his snack. He smeared a few crackers with peanut butter and took them back to bed. I thought briefly about crumbs in the bed sheets, but was loath to start a discussion, which would delay his exit from the kitchen. I didn't dare move my arms for fear that he would notice the envelopes. As far as I know, he didn't spot them. If he did, he had the grace not to ask what I was doing.

An hour later, I finished my task and fell gratefully into bed and that initial languor that promises a deep, satisfying sleep. As I did, a long glissando of a sigh rose from the other side of the bed and hung for a moment in the air. Ralph often produced unusual sounds in his sleep, but this one was especially musical. Smiling at this new addition to his repertory, I settled myself under the covers and was soon asleep.

Sometime around 2 AM, I awoke hungry—not an unusual occurrence. As I sat up and groped for my slippers, I noticed that Ralph wasn't in bed. I assumed he was in the bathroom and made my way into the kitchen for a snack. One slice of rye toast and a piece of cheddar later, I returned. He was still not in bed and there were no lights on anywhere in the apartment. I checked the bathroom, then the living room, then his study. Still no Ralph. Puzzled, I went back to the bedroom and turned on the light. It was several seconds before I noticed his feet extending from behind his side of the bed. I went to investigate.

He was lying peacefully on the floor, his head resting on his arm, apparently fast asleep. As was his custom on warm nights, he was wearing only a pair of jockey shorts. I stood there for a few seconds, absentmindedly admiring the curve of his back, while I tried to come up with a scenario that would explain this curious circumstance. I finally succeeded. While I was asleep, I reasoned unreasonably, our two cats had started a fight on the bed, and exasperated, Ralph had decided to sleep on the floor. Ridiculous as this explanation was, the cats did sometimes use our bed as the site of their frequent quarrels, so despite his never having done this before, there was some basis in reality. This unlikely fiction satisfied me sufficiently to send me back to bed.

Seconds later, I sat bolt upright. My arm had brushed against his pillow; he hadn't taken it with him. I shifted over to his side, leaned over, and poked him gently on the shoulder.

"Come on, sweetheart," I said. You can't sleep there all night."

No response. I poked him harder.

"Wake up, Ralph, you'll catch cold!"

I could hear the rising panic in my voice, but I still didn't feel it. I got out of bed and examined him more closely.

He was still on his side in a sleeping position with what appeared to be a faint smile on his lips. A thin line of spittle ran down the corner of his mouth and onto the rug, leaving a small damp circle. He looked uncommonly serene, and younger than he had in years. I realized later that the frown lines on his forehead and all other signs of tension, apparent even when he slept, had completely disappeared.

Now the panic took hold. I shook him hard, pleaded with him to wake up. Receiving no response, I raced to the phone, dialed 911, and screamed hysterically that I couldn't wake my husband. She asked if I knew how to find a pulse. Desperately, I tried to recall what I'd learned about finding pulses during the course in CPR that I'd taken shortly after Ralph's heart attack. Remembering, I dropped the phone and hurried to feel his carotid artery.

Nothing. I tried the other side.

Still nothing, except that his skin felt uncommonly cold.

I rushed back to the phone crying: "There's no pulse!"

She asked if I knew how to do CPR, and then, quite matter-of-factly, directed me to do, step by step, what I would remember in horrifying detail for the rest of my life.

"First, "she said, "You'll have to get your husband onto his back."

Impossible, I thought. Not only did Ralph outweigh me by sixty pounds, but he was lying against the bed frame in a narrow space bounded on the other side by a radiator. I would have to pull him away from the bed first, with little room to maneuver and no leverage. But desperation brought with it a rush of adrenalin—I could probably have lifted a light truck once it kicked in. I leaned hard against the radiator, and using more strength than I had ever been able to summon before, managed to pull him towards me and simultaneously roll him over.

Struggling not to gag, I placed my mouth on his, slimy with a film of mucus and vomit, forced that first breath into his body and heard a gurgling sound coming from deep inside his lungs. It sounded a bit like the sound children make when they blow with straws into the remains of their chocolate milk, a hideously viscous burbling. I knew the instant I heard it that my efforts would be futile, that he was drowning—or had already drowned—in his own fluids. But I could not stop.

Moments later, the doorbell rang. Dizzy from hyperventilation, I stood up drunkenly and ran to open the door. Then I rushed back to the inert body on the bedroom floor and tried to resume CPR. Two policemen accompanied by a couple of emergency medical technicians followed me into the bedroom. One of the technicians gently pulled me away. I was shaking uncontrollably. He asked me what position my husband was in when I found him, and with the help of his partner, turned Ralph back onto his side. He kneeled, pointed to some dark patches on his back, and said something I didn't catch. The other man nodded. They stood up in what seemed like slow motion.

"Do something!" I cried. "Why aren't you doing something?"

"Your husband has been dead for at least an hour, Ma'am," the first one said quietly. "There's nothing we can do."

One of the policemen eased me out of the bedroom and into Ralph's study where he asked for our doctor's phone number. In cases of sudden death, he explained gently, the coroner's permission was required to release the body to a funeral home without an autopsy. But the coroner couldn't be immediately located; it was Labor Day, and he was away. So, too, it seems, was our doctor, who, were he to become available, could certify Ralph's death as being from natural causes. We would have to wait for one or the other to call before the body could be moved.

And so we waited. The second officer suggested that I call my children. I said that since nothing would change over the next several hours, I would not wake them at three in the morning to give them such news; I would call them at seven. He said he wouldn't leave until I called them. Soon, soon, I kept repeating to myself over and over like a mantra. Soon someone would call. Soon everybody would leave. Soon I would go in and wake Ralph, and our life would resume.

At five o'clock, a new shift of police officers arrived. Neither the coroner nor our doctor had called. It seemed the night would never end. At six, the reality of the situation finally hit me. I returned to the room where Ralph lay, though the officers discouraged me. I needed to see if there were any traces left of the man I had lived with for forty-seven years, wondering how it was possible that this simulacrum of whitening flesh had ever been the glorious, maddening human being who had given me so much joy and pain.

Where are you? I raged at him silently. Why don't I feel your presence? Why didn't you tell me you were going to die, instead of sneaking away in the middle of the night without a hint that the evening we had just spent together would be our last? But of course there had been hints. I simply hadn't wanted to see them.

Ralph had made a miraculous recovery from two nearly fatal heart attacks and bypass surgery, returning to a full teaching schedule within two months and regaining enough strength to sustain most of his former activities. We had been told by his doctors that by rights he should not have survived the second attack, which followed the first by only a few days and destroyed two thirds of his heart muscle. When it became clear that he would survive, we were warned that he would probably remain a semi-invalid for the rest of his life. But Ralph found that prognosis unacceptable, and by sheer strength of will succeeded in reversing it. Lately, though, I had noticed a gradual slowing of movement, greater difficulty walking up hills, a diminution of strength and a subtle change in the timbre of his voice. Neither of us had acknowledged these changes, knowing that nothing could be done; there was so little functioning heart muscle left that for seven years it had been beating on borrowed time.

During those last few weeks, he had been uncharacteristically gentle—a welcome change from his usual prickliness—quick to praise and show affection, telling me how much he'd always loved and depended on me and apologizing for the unpredictable rages that had characterized much of our marriage. He said he had worked very hard that summer to give me an anger-free vacation. I was both touched and saddened to learn that it had been such an effort. A few days before he died, he called both of our children to say that he felt he had a lot to answer for as a father and ask their forgiveness.

The coroner's office called at last, the doctor shortly after. It was now late enough to call Emily and Paul. And though the two caring policemen tried to shield it from my sight, I watched as from a great distance as two funeral home attendants rolled the gurney bearing my husband's body down the hallway from our bedroom and out the apartment door. A short time later, Paul arrived, followed soon after by Emily, who had driven to the airport from her home in the Boston suburbs in record time and flown in on the shuttle. I had to relate the events of the night before many, many times before they were able to overcome their own stunned disbelief and accept the unacceptable: that their father was truly and irrevocably gone.

For the next couple of weeks I ricocheted between numbness and grief, railing at fate, or whatever it was that had taken my husband from me, certain I could never manage alone. I kept wondering where all that marvelous wit and intellect had gone, trying to reconcile the empty shell I had ministered to on that terrible night with the complicated man I had loved, fought and lived with for nearly half a century. If it is only electro-chemical energy leaping synaptic gaps that animates our bodies, why did I, a lifelong agnostic, feel that something very like the classic description of a soul had vacated his? Was it my long ago memory of Trixie, my grandmother's Chihuahua, that had kept the idea alive?

For weeks, I was utterly exhausted. It seemed that all I did between tackling the huge amount of paperwork that couldn't wait and answering the avalanche of condolence calls, cards and letters was cry and try vainly to sleep. Many times throughout the long days and nights that followed, I would ask aloud "Ralph, are you there?" half expecting an answer, alternately furious and inconsolable when none came. I missed him dreadfully—missed the tension, the delicate love-hate balance of our long marriage, the complexity of feelings that could have me say angrily, and yet with grudging admiration after he had just performed brilliantly at a film seminar on a day of awesome marital combat: "Damn it, Ralph, if you weren't my husband, I could fall madly in love with you."

That was the story of our marriage: I had fallen madly in love with him again and again for forty-seven years. How could you not love a man who'd offered to take up a collection for the Orchestra of St. Martin in the Fields so they could afford to rent a hall, or who, after having taken his first bite of the dessert known as Indian Pudding, asked the waiter to send his compliments to the Chief, or who, when asked by a television interviewer how he'd managed to stay married so long at a time when one of every two marriages ended in divorce, replied simply: "I love my wife."

Aftermath I

Ralph and I had spent the summer in Rockport, Maine, where Ralph was Artist-in-Residence at the Maine Film Workshops and where he had been teaching courses in film editing and directing. I was his camp follower. It was the end of August, and we were about to return to New York to resume our alternate lives, Ralph as a professor of Film Studies at Columbia University, and I as a writer—in May Sarton's phrase—of scant reknown.

Our old VW convertible was so jammed with our clothes and our collection of booty from auctions, flea markets and end-of-summer sales that we were afraid we'd have to drive home with the top down on a day that threatened thunderstorms. It was the Saturday morning of our departure, and we decided to take a swing through Camden and have a last look at Bayview, our favorite street, on which several art galleries were situated.

We were tooling down Bayview when Ralph slammed on the brakes, causing a near pile-up behind us. He pulled into a parking space opposite one of the galleries and sat staring out at a large piece of sculpture installed on a pedestal in an outdoor niche just to the right of the entrance. We had browsed this gallery many times—they had wonderful pieces—but were intimidated by their prices. We had bought many art works during our years together, though to be accurate, it was Ralph who proposed and I who disposed: he would buy a painting despite my protests that there wasn't an inch of wall space left, and then remind me that I had always found just the right spot to hang it no matter how impossible it seemed at the time, as indeed I had. But we seldom spent more than fifty dollars for any one piece, and usually a lot less. This gallery was in a different class altogether.

We sat there for several minutes, while I strained to see what he was looking at, my view mostly blocked by his leonine head. All I could make out were a few brilliant colors seemingly suspended in air. All at once, Ralph pulled the car back into traffic and made a right turn onto Elm. He was strangely quiet.

"What was that thing?" I asked.

"A weathervane," he replied.

"Why didn't you get out and take a better look?"

"Because I'll want to buy it."

"How do you know that unless you see it up close?"

"Why are you encouraging me?" he asked. "I thought we didn't have any more wall space."

"That never stopped you before," I said.

To my surprise, I heard myself using *his* argument. "I've found space for everything else you've bought. What makes you think I've lost my touch?"

He stopped for a pedestrian. The famous Maine civility seemed to be catching; he never did that in New York.

"Besides," he said, "It's too expensive."

"You won't know that until you ask."

We continued up Elm Street in silence. I braced myself against the rising tension.

"You've got a birthday coming. Buy yourself a present," I said.

"That's crazy," he said. "It's probably a fortune."

Five minutes later he swung around in an illegal U-turn and maneuvered himself back onto Bayview. Once again he parked in front of the gallery. Once again he sat looking intently at the piece. Then he got out of the car, crossed the street and slowly walked around it. I remained in the car, worrying. What if he decided to buy it, no matter what the price? Or decided *not* to buy it, thereby depriving himself unnecessarily of something he clearly wanted? Was there enough time before we had to leave for me to come back alone and buy it for him? As often panicked about finances as about wall space, I wondered if I should have my head examined. Reluctantly I got out of the car and joined him. The weathervane was magnificent. We circled it together.

Made of steel, a figure in a blue dress floated face down above a pyramidal base. Her hair streamed behind her in rigid black ripples, and the colors in which she and the base were painted were brilliant beyond description.

There was definitely no room for such a large piece in our already overstuffed apartment.

Ralph continued to circle her in a kind of hypnotic state, looking the way I imagine he must have looked at his first sight of Myrna Loy, his first crush. This went on for several minutes while I eyed him anxiously. I, too, coveted her, but despaired of finding a place for anything that big. We bought art voraciously; not only were there no walls left, there were no floors left either, as we tended to buy furniture the way we bought art.

Shaking himself out of his trance, Ralph disappeared into the gallery. I got there just in time to see him wince as the gallery owner stated the price: fifteen hundred dollars, plus tax and shipping.

"No way," said Ralph angrily.

I followed him into the car, not too happy about being with him when he was in such a fury. He sat in the driver's seat but for several moments made no move to turn the key. I suspect that like me, he couldn't erase that plucky lady's indefatigable expression from his mind. I hope he doesn't change his mind, I remember thinking. I would have had to hang the damn thing from the ceiling.

We went back to the campus for our last lunch of the season. Ralph brooded. I prayed he would exorcise the object of his brooding by the time he finished dessert—a slice of watermelon—which he had steadfastly insisted all summer to the chef, was not a proper dessert, but a garnish.

We said our goodbyes and took off. But instead of turning toward Route 1, he continued in the direction of Camden. I didn't have to ask why.

"I'll offer him nine hundred," he said grimly.

This time I waited in the car.

Ralph emerged, his face set in a scowl. "The bastard wouldn't budge," he said.

I waited.

Suddenly, he slammed his fist on the hood. "Damn it," he said. "In six weeks I'll be seventy years old. I'm buying myself a present!"

He went back in, wrote a check for the entire amount, arranged to have it shipped—it would take about a week—got in the car, and we were off. I made a vow not to think about where to put it until it arrived. There was enough to worry about before we got there, like keeping Ralph from imploding on the ride back through Wiscasset, which had too many stop signs, too many pedestrian crossings, and a policeman who looked to be twelve years old, extending what should have been a three-minute run through town into more than twenty.

*   *   *

Five days after our return, Ralph died. He had finally succumbed to the damage his massive coronary had caused seven years earlier.

Trembling in disbelief and shock, I'd had to decide quickly on a funeral home. I was able to remember the names of only three: Garlick's, Frank Campbell's and Riverside. The first sounded too redolent and the second was too East-Side, which left Riverside, where in a strange way I always felt at home, having attended the funerals of more friends and relatives there than I care to remember. So it was Riverside that I called at six AM to remove Ralph's body, as two sympathetic policemen stood by. I made an appointment to see an 'advisor' later that morning.

I dealt with my morning ritual in a kind of trance. It wasn't until I stood inside Riverside's front door with my two children that I was able to consider the possibility that this might not be a nightmare but a reality from which there was no awakening.

Waiting for my advisor to join me, I remembered that Ralph had once voiced disapproval of the elaborate coffins selected by families for loved ones destined to be cremated. He thought it criminally wasteful. In view of his having expressed his preference for cremation, I decided to buy the least expensive coffin in accordance with what I presumed were his wishes.

My advisor was a pleasant-looking woman in her fifties with the same faintly unctuous manner I remembered from when I'd arranged my mother's funeral twenty years before; it seems to be a prerequisite for the job. After extending her condolences and taking down some preliminary information, she brought up the matter of the coffin. She called it a casket. I told her I wanted a plain pine box. A look of consternation briefly crossed her features, but she quickly reverted to her previous expression of non-committal professionalism, and, unasked, embarked on a recital of the different styles of 'caskets' and their respective prices. I noticed with some amusement, surprised that I could feel anything so frivolous, that she used the same slightly oleaginous tone when quoting the costs of the various containers as she did when she alluded to Ralph. I was also aware of the euphemisms she sprinkled throughout her recital: never were the words 'dead', 'death', 'deceased' or 'coffin' spoken; my husband was always scrupulously referred to as 'Mr. Rosenblum', 'the departed' or 'the late', a misnomer, I wanted to tell her, as he'd always been twenty minutes early for everything.

She awaited my decision. Patiently, I repeated that I wanted a plain pine box with the no-frills cremation, and inquired when the 'procedure', as she called it, would take place. Her tone changed instantly from funereal to telemarket. Crisply, she advised me that the economy cremation was an unscheduled event that would take place any time during the next forty-eight hours. However, the deluxe package, which cost an additional thousand dollars, would entitle us to be transported to New Jersey in style and at a specific time to watch the 'procedure' from a comfortable seat in the well-appointed crematorium. If I hadn't already been sure of what I wanted, this settled it; I had no intention of watching my husband's body consumed by flames—it was enough that I would be imagining it in living technicolor for the rest of my life. So I reiterated my intention to stay with the less expensive package. Her disappointment was palpable; evidently, she worked on commission. After reluctantly accepting my decision, she told me that the 'remains' could be 'viewed'—she made Ralph's body sound like a museum exhibit—that evening.

With Paul and Emily, I returned to the funeral home at seven. Selfishly, I hadn't told anyone that Ralph could be viewed that evening, jealously wanting my last hours with him to be private ones. Emily and Paul each spent some time alone with their father while I paced the length of the corridor outside the chapel, dreading the moment when I knew that I would no longer be able to sustain the illusion that it was all a bad dream.

I spent more than an hour with Ralph, talking to him the entire time, but I can't recall a word of what I said. I stared at him intently, afraid of missing a sign—a flicker of an eyelid, a tremor of his hand—that a mistake had been made, that he was alive and ready to come home. At last, seeing none, I kissed his forehead, the tip of his wondrous nose and finally his lips, smoothed his beautiful hair for the last time, and left the chapel.

I spent the next several days wondering how I would get through the rest of my life. Having gone directly from my parents' home to the one I'd established with my new husband all those years before, I had never lived alone.

Ralph's ashes, I'd been told, would be Federal Expressed to me directly; they would arrive, I was promised, no later than Friday. Between sudden paroxysms of grief, waves of anxiety engulfed me. This was my first experience with cremation, and I had no idea in what form Ralph would be delivered into my hands. My mind refused to take me past the ringing of the doorbell and the first sight of the uniformed delivery man holding . . . . what?

Friday arrived; I spent the day steeling myself for the moment when the doorbell would ring and a Fed-Ex delivery man would leave in my hands all that remained of my husband. At five o'clock, I called Riverside to report that Ralph's ashes had not arrived. My advisor called back within minutes to advise me that she had contacted the crematorium, and that Mr. Rosenblum had been shipped out as per agreement on Wednesday morning. If he didn't arrive by Monday noon, she would put a trace on him. Given her insistence on referring to him by name, I began to wonder if I shouldn't be calling the police and filling out a missing person's report instead.

I do not remember the weekend. I sleepwalked through it, waiting for it to pass. Monday morning came and went; still no Ralph. The advisor was alerted again. On Tuesday, she called to say that he'd been located in a New Jersey post office; the crematorium had not only misaddressed the carton, they had sent it by parcel post instead of by Federal Express as promised. I was assured that it would arrive—albeit third class—by the end of the week.

The package was delivered on the following Wednesday, almost two weeks late, looking as bedraggled as a traveler who'd been forced to sleep a night or two at the airport. As my heart pounded audibly, the mailman placed the carton into my outstretched hands.

I walked into the kitchen holding it gingerly, trying to convince myself that this wasn't Ralph, only a few pounds of ash, and thus not a 'he' but an 'it'. Only an 'it' could I store for months on the top shelf of the bookcase to be confronted every time I reached for a book. (The ashes would remain there until the following spring, when I would drive them to Maine for interment, as he had requested.) This thought carried me through the cutting of the electrical tape and the careful tearing away of the corrugated cardboard. At last, a metal container six by six by six inches was exposed. Heart pounding, I lifted it out and carefully pried open the lid. Reverently, I sifted the ashes through my fingers. As I replaced the lid, I noticed the label for the first time. The names of the crematorium and the funeral home were displayed on one side of the container, and under them, the following legend: THESE ARE THE ASHES OF DAVIDA ROSENBLUM.

*   *   *

Two days after their arrival, the house intercom rang.

"The UPS man is here," the doorman announced. "He has two cartons for you."

"That's odd. I'm not expecting anything."

"Should I send him up? They're heavy, so he wanted me to check if you were there."

I couldn't imagine what they might be. "Well, if he's sure they're for me, let him come up."

While I waited, I wondered what I could have ordered that the UPS man, who was pretty heavy himself, would make a point of its weight.

The minute I saw the size and shape of the cartons, I knew: it was the weathervane. I hadn't remembered it was coming, much less Ralph having bought it. I was horrified. Panic-stricken over my financial situation, this was clearly not the time to have spent fifteen hundred dollars, plus tax and shipping, on something as non-essential as a weathervane, especially as I had no roof to put it on. The reality was that although I might have to cut back a little, I surely would have enough of an income to keep me out of soup kitchens. But at that point, not two weeks after his death, I could see my future only as a bag lady, living on the streets and pushing a stolen shopping cart containing all that was left of my worldly goods.

"I want to send it back," I said to the deliveryman, bursting into tears in spite of a promise to myself not to lose my composure in front of strangers. "My husband bought it, and it was very expensive, and now he's dead."

The poor man was clearly uncomfortable. "I can't do that, Ma'am. You'll have to call the office and arrange a pick-up."

I let him bring the cartons into the living-room, where they sat, huge and menacing, daring me to find a place to store them—I hoped temporarily—and threatening my future with the mocking paid-in-full stamp affixed to one of the boxes. I went to the phone, dialed the gallery in Camden and told my story to the owner.

"I'd like to send it back for a refund," I said tearfully

"I'm afraid we don't give refunds," he said. "It's our policy."

"But surely," I pleaded, "these are special circumstances."

"I'm sorry for your loss, I really am, but we never give refunds. For any reason. It's on your receipt."

He refused to make an exception. I was going to be stuck with that weathervane whether I wanted it or not.

I called Paul. He came over that evening, and together we managed to lift the lady and her triangular base out of the cartons. With some difficulty—I'm five-foot-three and he's five-seven, only a foot and a half taller than the weathervane was long—we placed her atop her base. And there she floated, as magnificent as I remembered her facing into the winds of Camden. I told Paul that the gallery wouldn't take her back, and that I wanted to sell her.

"You can't!" he said passionately. "It's the last thing Dad ever bought."
Hoping for support, I called Emily.

"You can't!" she said passionately. "It's the last thing Dad ever bought."

It looked as if I wasn't going to sell it, but with the apartment already crammed with furniture, paintings, small sculptures and other furbelows and gewgaws of various sorts and sizes, there was absolutely no room.

"Can you take it?" I asked Paul in desperation, knowing full well that he had even less room than I did, having a smaller apartment and at least as great a furbelow habit.

"If you really don't want it, I'll take it, but where would I put it?" He sounded pretty desperate, too.

I was about to call Emily back when I realized that in the last few minutes I had fallen in love with the lady all over again. I looked around the room vainly seeking a space large enough to hold her. Sighing in defeat, I maneuvered her onto the only floor space still unoccupied, a position that partially blocked the entrance to the bedroom. I did not care. I would keep that resplendent figure of a size and heft that would make her an inconvenience forever, because, in addition to my renewed infatuation, it was the last thing that Ralph ever bought.

More About Ralph

Ralph was a film editor for the first thirty-five years of his working life, a director for the next seven, and from then until he died at the age of sixty-nine, a professor in the Film Department at Columbia University. He had started his film career as an apprentice at the Office of War Information during World War II, excused from military service because of his father's recent paralytic stroke. With Jack, his older brother, newly married and in the army, he became his parents' sole support.

His first editorial job after the war was as assistant to Helen van Dongen, who was then editing Robert Flaherty's LOUISIANA STORY, a now classic documentary about the impact of Standard Oil's explorations for oil on the lives of the Cajuns who populate the bayous of Louisiana. His last as supervising editor, was Woody Allen's INTERIORS. By the time he left editing at the end of the 'seventies, he had raised the public's consciousness about the importance and often misunderstood function of the film editor through his book WHEN THE SHOOTING STOPS, with his collaborator, Robert Karen. By then, he had edited some of the most important and acclaimed films of the 'sixties and 'seventies. Ralph titled the last chapter of his book "Swan Song", and he meant it. With the exception of Woody Allen and Sidney Lumet, both of whom he praised without qualification, he decimated most of the directors he'd worked with, practically guaranteeing that no one in his right mind would be foolhardy enough to offer him a job as editor. What he really wanted to do was direct, and his book made certain that no one would be tempted to lure him back to the cutting room.

For the next few years, it looked as if his new career was taking off: among other television dramas, he directed three short stories for PBS, and SUMMER SOLSTICE, with Henry Fonda and Myrna Loy in their final appearances on film. Despite superlative reviews, SUMMER SOLSTICE would be Ralph's last film; the career he had longed for all his professional life came to a premature end. He never understood why, but I am convinced that it had more to do with his blunt assertiveness and his difficult and uncompromising nature, especially in his dealings with producers and network executives, than with a lack of directing talent.

In one of those happy accidents of timing, he was approached a couple of months after the airing of SOLSTICE by Frank Daniel, then chairman of Columbia University's Film Department, and invited to join the faculty as an adjunct (he became a full professor the following year). Ralph had always been terrified of speaking before an audience, having been a stutterer for most of his life. Despite having had many successful speaking engagements, he wondered how he could handle lecturing on a regular basis.

But far from being an end-of-life career reluctantly settled for, teaching became his greatest achievement and joy. His dedication and the affection he felt for his students, who idolized him in turn, was rewarded when they voted him the 'Great Teacher Award', the first ever given by the Alumni Association of the School of Fine Arts at Columbia. He looked upon this as his crowning achievement, second only to having been introduced by Myrna Loy at a screening of SUMMER SOLSTICE as "my director". Those words had thrilled him as no others could, coming as they did from the lips of his first real crush; he had loved her with an adolescent's passion since the age of twelve, after seeing her for the first time on the movie screen of Brooklyn's Marlboro Theater.

* * *

He was quite beautiful. Five foot eleven of one hundred and eighty compact pounds, hair enviably thick, dark and with regularly spaced waves that looked as if he'd labored over them for hours (I later discovered that they fell into place without any help at all, a cruel affront to a straight-haired, fine-textured individual like me), a short nose with a sweet, slightly bulbous tip that made me want to squeeze it gently to find out what kind of sound it would make, a broad boyish Russian face, and two things I found both exotic and erotically charged: world-class legs and a forest of coarse, tightly curled body hair, first revealed at the beach at Coney Island, where we went on our first date. This only added fuel to the cerebral fire that was already burning in my head, stoked by having discovered that although I'd been a music major in college, his knowledge of classical music was far more comprehensive than mine. (He also introduced me to jazz, which I had previously looked down upon, having been brainwashed by a father who abhorred any form of popular culture. Though he never proselytized, Ralph's enthusiasms were infectious.)

Having married in such haste—three months from the day we met—we hadn't had time to learn much about each other. Looking back, marrying after only three months was a brash and foolhardy thing to do, and I wonder at my (and Ralph's) innocence, not to mention our naïve confidence in our judgment. But in time, he began to unfold as a three-dimensional human being, rather than the Orson Welles clone I had fallen in love with.

As the child is father to the man, he had developed his intellect to make up for a chubby boyhood and a lack of athletic skill. He was an autodidact whose extensive reading of adult books from the age of twelve—no Hardy Boys for him—made him more knowledgeable than most of the formally educated people of my acquaintance. (In this way, he was an inspiration to me, a lackluster student until I went back to school in my thirties for a Master's in speech pathology, and again in my mid-forties for a doctorate.) Although he was a font of arcane information about a surprising number of subjects, one had to know him well to discover this; there was not a jot of braggadocio about him. In contrast, he was almost clownishly proud of my doctorate, bringing it up at every opportunity and insisting on our being introduced as Doctor and Mister. This didn't keep him from giving me a hard time during the four years it took me to earn it; he never got over his resentment about having had to leave college during his first year because of his father's illness. Though generous in many ways, he could never forgive others for being able to do what he'd been prevented by circumstance from doing himself. Unfortunately, this included his children.

By his account, there had been little physical affection shown in his household; his immigrant parents were too bedeviled by the economic hardships that dogged them all their lives to be overtly demonstrative. I didn't fully believe him until the day he visited his mother for the first time since his heart surgery. Although he had called her frequently during that period, she hadn't seen him for three months. Now recovered, he walked into her room in the nursing home wearing a big grin. If ever there was a time for a hug, this was it.

"Hello, Big Boy," she said, and solemnly shook his hand.

She never recognized his formidable talent, or understood that he was a giant in his field. Business success, like that of his brother, she could relate to, but the arts remained always beyond her comprehension. Whenever he told her about an upcoming television interview or a book or lecture tour on which he was about to embark, she would ask the same question.

"Tell me Ralph," she would say, and he would wince in anticipation, "How did they get wind of you?" This only fueled the anger that never ceased to simmer beneath the surface.

He could be both too trusting, and—another maternal legacy—almost paranoid in his dealings with people. This paranoia, directed mainly against salespeople, authority figures and government (he once said that the time to start working to replace the man you'd just voted into office was the day after he was sworn in), was a reflection of his mother's attitude about shoe salesmen. She truly believed that they received a large bonus if they talked you into buying a pair of shoes that didn't fit. On the other hand, some part of him refused to believe that other people weren't as principled as he was. I don't know how he dealt with the cognitive dissonance this must have produced, but somehow he managed.

He could be judgmental and unforgiving with even his closest friends. If anyone disappointed him—and there were many ways in which this could happen—the relationship was doomed. His intolerance for chronic lateness, or for any number of personal habits he found irritating, led him to abandon many friendships. I went along, if reluctantly, and in the process lost many valued friends. But in those years, a good wife didn't sustain relationships with people her husband disapproved of. Whenever I or anyone else attempted to rationalize the behavior of someone who had fallen short of one or another of Ralph's expectations, he would paraphrase a line from his favorite O'Neill play, LONG DAY'S JOURNEY INTO NIGHT.

"That's an explanation," he would say dismissively, "Not an excuse".

People were always disappointing him: a friend would speak rudely to a waiter; a novice film editor would fail to thank him for a recommendation that resulted in a job; another friend who'd asked for editing advice would forget to invite him to a screening of the finished film; his daughter would evidence too much interest in the opposite sex and not enough in her studies; his son would have wasted a musical talent by not practicing diligently enough, and so on.

Shortly before he died, he told me I was the only person who had never disappointed him, which, while flattering, wasn't true. At various times throughout our marriage I seemed to disappoint him a lot: the meals I made weren't interesting enough; I didn't entertain as often as I should; I didn't dress with enough flair, resulting in my looking exactly like the suburban housewife I was; my having gone back to school was interfering with my domestic responsibilities; I was no longer in the arts, having given up music and not yet begun to write—all of which, he insisted, caused him to be excluded from the show-biz social circles he longed to be a part of. Good friends who had dropped out of our lives (because of my shortcomings, I then believed), and who reconnected with me after Ralph's death, confided that while they enjoyed his wit and admired his formidable mind, they disliked his sharply critical tongue and intolerance of their failings. Tact was not one of his virtues.

Having played a fair amount of chamber music in my youth, I had imagined a good marriage as embodying the same kind of interaction I'd experienced making music, with the participants making frequent eye-contact to communicate a subtlety of phrase or a slight change of tempo. I had never played in a group in which there was one strong leader who seldom exchanged looks with the others, but went his own way with the expectation that the others would follow. To some extent, my marriage was more like the latter. But not completely, and certainly not in its later years. Whenever anyone asked me what I felt went into a good marriage—like mine, was always the unspoken tag—I would cite mutual respect, a sense of humor, a continuing (if necessarily attenuated) sexual heat, endless accommodation to whatever drives you crazy about your partner, and a realistic understanding of the alternatives. I never used the word 'love' because I believed then, and still do, that those are its elements. Ralph and I shared them all, which may account for the fact that our marriage lasted; unfortunately they had to co-exist with my over-sensitivity, his moodiness and ever-fulminating anger, and my inability to deal with both of these effectively.

Friends were especially mortified on my behalf when he criticized me in public. When I look back with wonder at having allowed myself to be humiliated in that way, I have to remind myself that this was before the emergence of the women's movement. By nature, Ralph was extremely domineering, and by virtue of his being a male and the mores of the times, he was expected—no, *entitled*—to dominate. It was only in our last twenty or so years that, bolstered by a raised consciousness and the rise of feminism, I began to protest this treatment and fight back. While my hard-won courage and the insurrection it inspired didn't eliminate our problems, it did level the playing field by making clear that I would no longer suffer his verbal assaults in silence. This led to horrendous arguments, but the fact that I was now giving as much as I got made the abuse more tolerable. For the first time, I was establishing myself as an equal, which did a lot for my sense of self; my father, who along with Ralph had been my strongest influence, was, like him, authoritative and uncompromising. I didn't need to have pointed out to me that in some ways I'd married the same man.

Ralph's tantrums were random and without an apparent external stimulus. My initial response was to either sulk or cry, reactions that only added fuel to the fire: an incendiary reminder that he'd once again committed the unforgivable. I now believe that what overtook him during those terrible moments was as irresistible as a tidal wave—a 'brain storm' in the most literal sense. Though I wasn't convinced at the time that his behavior was totally beyond his control, what kept me from leaving him—an option that I contemplated often—was that he never became defensive or tried to justify his behavior after it had blown over.

He could be extraordinarily generous, such as the time he paid for a series of expensive medical tests for one of his students who was very ill, but too impoverished by the cost of her thesis film to see a doctor, or when he spent the better part of a weekend helping to pack several hundred books for a newly widowed friend about to be evicted from a building scheduled for demolition. When our daughter's then inamorato, a college student at the time, was robbed of his beloved saxophone by a junkie who forced his way into their apartment, Ralph bought him a new one. (They broke up a year later, which made him think twice before he did anything that rash again.)

He was, however, less generous with himself. To Emily and Paul, he was the Holy Grail, forever unattainable. He had never wanted children, agreeing to have them only because I made it clear that having children was not negotiable. For whatever reason—I like to think it was love and not merely dependency—he capitulated. Because he had not himself received unconditional love (or thought he hadn't, which amounts to the same thing), he was incapable of giving it. It was only in the last years of his life that he came close to being the father he might have been. Our children were inconsolable for a long time after his death, knowing that he'd died just as he was learning how.

As dynamic and charismatic as he was in public, in private he was often angry and depressed. Emily asked me more than once why I stuck it out. Though she and Paul loved him, they, too, suffered from his unpredictable mood swings and the black depressions that poisoned the air for weeks at a time. During those periods, it was impossible for anyone in the immediate vicinity to concentrate on much else.

Fortunately, I had a safety valve to carry me through the worst; I would escape into memories of my love affair with Joe. Except for its ending, it had been idyllic, and my lover considerate, affectionate and tolerant compared to the moody and carping individual Ralph became during his many depressions. Because I had known about her from the start, but had hoped to change his mind, his choice of Peggy over me was neither perfidious nor totally unexpected, leaving his image untarnished in my memory, and useable for the purposes I put it to. I would summon him up for solace when I needed him, and relegate him back into limbo when I didn't.

I don't know if I did my kids a favor or a disservice by not leaving Ralph. I stayed because he and I shared so much that was valuable: a community of intellectual and artistic interests and a fierce commitment to the institution of marriage and to each other, a legacy from our progenitors and their history of sticking it out no matter what. It was because our children weren't privy to the more covert aspects of our richly textured relationship that they could ever imagine that we'd have been better off apart. To us it was clear, sometimes painfully, that like it or not, we were too closely connected—by love, anger, mutual dependency and respect to give each other up. (He once agonized to his therapist about wanting to leave me, but described me in such glowing terms that the good doctor had to remind him that love and admiration are not grounds for divorce).

Whatever problems we had, and some were never completely resolved, we managed to stay together, and dealt with them as best we could. In time, I realized that Ralph was not solely to blame. It is true that he was an unhappy, driven man, and it is possible that nothing could have reversed his deep sense of bitterness; certainly, years of therapy and anti-depressants failed in great part to do so. But it didn't help that I used my feelings of helplessness and a pose of martyrdom as a means to shame him. For most of our early years, I was too vulnerable, too reactive and especially too unassertive to make a difference. Beyond this, I will not analyze the role I played in the perpetuation of our difficulties; like most people, I am better at recognizing someone else's flaws than my own. Therefore, I can only acknowledge that my behavior contributed to our problems, and leave it for others to speculate, if they feel they must, on how I might have behaved more profitably.

Life with Ralph was part idyll and part ordeal. If examples of the latter come more easily to the pen, they were dwarfed in real life by what he nourished and sustained in me. I entered our union young, naïve and unsure of my worth, partly because of the outcome of my affair with Joe the year before. At the time, I was content to bask unnoticed in Ralph's reflected light: he was the star, and I a planet in orbit around him. I needed that time and those circumstances to mature, and eventually I did. Nietschze wrote that whatever doesn't kill you makes you strong, and despite—perhaps because of—Ralph's volatile and complicated nature, our long association provided me with what I needed. His resentments and need for control were ultimately a positive force in my development: whatever roadblocks he placed in my path forced me to find, fight for and make my own way.

I loved that complex, contradictory man, and twelve years after his death, love him still. Despite his faults—some of which were colluded in by me—his extraordinary mind, his dry humor and sense of irony, his deep and real love for me, his appreciation of my achievements and of the person I became, and not least, the incomparable experiences that his professional lives afforded us both, made me realize long before his death that while I would surely have preferred his unconditional acceptance and a less mercurial atmosphere, I wouldn't want to have shared those years with anyone else.

BoxArt

Ralph's taste in art ran to the ironic, to whimsy, and to any work that met either of those two criteria and also made a political statement. Among others, he loved George Gross, Ben Shahn, Joseph Cornell and Lucas Samaras, whose imaginatively, sometimes grotesquely altered chairs sent Ralph back many times to the Pace gallery, where Samaras exhibited. For me, beauty—or at least my definition of it—was paramount in whether I liked a piece of art, but being less set in my tastes, I soon incorporated many of Ralph's enthusiasms.

A visual creature, as reflected in his choice of occupation, Ralph had always been interested in art, even in its quirkier and less successful trends. But aside from a brief foray into photography during the early seventies—he'd had two photographic exhibits at the Museum of the City of New York—he never felt moved to paint or sculpt anything himself.

We were browsing in a Soho art gallery one day, when he spotted an assemblage of marbles and children's wooden blocks arranged in the shape of the Empire State Building and contained within a heavy aluminum shadow frame. The piece was described as a collage, but the materials used seemed too substantial for 'collage' to be an appropriate designation; 'construction' seemed more appropriate. He contemplated it for several minutes.

"How much?" he asked a nearby saleswoman.

"Two thousand," she said.

He contemplated it some moments more.

"I could do it for thirty," he said thoughtfully, to nobody in particular.

I was momentarily startled; he was sounding like a hayseed viewing a Picasso for the first time.

The next day he purchased a large number of marbles and alphabet blocks from the nearest toy store, and dumped them on the dining room table. After a period of trial and error, he fashioned a hundred or so of them into something resembling the Soho piece. Then, using a tape measure dug out from the disorderly depths of my sewing box, he determined its dimensions, and the next day ordered from the local lumber yard a drawer-like box two inches deep and three times as high as it was wide, which he later painted a deep shade of red. When it dried, he cemented into it the pieces that comprised his design. We looked over the finished product, and agreed that, though different from its inspiration, it was every bit as enchanting as the original. It had cost twenty-nine dollars and forty cents.

But he was only partly satisfied: he needed to prove that he wouldn't always be dependent on someone else's vision. And unlike the piece he'd just completed, he was determined to make a statement. Not for nothing had he been born just before the cresting of the wave of social commentary; in his unconscious, the WPA arts project was still alive and well. However, in a departure from the WPA's socialist realism style, he planned to style his constructions, which would become witty, visual commentaries on ethics, politics, religion and other contemporary issues, in a surrealist mode.

A week or so later, he arrived home from work, turned over his briefcase and dumped several used and very dirty cigarette packs onto the kitchen table. They looked as though they'd been stomped on in the rain with cleated shoes. I looked at him questioningly.

"My next box," he said, grinning broadly.

He had long wanted to memorialize his former cigarette habit, but until he embarked on this hobby—his first—he didn't have the means to express, in anything other than words, his ambivalent feelings about having had to give up smoking. (It had happened on the night of his first coronary, with three Emergency Room medics leaning over his gurney and piercing him with various tubes and needles, and a fourth gathering information that could just as well have been asked of me or read off his drivers license. This may have been to keep him from dying, on the theory that if someone is busy answering questions he will feel obligated to stay alive. He remembered being asked if he was a smoker. "I was," he answered without hesitation, despite having had his heart attack less than an hour before, just as he was opening his second pack of the day.)

He'd spent the better part of that afternoon collecting discarded cigarette packs from the streets of New York, stared at by scores of passersby, confounded by the sight of an elderly, obviously middle-class denizen of the Upper West Side apparently picking up used butts.

He sat down to examine his take. Not quite enough, he said. He needed more raw material and asked if I would help. Which was why, for the rest of the week, *two* elderly, middle-class denizens of the Upper West Side could be seen searching the gritty sidewalks of upper Broadway for the detritus of nicotine addicts too much in a hurry for their next fix to wait until they got to a trash basket to throw them out. Smokers, we decided, are a dirty bunch.

Surprisingly, we found a couple of dozen empty packs of Benson and Hedges—Ralph's former brand for verisimilitude—which he crumpled creatively until they were brought to the desired degree of dissolution. After ordering another box, he positioned the used packs in order of increasing decrepitude to the right of one that had been newly-purchased and left untouched, except for a small opening at one corner that offered a seductive peek at a few of its contents. The last pack, crushed to a state of near-anonymity, was glued to the bottom edge of the frame. He called the piece EARTH TO EARTH, DUST TO DUST, ASHES TO ASHES, and in a flash of inspiration labeled the genre 'Box Art'. When Emily saw it on her next visit, she insisted on taking it back to Beverly; she had just given up smoking, and badly needed a laugh.

His titles were an indispensable part of each work, so I suggested that he cut individual words from various magazines and newspapers, and paste them on the back of the box.

"You know I don't like scut work," he replied. "But if you want to do it, be my guest."

So with this invitation to interfere, I made the titles my responsibility. I set up a folder in which I collected cut-out words and letters of different colors and sizes. I did the same for each of the constructions that followed. Occasionally I would find one of the less common words intact, such as 'epistle' (discovered in a sub-headline in the Religion section of the Saturday New York Times), and pop it into the appropriate folder, awaiting the time when all the necessary elements had been amassed. The results were quite zany. The vari-colored and odd-sized letters of disparate type styles marched tipsily across the back of each box, which eventually came to range in subject matter from conformity in American life through political infighting, the place of bingo in religion and memories of his mother, to a take-off on Christo's Japanese umbrella installation, using Easter grass and a dildo donated by a friend.

Besides the titles, I did the gluing. This was a reflection of the difference in our characters; Ralph, a Libra, had no patience for details; I, a Capricorn, lived by them. He would lay the pieces out in a rough approximation of the finished design and walk away, one of the few things in life he wasn't compulsive about. I would then line them up more precisely, following his prior instructions, make suggestions for small changes, reach for my glue gun or the rubber cement—whichever I thought had the best chance of adhering for the rest of eternity—and go to work. I referred to myself as his atelier. He was grateful as well as amused by the results, but always a collaborator in his work as a film editor, he was loath to admit that anyone else had played even a small role in bringing each piece to completion.

He finished his most ambitious construction in May of '95, a month before we left New York for Maine at the beginning of what would be his last summer. He called it THE EVOLUTION OF MARRIAGE or I DO, I DO. By then he had collected hundreds of unrelated objects, some found, others bought at street fairs, flea markets and botanicas. At country auctions, he would bid a dollar on a 'box of contents', as we once heard them described, and return home with armloads of unrelated treasures, which he placed in large cardboard hatboxes to hibernate until some quirky inspiration dictated their resurrection. They were the last of his things to be disposed of after he died; to me, they embodied Ralph more than any other of his possessions. I kept seven of the twenty-two pieces he managed to complete in those last two years; the rest went to Emily, Paul and a few cherished friends.

In THE EVOLUTION OF MARRIAGE, small figures, the size of those placed on the top tier of old-fashioned wedding cakes, are arranged in groups of two or three. The middle figure, if there is one—he didn't have enough officiators for every set—was always a priest or a minister. In the first set, a small girl and boy, dressed fancifully as bride and groom, play at getting married. Next are three nuptial couples, one Caucasian, one interracial, and one black, the latter a shotgun wedding in which a plastic rifle is pointed at the groom's head. This is followed by a pair of nuns flanking a picture of Jesus, whose eyes follow the viewer as he or she moves along the length of the box. Next are a generic couple, between whom stands a priest in full regalia; the bride is decked out in a billowing white wedding dress and is carrying an infant. And so on, through a gay and a lesbian wedding and ending with a man about to be united with a gorilla, this last, according to Ralph, the ultimate fate of the institution of marriage, considering how its definition was being expanded daily.

I asked him which one he thought of as ours.

"That one," he said, pointing to the children. "We make it up as we go along."

He placed the new construction on the closed lid of the piano I kept until recently out of nostalgia for my musical past. It was almost as long as the keyboard.

"What's next?" I asked, looking at it admiringly.

"No idea," he replied. "Something will come up."

A week later, he started collecting oxymorons. The only ones I can remember are 'black light', 'the smaller half' and 'jumbo shrimp'. He had no idea how to visualize them, he said, but he'd think about it. He would be too busy teaching over the summer to do any work on it, so it would have to wait until fall.

*   *   *

Summer was upon us. My packing, as usual, started a month before we were due to leave, with a check of all the bathroom items I planned to bring along. It was a ritual I performed every June, and this year would be no different. Looking through the dozens of items I'd dumped on the bed from the overstuffed toiletry bag that resided all winter in the linen closet, where I always forgot I'd put it, I remembered wistfully the long ago days when all I needed to pack, for however long a stay, was some shampoo, a toothbrush and a bottle of aspirin. Now, an entire suitcase was required to accommodate the makeup, powders, lotions, deodorants, vitamins and medications, both prescription and over-the-counter, that had become indispensable over the years. The largest carry-on bag I possessed couldn't be zipped closed once I'd put everything in. Of course it didn't help that my hairdryer, an absolute necessity, had a diffuser attached.

Clothing was no different. In July and August, temperatures in Maine can vary from the high nineties to the low forties, with conditions ranging from clear to windy to stormy, sometimes on the same day. That meant taking almost every piece of clothing I own. And a portable ironing board and steam iron to keep them looking presentable. And a stick vacuum cleaner to keep the *house* looking presentable. Plus an electric fan. Ninety-five degrees is ninety-five degrees in whichever State you happen to be vacationing.

And last, but certainly not least, my writing tools. It used to be that Strunk and White's Elements of Style, a thesaurus, a dictionary, a couple of dozen lined yellow pads, some number two pencils, a sharpener and later, a portable typewriter were all that I required to pursue the writers' craft. Now, it was all those things minus the typewriter but plus a computer with monitor, a printer, floppy discs for backup, several reams of Xerox paper, and as much of my latest work as I'd already written, including previous drafts that might end up being better than anything I might turn out that summer. And oh yes, my address book, a calendar and a carton of books for each of us. The spice rack. A non-stick frying pan. The coffee maker. The salad spinner. My favorite kitchen knife. You get the idea.

We usually left on the first Saturday in July. As usual, by that Monday, the living room was so jammed with piles of STUFF that we could barely make our way past them to get to the front door. And this is before Ralph had done any of *his* packing. Each day, as things occurred to me, I added more to the piles, and by the middle of the week, every time one of us had to pick our way through them, I would break into helpless laughter.

Ralph's reactions were the same every year. First, he would get angry (his initial response to almost everything), shouting that I'd have to leave half of it home or he'd refuse to go. But in a day or so, he too would be infected by the ridiculousness of the situation, and we'd both laugh hysterically whenever either of us added another item to the burgeoning heap. And then, just before we were ready to leave, when getting it all into the car seemed truly impossible, his anger would take over again, and we'd spend the last day not talking to each other.

On the designated Saturday morning, we would move it all down to the lobby. By this time, Ralph would be in a state of fury, and I beside myself with the absurdity of it all. I would break into uncontrollable giggles every few minutes, like a hebephrenic who laughs aloud at things not apparent to anyone else. This, naturally, did nothing to improve Ralph's mood. Livid, he would leave to get the car, while I stayed with the goods. We would then pack everything into our VW convertible and take off in angry silence. As always, there was room to spare.

This year was no different. As usual, we were talking to each other again by the time we reached Yonkers.

A Bird's Life

The trip to Maine was uneventful, enlivened only by the hour-long tie up that always occurs just south of Wiscasset, which advertises itself by banner and sign as the prettiest town in Maine. They neglect to mention, however, that the two-block shopping area, lining both sides of Route 1 with seductive antique and bric-a-brac emporia, has several pedestrian crossings without lights, and that Maine drivers, evidently the most courteous in the entire country, will stop for everyone who wishes to cross, even if some of them haven't yet reached the intersection. And because it is, by self-acclaim, the prettiest town in Maine, it attracts many, many tourists, none of whom ever seem to walk on one another's heels. This makes for a steady stream of shoppers strolling in loosely constituted groups, each separated by several feet. It also makes for a line of cars stretching back for at least a mile, and near hysteria on the part of any driver unfortunate enough to be Type A, like Ralph.

To complicate matters, just before the narrow bridge that crosses the Kennebec River and blessedly takes one onto a long, clear stretch of northbound Route 1, is stationed a policeman, who, like traffic cops everywhere in the world, more often delay traffic than expedite it. The officers in Wiscasset appear to be teenagers, and don't have the authoritarian manner necessary to direct traffic properly. As a result, they will let what seems like an endless number of tourists cross to the other side before a single car is allowed to pass.

Ralph could always be counted on to make a fuss about the wait. But this time he was inconsolable. It was our fifteenth year of trying to get through Wiscasset on the Fourth of July weekend.

"I can't stand it anymore!" he shouted, his face turning an alarming shade of crimson. "We're finished with Maine. I will never, ever make this trip again!"

I believed him. (The first time we saw Fellini's "8 ½", Ralph poked me at the point where Marcello Mastroianni fantasizes floating up and out of his car and remaining suspended above a monstrous traffic jam. "That's exactly how I always feel," he whispered.) Then I remembered that he made the same statement every year at this same spot. Knowing that nothing I could say would calm him, I heaved my usual sigh and settled down to biting my nails. Ordinarily I wouldn't have worried, but I didn't like his color. People with heart conditions should trade in their type A for a different letter.

At last we passed the baby cop, my hand clamped tightly over Ralph's mouth lest he shout something insulting out the window and get himself arrested. An hour later we were in Camden, entering the house we'd contracted to rent the summer before.

It was a lovely sprawling house of no identifiable style about a half mile from town, set part-way up a steep hill on a street that led to the sea. Camden Harbor was visible from our bedroom under the dormers on the top floor, as near to heaven as I'll ever get. A small area off the kitchen had been made into a greenhouse and filled with several dozen exotic plants, the care of which I'd been carefully instructed about by the owners. They had also written us about a robins' nest newly built on the wall of the house that backed the front porch. By the time we got there, five blue eggs, newly laid, would have hatched.

The first morning, with the air as crisp as a not-quite-ripe apple, I tiptoed onto the porch and approached the nest. It had been constructed inside a decorative wreath hanging just above eye-level. Many of the materials from which it was made had been taken from the wreath itself, with the result that one flowed seamlessly into the other. A loud, insistent cheeping could be heard coming from its interior. From the corner of my eye I could see a large robin pacing the driveway of the house opposite and eyeing me suspiciously. I lowered myself into the nearest chair, sat down quietly and waited. A minute passed. Then another. The robin was becoming more and more agitated. Suddenly, unable to wait any longer, she swooped under the roof of the porch and landed on the nest. The cheeping became louder as her head ducked this way and that, feeding her large brood pieces of the indefinable object she'd brought aboard. When they were finished, she gave me what seemed to be a sharp look and flew back to the other driveway to resume her pacing. I rose slowly and approached the nest. Standing on tiptoe, I looked in.

Five scrawny necks stretched skyward, at the end of which were five wide-open beaks clamoring for more. I was enchanted; I'd never been this close to birds before if you don't count canaries, and certainly never such young ones. One was somewhat larger than the others (I assumed it had hatched first), three were a bit smaller and roughly the same size, and the fifth was what I came to think of as the runt of the litter: it was only a little more than half the size of its nest-mates and looked puffy and weak in comparison, its feathers bedraggled and irregularly fluffed. I hoped it would catch up to the others in time.

The mother—and father, for he did his part with the brood—soon grew accustomed to my presence, and one day about a week later, I was able to get quite close to the nest during a feeding. Standing on a small wooden box, I had a perfect view of the inside of the nest. I was shocked by what I saw. The four healthy birds were getting their craws well stuffed, but the smallest one, desperately struggling to get close to the source of the food, was being elbowed aside (if that's the proper word) by its stronger siblings. And worse, the parent was totally ignoring it, paying no attention to its anguished cries and plaintive efforts to be fed.

Each day I watched as it grew weaker, becoming smaller and smaller in proportion to its more robust brothers and sisters, who were now beginning to test their wings on short flights. One morning, I watched as the largest of the fledglings flew onto a branch of a nearby tree, sat there a while, then took off and disappeared completely. The mother returned several times that day to feed those that were left. By the next afternoon, all were gone except for the sickly one. Now alone in the nest, it let out a faint, forlorn peeplet and settled into a pitiful ball of dandelion fluff, its head tucked under its wing.

A few minutes after the last of its siblings had left, I saw the mother pacing in her usual manner, with a fresh supply of food dangling from her beak. She seemed oddly hesitant to make the crossing. I retreated to a chair several feet from the nest and continued my watch. After what seemed an uncommonly long time, she flew to the nest. Perching on its rim, she looked in. A nearly inaudible peep issued from inside, and an open beak slowly became visible. At last! I thought happily. Now that the others were gone, the poor neglected leftover would finally get the nourishment it craved. Boy, was I wrong! When she realized which one of her babies remained, she tossed the food onto the porch and left. Simply flew away! Abandoned her own flesh and blood (do birds have blood?), sentencing it to death. Some mommy!

I looked into the nest, uncertain what to do. The bird was clearly moribund, certainly too sick to be rescued. But I couldn't bring myself to kill it, while at the same time, I couldn't bear the thought of its continued suffering. Ralph, ever the cynic, didn't understand why I was so upset. He suggested that I not let it ruin my sleep, as it would probably be dead by morning. His prediction helped ruin my sleep.

Early the next morning, I ran to the nest. The bird was still alive, taking small, shallow breaths and shuddering pitiably. I turned away in anguish, wondering what I could do. Suddenly, there was a flurry of small wings. Summoning just enough strength to heave itself out of the nest, it landed with a thud on the porch. Then it staggered off the edge, leaving a sickly green trail of excrement behind, and fell into a flower bed. Slowly, I made my way to where it had landed. It was lying on the lowest branch of a pink rhododendron, its neck twisted at an unnatural angle. One unblinking eye stared up at me. It was, I noted gratefully, quite dead.

For days I thought about those birds and the pleasure they had afforded me. I mused about the cruelty of nature as opposed to its sometimes unbearable beauty and the feeling of euphoria my first sight of those fledglings had evoked.

I made my way back to the empty nest a few days later, and looked in. Its interior was covered with bits of down and congealed droppings. I followed a greyish-white line down the wall to where it ended in a small, desiccated mound of excrement. In all those weeks, I'd been so entranced by the developing drama taking place inside the nest, that I hadn't noticed the large pile of droppings beneath it. I got a putty knife and spent the better part of an hour scraping it off. Then I mopped the porch floor clean.

Every afternoon, resting from the exertions of writing, I came out to the porch and contemplated the nest, wondering whether I should remove it and clean up the mess that surely fouled the wall behind it. Finally, I decided to leave it for the owners of the house to contend with. It was, after all, their property.

About two weeks after having witnessed my first, and I hoped, last avian tragedy, a different robin, larger than the first, flew onto the porch and made several passes over the nest. She appeared to be casing the joint. I expected her to reject it due to its sorry condition. But she kept coming back, sometimes bearing bits of twigs and what looked like tiny pieces of cotton. Once, she and her mate worked on the nest at the same time.

Curious to see how they were getting on, and with both robins momentarily out of sight, I stepped up on the wooden box and looked in. The nest had been cleaned right down to its base. It was immaculate; all traces of the family that had occupied it earlier that summer were gone. And wonder of wonders, smack in the center of that newly renovated condo lay one perfect egg!

Two more were added in the next week or so, and there was just enough left of the summer to see them hatch. Watching for the event provided no small excitement, and the ultimate emergence of those three fledglings gave me my greatest thrill of the summer. At the same time I noticed, with a frisson of disgust, a hill of fresh droppings collecting anew under the nest. This juxtaposition of fair and foul seemed to parallel much of what I know about life: the highs and the lows of creative work, the pleasures and the travails of relationships, the joys and the agonies of raising children. It is, I reflected, the one certainty of existence, and a perfect metaphor for life in general: Wherever there's birds, there's bird shit.

Omen

The summer was progressing well. I was writing and overeating, as I always did, at the Workshops' lavish buffet, Ralph was teaching his classes and happily playing the role of resident wiseacre and elder statesman, and both of us were being tapped for parts in student films that no one else on campus was old enough to play. A squirrel disrupted TV reception for us and several thousand viewers by barbequing itself while gnawing its way into the main power plant of the local television station, we finally mastered the Dispose-All and the landlord's recycling rules, which had us separating our garbage into no fewer than eight bins, and foolishly, I had just bought a painting at a gallery auction that I wasn't sure I really liked and that I *was* sure we had absolutely no room for in our New York apartment.

The Sunday before we were due to return to New York, Ralph and I were walking on the main street of Camden, discussing my latest essay. Ralph had read it that morning, and had just come up with a solution for a problem of structure that had eluded me for weeks. As we crossed Main Street, still deep in conversation about the essay, he suddenly stopped.

"I need to tell you something important," he said.

We were in the middle of the road. Those wonderfully polite Maine motorists waited patiently.

"When my time comes," he continued, "I want to be cremated, and I don't want a funeral service. Then I'd like my ashes scattered on the Workshop's campus."

I was stunned. Not only had we been talking about something else entirely, but this was a subject he had steadfastly refused to discuss, short of naming two jazz pieces he would like played at his memorial, if, he'd added, anyone thought to do one. And that had been thirty years before, when we were both sure that neither of us would ever die.

At that point, one of the waiting drivers gently beeped—his license plate identified him as a Vermonter—and we made our way to the other side.

"Understood?", he asked.

"Understood," I replied, still baffled.

We resumed our walk. After a while, I forgot how strange that conversation was, coming out of the blue as it did.

That night he reached out to make love for the first time in years; his potency had been compromised by the severe damage to his heart and the high doses of the medications he needed to keep him alive. It would be the last time.

Countdown

By the time we got to the New Hampshire border, Ralph was feeling so exhausted that he asked me to drive. Ordinarily, he did most of the driving himself, no matter how long the trip. He said my reflexes weren't fast enough. I came to prefer being a passenger: his attitude about my driving made me so nervous that I'd make mistakes I never made while alone, like passing stop signs, pulling back into lane too soon after passing, and tailgating, something I wouldn't tolerate in anyone else.

As soon as I took over the wheel, Ralph fell asleep. This worried me a little. He could usually drive for hours without stopping, and never dozed off while I was driving; he felt he had to stay awake to save our lives. I wasn't sorry he slept, though. Without him sitting as taut as an E string in the seat next to me, and with the tension level at zero, I could relax. I got us there in record time and in one piece.

By the time I pulled into the motel parking lot, he was awake and seemingly revived. We registered, locked the car and brought the night's necessities up to our room. It was now six o'clock. After a short walk to get the kinks out, we had a light dinner and repaired to our room. I read for a while, then fell into a deep sleep.

It seemed only minutes later that I was being shaken awake.

"It's almost six-thirty. Let's get going."

"What's the hurry?" I groaned, pulling the covers over my head. I'd been deeply asleep, and resented being forced to rejoin the living so soon.

"I'm feeling too restless to stay put. Please, let's go."

I heard the urgency in his tone. My eyes flew open.

"Is something wrong?" I asked.

"No, but I think I'm having a panic attack."

Ralph had always suffered from mild claustrophobia, a condition that had caused him real distress only once. It happened the first summer after his heart attack. We'd rented a cabin in a heavily wooded area of the Catskills, and towards the end of our stay, it began to rain. It rained steadily for two days and two nights without let-up. Ralph seemed fine until the third morning, when he woke me with the same urgency I was hearing now, to insist that we leave immediately. I'd asked him if I had time for a shower. He said, no, he needed to leave that minute. Until we got in the car and drove out of the woods, I thought he would burst out of his skin.

Now I asked him the same question and received the same answer. I quickly pulled on my clothes. Instead of doing the same, he staggered to the door, opened it a crack, and stood behind it, gulping in air.

"I'm calling the house doctor," I said.

"It's just a little panic," he said. "It'll get better."

"There's no such thing as a little panic," I said angrily. "It's like being a little pregnant."

He started to get dressed, but had to sit down. His breathing became more labored. I helped him into his clothes and pulled him into a standing position.

"Sweetheart," I said, by this time a little panicked myself, "I think we'd better get you to a hospital"

"Don't bug me," he whispered, too weak to shout. "It'll pass."

He slowly bent to pick up his overnight bag, and placed the room key on the dresser as if it might break.

"Don't worry, I'll be fine."

I grabbed his bag and shifted mine to my shoulder. From the way he looked, I didn't think he'd make it to the lobby. He inched his way along the corridor and fell heavily into the first chair he came to.

I glared at him, furious at his obstinance.

"*Now* can I call?"

He nodded, too weak to answer.

I asked the room clerk to send for an ambulance. There was no protest from behind me. What felt like hours later, but couldn't have been more than a couple of minutes, an ambulance pulled up in front of the inn.

This was no panic attack, I suddenly realized, as the medics put him on oxygen and inserted an IV needle; it was heart failure. He'd had two such episodes just after his second attack, which was one of the reasons he'd had to have the bypass. Fluid was building up in his lungs, and if it wasn't treated immediately, breathing would become impossible. If he reached the hospital in time, he'd be given a strong diuretic through his IV line, and within a short time he would be breathing normally.

The hospital was only five minutes away. I had followed the ambulance in our car, and was at the entrance to hold Ralph's hand as he was wheeled into the tiny emergency room. He looked frightened and vulnerable.

The diuretic worked quickly. In less than half an hour, he was breathing without difficulty and asking when he could leave. An EKG documented the extensive damage his heart had already sustained, which, plus his history, made the doctor on duty reluctant to discharge him. Although his vital signs were now normal, the doctor felt it would be prudent to speak to his cardiologist in New York first. The trouble was that Ralph had fired his cardiologist just before leaving for Maine—he was the only person I knew who fired doctors besides me—and was being cared for by our internist, aka family doctor, an excellent diagnostician and a nice guy, whose medical philosophy was that since everything would be all right eventually—or it wouldn't—why hurry. The nice guy was located at home, and promised to fax a copy of Ralph's latest EKG first thing in the morning.

In the meantime, Ralph was complaining loudly. There was nothing to read and nothing to eat. Besides being bored silly, he moaned, he was starving. So was I. Though I suspected he wouldn't be allowed to eat anything, I told him I'd see what I could do, and left.

I remember opening the car door and thinking that I was on my own in a strange town with nobody around to help, and somehow I was managing.

Feeling extraordinarily competent, I started combing the neighborhood for food and a bookstore. Fate was on my side, at least as regards food: I found a pizza parlor, at which I consumed a large pepperoni pizza, not having had anything to eat or drink since six o'clock the evening before. Ralph, at least, was being fed by IV.

I returned to the hospital sated but bookless—it was Sunday, and nothing was open, not even the supermarkets. A slice of pizza, just in case, oozed its topping into my tote. When I asked the nurse if Ralph could have it, she forbade him even to smell it. His level of frustration at its apex, he demanded that the television be connected. But alas, the TV technician wouldn't be arriving until after twelve the next day.

I asked the nurse if a cot could be brought into Ralph's room so that I could spend the night. She said sternly that such a thing was never done, even if the patient was dying, which was not the case with my husband. I said that since the hospital appeared to be almost empty, one more healthy person shouldn't be too much of a burden, but that didn't work.

At eight-thirty I was asked to leave. I promised Ralph I'd be there first thing in the morning, which in hospitals of my acquaintance is five AM if you're a patient and eleven if you're visiting. He asked me to try and spring him then and there, but it was only a gesture—he'd been thoroughly frightened by the events of the day—so I didn't take him seriously. I did promise, though, to call the next morning just after the changing of the guard and ask the doctor in charge what his plans were.

"If you've had a calm night," I warned, "without any temper tantrums or blood pressure spikes, maybe they'll let you go." Hoping that the possibility of freedom would keep him quiet for the night, I kissed him goodbye and set out for last night's inn.

*   *   *

By noon the next day, the fax had still not arrived, and the doctors were reluctant to release Ralph without having had a chance to look at it. He was in a fury at being confined and I was beside myself with anger at our doctor in New York. The day nurse had tried to get him on the phone every hour on the hour, but had so far not been successful.

I decided to call him myself. His secretary picked up.

"He spoke with the doctor up there yesterday," she snapped, "And he's at the hospital. It's his teaching day."

"So when will he be back in the office?"

"Tomorrow after eleven."

"We will *not* spend another night here without any treatment and without knowing when we can leave. Where the hell is that EKG?"

"Our fax machine is broken." I was beginning to feel like Kafka's Joseph K.

"So send it from outside! There's got to be a fax machine somewhere on Madison Avenue! You're in the middle of a big city!"

"I'm the only one here." she said primly, "and I can't leave the office. I'm expecting the repair man."

"When, for God's sake?"

"Late this afternoon or tomorrow."

This was getting beyond ridiculous. I was an experimental rat in an unfamiliar labyrinth and couldn't find my way out. I slammed down the phone and asked the nurse if I could speak to the resident.

"Is my husband in any danger?" I asked, when someone resembling Doogie Howser made his appearance.

The mini-doctor shrugged, walked across the hall to Ralph's room and picked up his chart. "His vitals are OK."

Then he looked at Ralph and smiled professionally.

"How are you today, Mr. Rosenthal?" he said.

"Rosenblum," Ralph replied with his teeth clenched.

"Yes. Can you tell me if you had anything with a lot of salt on it the day before yesterday?"

"Not that I can remember. Why?"

"Because if you'd had a whole bag of potato chips or pretzels or anything like that, your regular diuretic might not have been able to handle it, and that could explain the fluid."

'Oh, God," Ralph said. "I forgot to take my diuretic!"

"When?" asked the mini-doctor.

"Saturday morning before we left Camden."

That was it. An explanation had been found and the mystery was solved. Ralph was sprung within the hour.

We had a quick lunch, got back in the car only a little the worse for wear, and continued our trip home. Ralph, despite my protestations, insisted on driving.

That Saturday night, we attended the wedding of a cousin. Ralph's behavior at the reception was most unusual: he rose, ostensibly to make a toast, but instead told a gross, off-color joke. For as long as I'd known him, his humor had always been informed by wit and good taste. Never before had I heard him deliver the kind of wedding joke, commonly told by an uncle in his cups, that refers leeringly to the coming defloration of a virgin bride. I have a photograph taken at that very moment: Ralph is holding a glass of champagne and grinning with self-satisfaction as our table-mates look at each other in embarrassment. Mortified, I am covering my face with my hands. He would live only another thirty-six hours.

In retrospect, I should have put that uncharacteristic behavior together with the episode of heart failure in Massachusetts, his request for cremation on the streets of Camden and his physical decline in the last weeks of the summer. In retrospect, I should have sensed that the time was drawing near when there would be no more prizes to win or battles to fight, an end to a lifetime of tilting at windmills.

In retrospect, I should have known that my dear warrior was dying.

Aftermath II

Four weeks after Ralph's death, and against my better judgment, I was on the train to Boston. Before leaving New York, Emily had insisted that I visit her for a weekend. She'd suggested a date in early October, and scarcely listening, I'd agreed. Since time was standing still, I figured that October would never arrive. In each of her daily calls she reminded me of my promise, making it impossible for me to claim that I'd forgotten and made other plans. I resigned myself to having to spend forty-eight uncomfortable hours before I could retreat into the solitude that suited me more.

I got to the station early to secure a window seat; if whoever sat in the seat next to me wanted to make conversation, I could turn and look out the window. I feared it would be impossible for me to sustain a casual conversation; I would blurt out my pain at the first provocation and make a fool of myself. Fortunately, the teenager who sat beside me had as little desire to chat as I did.

The trip seemed unbearably long, though it was the same four and a half hours it takes by car. Emily was waiting for me at South Station. As soon as I spotted her scanning the arrivals in the waiting crowd, the waterworks began. They were becoming embarrassing, those unexpected floods. But no one seemed to notice, a benefit of the anonymity bestowed by travel. I was still wet-eyed when I reached her, which immediately set her to crying as well. We hugged until we could speak, then walked arm in arm to where she'd left her car.

She asked me about the trip, and I about Mike, my son-in-law, and their cats. Besides that, we didn't have much to say. Our daily phone calls had used up any news that might have otherwise accumulated.

"Oh, yes," she said, as she edged our way onto the highway. "A friend of mine in Cambridge is giving a party tomorrow night and asked if we'd come. I said we would."

I was appalled. I couldn't conceive of socializing, especially with people I didn't know. My protestations didn't move her.

"It'll be good for you," she said firmly. "I know who's coming, and they're good people. Besides, they're all therapists, and they'll understand if you don't feel like talking."

I hardly found this reassuring; they would covertly examine me for one of the five stages of grieving, with a prize of a week in the Bahamas for the person who guessed correctly which one of them I was currently in.

"We'll see," I said gloomily, knowing in the end I would go. In our shared lexicon, 'we'll see' usually meant 'yes'. I didn't have the strength to resist.

I had agreed to stay for two days; the morning after the party, I would be taking the train home. I longed to get back to New York. Having to be with anyone for so long a time, even people I loved, filled me with anticipatory exhaustion. For the rest of the ride, I tried to figure out how early I could gracefully go to bed, and how late I could reappear the next morning. The number of hours left for togetherness seemed daunting. I felt that I was regressing into the depression I had for a short time seemed to be coming out of. Somehow, we got through Saturday; I spent some of the daylight hours talking to the cats and the rest accompanying Emily and Mike on errands. That evening we looked at a video tape. I couldn't remember a thing about it in the morning

The next day was scarcely better. The three of us tried valiantly to talk about something other than Ralph's death, but we finally gave up. I worried aloud about my future, at the same time assuring them—though not completely believing it myself—that once I got past the next few weeks, I'd be fine. Em and Mike told me that they had talked about adding a wing to their house if I would consider moving in. I was touched by their impulse, but inwardly I shuddered. The offer was its own reward. To accept would be a kind of suicide; I would be abdicating my life. However, it did put things in perspective: only recently able to think of autonomy as a promise instead of a threat, it made me consider the alternatives. That night, I found on my pillow a gift from one of the cats: the head and liver of what Mike later identified as a vole. I took it as an omen of sorts and tried to divine its meaning, but its exact significance eluded me.

I can't remember what exactly was being celebrated the next night—our hostess' birthday, her cat's birthday or *Roshashona*, but whichever it was, to me it was a nightmare. To start with, the streets of Cambridge were impassable; a carnival had been held that afternoon and was in the process of being dismantled. Traffic was so heavy that despite having allowed sufficient time, we were almost an hour late.

I wanted to leave as soon as we stepped into the apartment; it embodied all my as yet unexorcised fears about the future. The hostess, whom I will call Abigail, was just as Emily had described her: warm, chatty and interesting. But I could see nothing beyond the surroundings. The single room was too small to hold the eight or nine guests already there, much less the worn furniture that filled every last inch of floor space. It was garishly lit by a ceiling fixture that held a bare bulb, the glare of which was only partially diffused by a torn paper globe. Two dented pots sat on the chipped enamel stove that leaned at an angle against the far wall, and not one of the rickety, mismatched chairs set around the ancient table that dared anyone to call it an antique, seemed sturdy enough to hold even my reduced weight. The room looked poverty-stricken. This is what I'd been seeing in my dreams; this was my destiny after the money ran out. Abigail, I'd been told, had been divorced for many years and was an interior designer currently down on her luck. My fate, I feared, would be worse; unlike Abigail, I didn't have an ex-husband in the wings to lean on in a pinch, nor did I have any work I could be out of. Besides, I was at least twenty years older than Abigail. If *she* had to live that way, how would I, a woman nearing seventy, manage?

Somehow I got through the evening. While the company was pleasant, I was devastated by this preview of my future. One of the guests complimented me on how well I was doing so soon after losing my husband, which seemed like a strange observation for a psychotherapist to make; she should have been able to see past the dark eye makeup and the slim figure to the ever-threatening tears and the too-rapid weight loss. I didn't sleep at all that night; in a show of sympathy, two of Em's cats jumped on the bed and lay against me, one on each side. It wasn't too comfortable, but at least it kept them from collecting more voles.

The next morning, Emily drove me to the train. Somehow, I managed to keep from breaking down, even during the long goodbye hug. But I cried into the streaked and clouded window all the way home.

Some days later, I received a call from Lewis Cole, chairman of the film department at Columbia University, where Ralph had taught for the last seven years. He said that the dean of the School of the Arts wanted to sponsor a memorial service at Columbia's Miller Theater. When would be a good time? I wanted to say that there was no good time, that all I wanted to do was bury myself under the covers and not have to deal with it, and that a memorial service for Ralph would only make it more difficult for me to deny that he was dead. I told Lewis that I couldn't face a memorial just then, but he might try scheduling it in six or seven weeks, a figure I pulled out of the air. Having lost all sense of time, it sounded sufficiently distant never to arrive.

My days were filled with trivia. I went through Ralph's files and discovered that I was entitled to several small pensions from various unions. In order to activate them, letters had to be written and phone calls made. Social Security had to be notified. So did the stockbroker who handled our IRA's. Bills had to be paid. I would need some cash to tide me over. A life insurance policy from Columbia would take me through the following summer, but I had to fill out half a dozen forms and submit an affidavit before it could be paid. Ditto with an annuity I never thought I'd live to redeem. Everything, it seemed, called for an affidavit, each of which necessitated a visit to a notary. Acknowledgments had to be sent to everyone who wrote in condolence. The phone wouldn't stop ringing: from people I hadn't heard from in years, from people I hadn't called but who had learned of Ralph's death through his obituary in the Times, from friends who wanted to know how I was doing, daily from Emily and Paul. One morning, copies of the death certificate arrived in the mail, sending me back to bed for the rest of the day: Ralph's name was so prominent on the page that it seemed to be printed in neon.

I had appropriated his massive rosewood desk for the enormous amounts of paperwork that suddenly engulfed me, as my smaller one was completely taken up with my desktop computer. The desk was six feet long and three feet deep and it offered more room to work on, despite being a microcosm of his penchant for carefully arranged clutter. Two thirds of its surface was hidden under a bevy of miniature picture frames into which he'd inserted his favorites among our family snapshots and photographs taken with some of the luminaries he'd worked with.

One night, writing replies to the mountains of condolence notes that had arrived within the past two weeks, I noticed a photograph that I was sure hadn't been there the last time I'd looked. It was an old, faded print of a young man and woman, set in a frame I didn't recognize. I leaned forward to examine it more closely.

It was a snapshot of the two of us taken just after our marriage, forty-seven years before. I am gazing up at him in adoration; he is looking down at me with a slight smile. I remembered where it was taken: on the boardwalk at Brighton Beach. The photo was a color print that had faded almost completely to brown.

As a child, I would spend hours going through our family album. The sepia-toned prints of my grandparents as newlyweds and my parents as babies would transport me to another time. 'Yesteryear', 'yore' and the crossword puzzle word 'erst' have always bought to mind the color of those photographs. For me, brown and buff were the colors of the past, and if enough time had elapsed between viewings, the creams would have edged further towards yellow and the browns towards rust. I, on the other hand, existed in the here and now, the moments of my life and those of Ralph and our children preserved in color and black and white. This difference had so far assured me that despite my advancing age, I was still a child of modern times, an era that began for me in 1927, the year of my birth. But when I saw that faded photograph of my young husband and myself, I knew that I, too, had become a scrap of yesteryear and yore and erst. The past now included me.

With this realization, I began to see myself as fragile. I was in reasonably good health at the time. But what if I fell or had a stroke and wasn't able to reach the phone? And what was my actual financial situation? Would it be enough for my needs? (I could expect to live another fifteen years according to the actuarial tables, even though I didn't much want to.) How soon would I have to move from my apartment in order to postpone, for as long as possible, the inevitable state of penury? I would have to live on whatever income I had; my writing couldn't keep me in cashew nuts.

I couldn't read, hardly slept and barely ate, losing fifteen pounds in as many days. I reversed day and night, sleeping fitfully during the day and staring into the dark until dawn. I misplaced everything I touched, the most important of which was my driver's license, for which I had to apply again. Taking the subway to the Motor Vehicle Bureau was a nightmare; people seemed to travel only in two's, making every public conveyance a parody of Noah's Ark. I forgot my keys twice and had to call a locksmith, because Ralph hadn't believed in leaving keys with superintendents. When the Con Ed meter reader rang at eight o'clock one morning, I refused to let him in, fearing he might be an imposter bent on mayhem or worse. I left the apartment only during the daylight hours, and infrequently at that, too fearful to brave the streets after dark. Whatever time I spent away from Ralph's desk, I spent in bed. My initial anger at Ralph for having deserted me began to abate, to be replaced by a disconcerting habit of dissolving into tears for no apparent reason.

I felt as though I were living someone else's life. My days were suffused with an air of unreality: lights seemed brighter, natural light more dim. Friends called to ask me for dinner, for a walk, for a movie; I always declined. I spent days moping around the house listening to Bach's unaccompanied violin sonatas, as I had done years before when Ralph had left me, I'd thought, for good. Sometimes I would say the word 'widow' aloud over and over until it lost all meaning, the way my life had. In a strange way it was comforting to wallow in gibberish and not have to think. I wondered how long this would go on.

One morning, I received a call from Ralph's cousin, Estelle. She and her husband, Amos, friends as well as relatives, were planning to visit the Edward Hopper exhibit at the Guggenheim that afternoon, and asked me to come along. By that time I had sunk back into my lethargy and would have preferred doing nothing. But partly out of gratitude, and partly because I didn't know how to refuse graciously, I agreed.

As it turned out, their enthusiasm for Hopper evaporated when they saw the long line of people waiting to get in. Amos remembered having read about an interesting exhibit at the Asia Society, so we set out for Seventy-first Street and Park Avenue. So far, the day's excursion had failed to lift my spirits; never during all my years of marriage had I spent time with the two of them without Ralph at my side. I felt split down the middle; one part of me continued to participate in the conversation, while the rest couldn't wait for the afternoon to end.

When we arrived at the Asia Society, the receptionist informed us that the exhibit we'd come to see had just closed. But, she added, we were just in time for a complementary bus that would take us to the Noguchi Museum in Queens and bring us back to Manhattan two hours later.

Now, while Queens is one of five incorporated boroughs that constitute the city, privately I had never acknowledged it as part of New York. In my parochial estimation, Manhattan was the only real New York and the other boroughs mere appendages. Traveling to Queens when I was already feeling so deracinated was unthinkable.

"Why don't you two go, and I'll take a cab home, " I suggested hopefully. The effort of keeping up my end of the conversation was exhausting me.

"If you don't want to go there, we'll do something else," Estelle said. I was disappointed, hoping that because my discomfort was showing, their good deed was becoming as much of a strain for them as it was for me.

"I don't think so," I said, wishing everybody would leave me alone. "We've done a lot of walking already, and I'm really tired."

Amos took my arm. "Why don't we have some coffee and we'll talk about what to do next."

I sighed deeply and capitulated. It might as well be Noguchi as anything else. Fortunately, we couldn't find seats together on the bus, so I didn't have to talk. I felt all talked out. What on earth would we say to one another for the rest of the afternoon?

The moment of my entrance into that cool, tranquil garden with the stone sculptures and fountains dotting its minuscule confines was an epiphany. It was a long time since I'd experienced such a visceral sense of beauty. It took me completely by surprise. Faint with delight, I lowered myself onto one of the benches lining the narrow path and allowed myself to melt into the scene. For a few seconds, I completely forgot the circumstances that had brought me here. Amos and Estelle had tried to take me out of myself for an afternoon; they'd accomplished that and more. Sitting in that lovely garden, I was suffused with a sense of serenity and wholeness. It was—and I've always hesitated to use the word—a spiritual moment, one that marked the beginning of my recovery. The feeling didn't last, of course, but for that hour my solitude seemed a bit less oppressive and my future less dire.

Little by little, the more positive possibilities inherent in living alone began to occur to me. I began to anticipate some of the ways my new independence might manifest itself. If I ever developed an appetite again, I reflected, I could eat anything I wanted at any hour, no longer tied down to preparing Ralph's set-in-stone three-course, seven o'clock dinner. Furthermore, if I ever worked up the energy to move to another apartment, anything I might buy—a lamp, a chair, a new set of dishes—need please only myself. And never again would I have to walk out of a supermarket because I couldn't bear hearing my husband shout at the clerk for checking out someone with eleven items who had dared to get on the ten-items-or-less line. Never again would I have to question my own worth because Ralph, in an ugly mood, had denigrated me before others. Never again would I have to stand in the shadow of someone bigger than life.

Friends who had been privy to the difficulties in our marriage could see the change and complimented me on 'not overplaying the widow thing', as one of them characterized it. They mistook my new perspective for relief, not realizing that I was mourning Ralph as much as before, but without the sense of desperation I'd felt previously. For the sake of domestic peace I had sublimated much of my anger and my need for autonomy to Ralph's need to dominate. Though things had been much better between us in the last half of our marriage, we were still, with some important modifications, the same people we were.

My unaccustomed sense of freedom was a counterbalance to the grief, not a substitute for it. A measure of my new confidence was that I didn't feel it necessary to explain to anyone what might have seemed an unnaturally quick recovery. If any of my friends could have observed me in my private moments, they would have seen me continue to burst into tears over nothing, drag myself out of bed every morning and fight to keep from getting back in, lie awake at night for hours, too catatonic even to reach out to put on a light. But the inner reality was more complex. I was slowly reinventing myself. Neither my evolving self nor my feelings of loss were diminished by this metamorphosis. On the contrary, in their balance was my salvation.

Inexorably, the day of the memorial drew closer. The positive feelings aroused by my afternoon at the Noguchi resurfaced occasionally, but always left as quickly as they had arrived. My eyes were still bright with fatigue. I had lost another ten pounds and my flesh no longer filled my skin. I wondered how fashion models managed to stay alive; I'd been eating next to nothing and still wasn't in their league. As yet unable to concentrate, it was necessary that I try, for I had decided to write—and what's more, deliver—a eulogy.

Ralph had always railed against light-hearted memorials, perhaps peculiar to show-business, where the frailties of the deceased are paraded as if they were virtues, and the laughs outnumber the tears. And with Anne Meara and Herb Gardner scheduled to speak, I worried about the tone. I felt I owed it to Ralph to inject at least one note of mourning into the proceedings, and because he so admired personal courage, I was determined to read the eulogy myself. By this time, the bulk of the paperwork was behind me, and with little else to do every day besides assuring each of my children that I had survived the night, I was able to write it in three hours.

For the next two weeks, I practiced reading it aloud. But no matter how hard I tried, I always broke down in the middle of the first paragraph. Finally, I was forced to admit defeat. Using an old Walkman, I taped it, two and three sentences at a time, waiting until I'd regained my composure before recording the next few. It took two days to complete. I was ashamed at having capitulated to my weakness, but if I was unable to read it in the privacy of my own apartment without breaking down, I knew I would never get through it standing on a stage in front of five hundred people.

The week before the memorial was frantic. This being a form of show-business, Lewis had appointed one of the students as stage manager and invited me to his office to meet her. For the first time since Ralph's death, I found myself on the fifth floor of Dodge Hall. I kept my composure until I heard a familiar voice and followed it into one of the editing rooms. There, on what had been Ralph's desk, was a framed promotional poster for his first photography exhibit. Unable to resist the wave of grief that overcame me, I crumpled into the nearest chair and started to wail. The time of that exhibit had been a heady time in our lives, and a source of joy for both of us. Lewis, who had been waiting for me in an adjacent office, heard the commotion and came to get me. Gently, he led me to his office, where, after allowing me a few minutes to recover, he introduced me to the stage manager. She was a frighteningly competent young woman in her first year of film school. Beneath the professionalism she brought to the task, I sensed awe that she was the one chosen to stage this tribute to a man whose work had so impressed her that she had applied to Columbia largely because he taught there. She had missed meeting him by two days.

She took me down to the Miller Theater, showed me its sound and lighting capabilities and asked what I had in mind. I listed the few things I wanted included, and we discussed their possible order. I had hoped that putting the memorial together would be simple and that the school would take care of the details. I was wrong; nothing about it was simple and my involvement was taken for granted. The number of decisions to be made astounded me. They included where the lectern should be placed; how large the rear-projected picture of Ralph should be; from which side of the stage the participants should enter and how much time should be allotted to each; what kind of equipment would be necessary to show the videos already in preparation and to play my taped eulogy as well as the music Ralph had specified, and on and on and on. Additionally, the typography and layout of the printed program had to be decided upon. So did the wording of the memorial notice that the film school would be placing in the Times.

There were other tasks as well, which were mostly my responsibility. The most difficult was having to go through dozens of old photographs of Ralph in order to find two that I liked most. One was to be printed on the back of the program, and the other would be projected onto a screen that was to serve as a backdrop throughout the proceedings. The memories aroused, both pleasant and otherwise, caused me excruciating pain at a time when I was least able to handle it. Everything else was easy. I was too busy to think, which was all to the good. Besides the choosing of the pictures, I welcomed the distraction; there would be plenty of empty days ahead.

Miraculously, it all came together, and the day I had dreaded for weeks arrived. As soon as I stepped out of the cab, I was surrounded by people: film students, friends, relatives, students of mine from my years at Lehman College, neighbors from the many places we'd lived, high school friends of Paul and Emily from New Rochelle, even people Ralph had been estranged from for years. The street in front of the theater looked like a first night; hundreds of people waited to enter.

The doors opened. From inside, I could hear the strains of Just a Closer Walk with Thee, a traditional New Orleans funeral march both in dirge and up-tempo, played by the jazz clarinetist George Lewis and his group. It was one of the two selections Ralph had requested years before. We took our seats and the lights dimmed.

The dean of the School of the Arts opened the ceremony by noting that when he had announced Ralph's death to the faculty on the first day of the new semester, he'd asked for a rousing three cheers instead of a moment of silence. I was deeply moved; three cheers captured Ralph's spirit in a way that silence never could. Herb Gardner and Anne Meara spoke, and then Lewis showed slides of most of Ralph's BoxArt constructions. Ralph had tried to have them exhibited, but without success; this would be their only public showing. Each piece was greeted by the audience—for the memorial was, from start to finish, a show in the best sense of the word—with appreciative giggles and applause.

There was a video scroll of some of Ralph's best aphorisms, eulogies from students that were powerfully affecting in the tearful expression of their appreciation and love, some gently humorous speeches by former colleagues from the film industry, an achingly evocative video of excerpts from filmed interviews done with Ralph at the Rockport Workshops, a tribute by David Lyman, the Workshops' director and a friend of many years, a tender speech by our son, who was petrified of speaking in public, but did so anyway with grace and courage, and then it was my turn.

With a spotlight on an empty lectern, reminiscent, I realized later, of the riderless horse at the funeral of a president, my disembodied voice issued from the loudspeakers. There was a collective gasp from the surprised audience, who had expected me to appear on stage like everyone else. My eulogy was short.

"When Ralph and I first met," it began, "I was enchanted by his vaguely depressed air and the artistic angst that I could sense lay not far beneath the surface. He seemed to me a regular Jewish Byron. In the days that followed, I discovered his other more felicitous qualities, and fell in love. We met in late June of nineteen forty-eight, became engaged three weeks later, and were married in November of that same year. It may have been the most precipitous act of Ralph's life. His family was scandalized. Given our short acquaintance, they never expected it to last. True, our marriage was a tumultuous one. But to everyone's surprise but ours, it grew, deepened and flourished for nearly half a century.

"Ralph was an understated man, a man of talent, generosity and wit. His greatest strength, as well as his greatest fault, was his uncompromising nature; he was a hard taskmaster. He despised these things above all: ignorance, arrogance, incompetence and sham. His standards were almost impossibly high—and they were non-negotiable. His saving grace was that he held himself to the same high standards as he held others, and gave himself every bit as hard a time. He toughened people, knowing that toughness is a necessary attribute in any creative field. He did this by seldom taking time to praise what was good; like the master editor he was, he cut to the chase. I for one will miss him as the one person whose honesty about my work could be counted on, and whose praise, when it came, was a benediction. For Ralph, whether as editor, director or teacher, it was only the work that mattered. Ego never entered the equation.

"He died young in spirit, and much too soon. But I suspect that after his coronary, which left his heart more severely damaged than he wanted known, he struck a bargain with the powers that be. He would give up a few years of life in exchange for three things: the strength to continue teaching with his usual intensity and brio, a twice weekly cigar, and an occasional corned beef sandwich. I think this was less self-indulgence than a way of living out his abiding belief that less is more, which, when you think of it, is merely a restatement of that old show-biz motto, 'Always leave them wanting more'. He did."

The music resumed, this time with Buck Clayton's recording of Duke Ellington's Limbo Jazz, a piece that inspired us, one rainy afternoon in our youth, to abandon our plans to see a movie and make love instead. I like to think he had that afternoon in mind when he asked me to have it played at his memorial.

There was a buffet set up in the lobby of Dodge Hall that I was eager to get over with. It would be my last obligation of the day, and then I could go home, though between Emily, Paul, Mike, Mike's sister, his son and daughter and sundry other friends and relatives, I wouldn't be getting much privacy. As I made my way through the crowd, a woman Ralph had once worked with came over to greet me. Her expression, as befitted the occasion, was mournful.

"I know just how you feel," she said somberly. "I went through it myself six years ago. It's terrible."

I nodded, waiting for her to go on.

"It gets worse," she said squeezing my hand, and disappeared in the direction of the food.

Dodge Hall was packed. It was like the opening night party for an Off-Broadway production. Taking a deep breath, I plunged into the crowd. David Lyman noticed my entrance, and elbowed his way toward me.

"How're you doing?" he asked, giving me a quick hug.

"OK, I guess. But I'm going to miss my summers in Rockport."

"Don't be silly," he said. "You'll come and visit. I'll put you up for as long as you like."

"Thanks David," I said regretfully, "But I don't think so. Rockport was Ralph's territory, and I have no role there anymore. After I come up in June with his ashes, I'll be on my way."

He looked thoughtful. "You know, there's a book I've been trying to finish for a couple of years now. Why don't you plan on spending a few weeks at the Workshops next summer and help me put it together?"

It took me less than five seconds to make up my mind. Here, at last, was both the promise of continuity and the possibility of something new. The abrupt cessation of my previous life had been giving me the emotional equivalent of the bends. True, I had never done any book editing, but I was pretty good with words and had a feeling for structure. I'd learned, after all, from a master.

"Deal?" David asked. I searched his face for any sign of equivocation. There didn't seem to be any.

"Deal," I said, and we shook hands. I felt better than I had in weeks.

So, I thought happily, next summer is taken care of. All that remains now is to fill the time between.

Joe

The days began to seem less empty with the prospect of a summer in Maine to sustain me. Between the now-familiar bouts of depression and panic about the future, I had pipedreams about my work on David's book becoming the start of a new career. In anticipation, I bought a text on copyediting for the purpose of learning the requisite shorthand. I'd seen editors' marks on the manuscript of my first book, but except for a few of the more common ones, like stet and dele, they might as well have been in Sanskrit.

I set about trying to read it, but it was apparent that I was not ready to take anything in; I still couldn't focus my attention on the printed page for more than a few minutes at a time. Undiscouraged, I put the book aside, knowing that at some point I would once again be able to process what I read and retain at least some of it. Though I still passed much of each day in a state of near-somnambulation, I was beginning to imagine a less dismal future. All I needed was time.

I was most concerned about my listlessness. My appetite had fled: I ate no more than a can of fruit and a bowl of cereal a day, which was probably as much responsible for my lack of energy as depression. Because I was looking so drawn, I made a resolution: I would start to cook again. Having a few of my favorite dishes at hand might tempt me to eat.

I rolled my shopping cart to the supermarket for the first time in weeks, my eyes welling up every time I passed an older couple. It was becoming annoying always having to squint through tears to see where I was going. I bought enough barley, onions, carrots and celery to make a huge pot of vegetable soup, a large selection of fruits for a major fruit salad, and a variety of exotic greens. Then I pushed the cart to Jake's, an upscale fish emporium, and bought a salmon fillet. The fact that the salmon was expensive would be added incentive to eat it before it went bad.

When I returned home, there was an anguished message on the answering machine.

"Tell me that what I just heard about Ralph isn't true," wailed the voice on the tape.

It was the second wife and now widow of our late accountant, Sam. I hadn't called Greta about Ralph because she and I had never really been friends, and I had contacted only relatives and my closest friends. Anyone else, I expected, would either hear about it through the grapevine or read about it in The Times, which had published not only my paid obituary and Columbia's, but also an article about Ralph's career. A few weeks later, there had been an item about the memorial. I couldn't imagine anyone not knowing. But Greta, more depressed than I and for a longer period, had insulated herself from the outside world. She had heard about it only by chance, through the accountant both she and I had been using since Sam's death.

Sam's first wife, Lois, was my mother's closest friend. She was also the elder sister by fourteen years of Joe, my first lover. It was Lois, in collusion with my mother, who had brought Joe and me together. Halfway in age between my mother and me, Lois later became my friend as well, and throughout the years she casually kept me apprised of the major events in Joe's life. I knew that he'd earned a Masters degree at NYU and become a science teacher in the New York City school system, that he had three sons and a Scottish terrier, and that he'd moved out of Manhattan to somewhere in Queens, a borough composed of a huge number of disparate neighborhoods, separated from Manhattan by a moat called the East River.

Once, in the early 'seventies, I'd seen his face reflected in the mirror of a midtown Chinese restaurant, but though we briefly touched glances, he failed to recognize me. I had also seen the back of his head from the last row of the chapel at his sister's funeral service ten years before. But those two sightings were the limit of our contact; we hadn't spoken in almost fifty years.

After Joe's sister died, Sam married Greta, then his secretary, and fifty years his junior. Greta stopped working after her marriage to devote herself to Sam's care. He was a frail seventy-five at the time and an even frailer eighty-two when he finally succumbed to heart failure. Greta was inconsolable; she had genuinely loved Sam, despite the difference in their ages. Though only thirty-two, she was convinced that her life was over. It was a self-fulfilling prophesy; she remained so depressed and talked so obsessively about Sam's death, that her friends finally stopped calling. With no financial incentive to work, she had spent the ensuing six years sleeping all day and nursing her grievances at night. She would call me once a year to complain at length for as long as I could tolerate it—sometimes I would let her go on for an hour or more because I felt sorry for her—about the perfidy of her friends, about how much she missed Sam, about how he had died alone because of the inhumanity of the hospital staff, and about how miserable and lonely her life was now that he was gone. Though I felt for her, I avoided calling, because it was the same hysterical litany every time we spoke. My resolve not to end up like Greta may have been my major incentive to start cooking again.

After a few words of condolence, she embarked on her usual monologue. This time, there was something new.

". . . . and Sam's family has been rotten to me ever since he passed away. The only one who ever kept in touch was Peggy, and now that she's gone, I'll probably never hear from any of them again." She continued to talk, but I had stopped listening.

"Hold on, Greta," I said, interrupting her. "Back up a couple of sentences. Now that *who's* gone?"

"Peggy. Joe's wife. She was the only good one."

My heart was beating wildly. "What do you mean, gone?"

"She died two months ago. In August."

"Oh, God. What from?"

"Ovarian cancer. She had it for more than a year. They never even called to tell me she died."

I barely heard her as she continued to vilify her late husband's family. All I could think of was that although Joe and I had suffered a similar loss, Peggy's dying had taken a long time and must have been terrible to watch. I'd had it easy by comparison: Ralph's death had taken place in an instant, and I hadn't even known it was happening. How awful it must have been for Joe, I thought, as Greta droned on. It struck me as eerily coincidental that in light of our history, we had not only married within two months of each other, but been widowed two weeks apart.

My immediate impulse was to send him a note of condolence, but I hesitated. To begin with, he might not remember me; I had no assurance that Lois had kept him informed about my life the way she'd kept me informed about his. I doubted he even knew my married name, making it unlikely that he would connect me with Ralph's obituary, even if he'd read it. I was also concerned that he might interpret a note from me as an attempt to reestablish our relationship which might have been the case, although I was aware of no such intention at the time. I didn't want to see him as an old man; almost half a century had passed since our affair ended, but in my memory he was twenty-four. Still, for old times' sake, I felt that I wanted to communicate my feelings of empathy.

Sentiment finally triumphed over reticence. I wrote a short note expressing my sympathy as someone who had suffered a comparable loss. I followed this with a three-word sign-off, the exact configuration of which eluded me for the better part of an hour. I chose, finally, 'With remembered affection'. Too shaken to cook, I froze the salmon, washed and rinsed the greens, and stored the vegetables in the vegetable bin. Everything would keep until I regained my composure. I had stopped thinking about Joe after Ralph's death, the raison d'etre for his periodic emergence from my unconscious having ceased to exist. But Greta's call had brought back memories of our shared past and unsettled me more than I liked to admit. It took me three days to recover enough to thaw out the salmon.

When I opened my mailbox that day and saw an envelope with my name printed on it in a vaguely familiar hand, it was a minute before I realized whom it was from. There was no name on the return address. It was the Queens postmark that gave it away; I didn't know anyone else who lived in Queens. I went upstairs, my heart beating wildly, and placed the letter on the table. It lay there a long time while I debated whether or not to open it, wondering, a la Dorothy Parker, what fresh hell this might bring.

Every possible 'suppose' jostled for space. Suppose he thanked me for writing, but didn't remember who I was. When he hadn't recognized me in the restaurant mirror fifteen years before, I had smoldered for weeks. Or suppose he suggested that we get together. Was I prepared to face the reality of a seventy-two year old Joe? To carry it ridiculously further, suppose that out of loneliness we started to date again, a ludicrous concept at our age. Besides, it was only two months since Ralph's death; what would my children say? There was one final, unthinkable suppose: suppose some of the old feelings resurfaced and I found myself becoming emotionally involved again. Impossible, of course: who could feel romantic about an old man, even if he *had* been my first love and comfort fantasy for the past forty-seven years? And would I be willing once again to sublimate my own wants, compromise in all the ways a relationship demands, reassume all the household obligations I was just starting to enjoy being free of, now that I had taken inventory of my new life and seen its possibilities? The answer to all of the above was a resounding "Not on your life!" I toyed with the idea of discarding the letter unopened, but soon my pulse returned to normal and curiosity won out.

Joe's note was even shorter than mine. He expressed thanks for my letter, added a few words of condolence and ended with the following lines: Perhaps we should meet. At the very least it could be therapeutic, and at best, enchanting. If you agree, please call.

He included his phone number, which, aside from the area code and one digit in the exchange, matched Emily's exactly. Another coincidence.

Damn! I said aloud. Why couldn't he simply have called me himself and not left the ball in my court? Then I remembered his defining characteristic: diffidence was his middle name. Unless he'd changed radically in the intervening years, it would be out of character for him to act otherwise. He had taken my letter exactly as I thought I'd intended it: as an expression of sympathy and not an invitation. In his quiet way, he was signaling his interest, but leaving the decision up to me.

I started the soup, took the salmon out of the freezer and prepared the marinade. Then I washed my hands and dialed his number.

His voice hadn't changed. Along with its Irish tenor overtones and the faintly Bronx-inflected consonants, the past came flooding back with the force of a tsunami. He asked if he could take me to dinner. After a moment's internal struggle, I suggested he come to my apartment instead; I had bought provisions enough for a small army. Between the two of us we might eat enough to have made it worthwhile.

"How about tomorrow?" he asked.

"Fine" I said, thinking there was nothing fine about it. I'd acted impulsively and now I was stuck with the consequences. We set his arrival for six o'clock.

My mother had taught me how to make her ambrosial fruit salad the day before her hysterectomy; she was afraid she wouldn't come out of the anesthesia and wanted to pass it on. She actually survived for another thirty-two years, but because of her foresight, I acquired not only a great recipe, the secret of which lay in lemon juice, sugar and a shot each of Amaretto and Banana Liqueur, but something else that I discovered serendipitously: an unbeatable therapy for stress. This benefit lay specifically in the squeezing of the lemons. I always juiced far more than were needed, just for the calming effect. A great many lemons may have been wasted in the pursuit of my mental health, but I'm convinced that the act of squeezing them saved me from several breakdowns.

I use an old glass juicer to do the job, a round one with a ridged dome rising from the center and a depression around the base of the dome in which the juice collects. Squeezing half a dozen lemons, as is my habit, requires both digital and upper arm strength. I realized early on that if I ever developed arthritis, I'd have to retire that marvel of functional design or give it to one of my children, neither of whom can tolerate fruit salad anymore, and check myself into Payne Whitney. Reconstituting frozen lemon juice just doesn't do it for stress.

Squeezing the lemons worked that day as it always did: I was feeling much calmer by the time I finished. But still, I was worried. Despite the slowing of time to a near-standstill, both the evening of Abigail's party and the afternoon of the memorial had indeed arrived. I was anticipating Joe's arrival with the same anxiety, and there wasn't enough time left for the hours to drag. They would pass, and at whatever pace, it would be too fast for me. The doorbell would ring, I would open the door and there would be . . . . I couldn't imagine.

First Love

I met Joe at the end of 1945. Both my mother and Lois, who felt more like his mother than his sister because of the difference in their ages, had their own reasons for bringing us together. My mother's was that I was almost nineteen and about to enter my marriageable years at a time when there was a dearth of available young men, World War II having occupied them elsewhere. Lois's was a concern that Joe might be becoming serious about a young woman he had met in England, where he had spent the war years. Though he'd downplayed the attachment, she didn't want to take any chances. Her only objection to Peggy was that she wasn't Jewish; her main reason for introducing me to her brother was that I was.

As Joe was being shipped back to the states in August of 1945 with the expectation that he would be sent to the Far East, President Truman dropped atom bombs on Hiroshima and Nagasaki, thereby ending the war. Instead of the Far East, Joe would be sent to Fort Dix, New Jersey to be discharged. In the meantime, he became an unwitting participant in Lois' plot.

The week before Joe and I were introduced, I'd met Andy, another soldier about to be demobilized, who had asked for my phone number and promised to call. I was much taken with him and prayed that he would. That may be why I wasn't especially impressed with Joe the first time we met.

Lois called me one evening to suggest I come by the following afternoon to pick up her copy of a two-piano piece that my mother had requested. I discovered that she had asked Joe to come over at the same time on another pretext. Our meeting, though planned to the minute, would seem accidental enough not to arouse our suspicions. I barely glanced at Joe when we were introduced; I was more interested in getting home to Brooklyn, where a message from Andy might be awaiting me. When I got up to leave, Joe asked if he could walk me to the subway. I agreed; it was a bright autumn day, just right for a stroll, and there was no reason for me to go right home. We strolled through Riverside Park, kicking idly at fallen leaves and making desultory conversation.

At first, it didn't come easily. Joe was the personification of laid-back, though the phrase wouldn't come into currency until several decades later. He was content to walk in silence for many minutes at a time. This was not my style at all; I was a chatterbox, and silence made me uncomfortable. But things eased up after a while, and we ended by spending a pleasant, if unspectacular hour together. After we said goodbye, I promptly forgot about him and hurried home to what I hoped would be the much anticipated message from Andy. He hadn't called.

Two weeks later, a friend offered me two tickets for a chamber music concert that she was unable to attend. By that time, having given up on Andy, I wondered aloud who to ask. My mother saw her opportunity and suggested that Lois' brother might enjoy going—she'd heard that he liked classical music. I called Lois for his number and asked if he'd like to go.

That night, I fell in love. I'd been too distracted to pay much attention to Joe that first afternoon; now I was seeing him more clearly. What I saw was a big, sturdy twenty-two year old with the sweetest expression I had ever seen on a man; the two most influential men in my life so far had been my father—short in stature, demanding and something of a despot—and my brother, otherworldly and well on the road to the schizophrenia that would dog him all his life. Joe, in contrast, was ingenuous, good-natured and serene. He was tall—six-foot-one, the antithesis of his sisters, neither of whom were able to attain the height of five feet without standing on their toes. A gentle giant, he was large-boned without being overweight, with thick, wiry hair that at first glance seemed a darkish brown, but which was revealed in sunlight to be a rich, burnished copper. He had the pale complexion typical of redheads, and light blue eyes under epicanthic lids. The slightest hint of a smile caused them to narrow into slits, the heritage, perhaps, of Russian ancestors who might have lived near the Chinese border. His expression was mostly serious, leavened by an occasional, barely discernible twinkle in those disappearing blue eyes.

He had beautiful hands, I noticed for the first time that night: long, narrow violinist's fingers (sadly, he didn't play an instrument), in total negation of the rest of him, which looked comfortably soft and cuddly. And in a total reversal of my first impression, he revealed himself to be an amusing and knowledgeable conversationalist, a fact I discovered during the hour's walk that preceded the concert and included a dinner of two Nedicks hot-dogs with mustard, sauerkraut and an orange drink. He took me home that night on the subway, but to my disappointment, made no attempt to kiss me goodnight. Though kissing a boy on a first date was frowned upon in those days, I was upset not to have been given the chance to flout convention.

Two weeks later, he called again. He said he'd be leaving for Fort Dix in a few days to receive his discharge and wouldn't be back for a couple of weeks. Would I like to go for another walk?

"Oh, yes," I replied immediately, trying not to sound too eager and failing utterly.

"Fine," he said, apparently unfazed either by my enthusiasm or the prospect of the long trip to Brooklyn. "I'll be there in an hour."

Not for a minute did I contemplate playing hard to get, despite my father's admonitions. My father had a philosophy about everything. For male-female relationships, it consisted of the following: never tell a boy you even like him until he has proposed, never let a boy touch you below your earlobes until you're married, and always remember that it's just as easy to fall in love with a rich man as a poor one.

By the time Joe arrived, I was in a fever and more than a little desperate, knowing that I wouldn't see him again for several weeks. During our walk, I asked him a thousand questions; here I was, head over heels in love with someone about whom I knew nothing at all.

His mother, he told me, had died when he was ten. Lois was living at home at the time, but she worked and was also courting, which resulted in her being out most of the time. His other sister, already married, had moved into her own apartment. And his father, a sewing machine operator in the garment trade, worked long hours and seldom came home before ten.

"So if no one was around, who brought you up?" I asked, feeling distinctly over-familied.

"I did," he answered without a trace of resentment. My heart began to melt.

"What about meals?"

"I learned to cook, after a fashion."

"At ten?"

"Well, it wasn't gourmet."

"And school?"

"I played hooky some, but I went most of the time. I remember feeling really proud of myself for showing up and doing my homework without anyone telling me to."

My heart was now a puddle of molten lava.

Peripatetic from the age of four, he had wandered over half a mile from home when he was five, to explore the interior of a cathedral in Bay Ridge. He was lost to the world for several hours, while his parents scoured the neighborhood with rising panic. By the age of six or seven, he was satisfying his wanderlust via public transportation, which may have been the genesis of his lifelong interest in trains. Later, during the war, he traveled every part of England by rail and bicycle until he knew it better than most natives.

When he wasn't exploring the city, he was reading. By the time I met him, he knew, it seemed to me, just about everything about just about everything. I was dazzled by his erudition.

When it was almost time for him to go, he kissed me lightly on the mouth.

"Tell me about Peggy," I said, in a burst of bad timing. I should have been savoring the afterglow of that kiss, but it was important that I know how serious he was about the girl he'd been seeing in England. If he said he was in love with her, I would end it now and be spared both missing him while he was away and daydreaming about his return.

He looked startled. I explained that Lois had told my mother that he'd had a girlfriend in England.

"What do you want to know?"

Since I'd gone this far, I might as well go for broke. I took a deep breath.

"Are you in love with her?"

For a long moment, he didn't answer. "I'm not sure," he said, finally.

I searched for a less direct phrasing. "Well, do you have . . . . an understanding?"

He looked me straight in the eye. "We talked about the possibility of her coming here, but nothing's definite. Anyway, it wouldn't be for a couple of years. There's all kinds of red tape."

"How come you didn't get engaged before you left England?"

"The subject never came up."

I took a deep breath. I was about to break one of my father's cardinal rules. "I really like you a lot," I said. "But I don't want to see you again if you're planning to bring her over."

Another long pause. "I'm not absolutely sure."

I wasn't happy about that 'absolutely', but Joe seemed incapable of guile; if his responses were equivocal, the equivocations were, I decided, unconscious.

Then he added "I don't even know how I'm going to make a living."

He had answered a question I hadn't asked, and in retrospect, I should have intuited the implied antecedent, as in "How can I make definite plans to bring her here when . . . ." But on balance, I was encouraged: he wasn't sure he loved her, they weren't engaged, it would be years before she could come over, and anyhow, such a decision hadn't yet been made. Plus we'd had a lovely afternoon and he'd kissed me goodbye. On the other hand, he hadn't called for two weeks. I interpreted this as reflecting a fearsome struggle between wanting to see me again and his feelings about Peggy, and that somehow I had won the battle, if not yet the war. Curious to learn as much about her as I could, and sensing that the subject should not come up again, I asked if he carried her picture. From his wallet, he drew a small photograph and handed it to me.

She was lovely. High-cheekboned and wasp-waisted, she had a gentle expression and eyes the color of turquoise and the shape of tilted almonds. If I were smart, I told myself, I'd give up now. Gentleness was not one of my qualities, I had no waistline to speak of, and my cheekbones could only be inferred. But, and this is what decided me to stay the course, my competition was three thousand miles away, I was here, and there was plenty of time. Looking back, I think that trying to disengage Joe from Peggy is the only deliberately unethical thing I have ever done. But I wasn't thinking ethics just then. This was the man I wanted—to marry, have children with, and live with for the rest of my life. That's the way young women thought in those days.

"Write to me," I said, as he started down the subway stairs.

"I will," he replied, and disappeared into the bowels of the IRT.

Joe left for Fort Dix that weekend. As promised, he sent me a letter. I remember nothing about it except that he used the word 'ubiquitous' in referring to the comic books most of the servicemen read to pass the time. It was the first time I'd ever encountered it, and to this day, that word carries a vaguely sexual aura. By the time he returned, I was more taken with him than ever.

He introduced me to his friends. With one or two exceptions, they weren't especially warm, but having never been part of a crowd, I was having my own problems relating to them. One thing did strike me as strange: whenever I made an entrance, one of the young men in the group would sit down at the piano and play the same two songs. I didn't know their titles, having almost no knowledge of popular music. (Some thirty years later, I heard them broadcast in the same order on an FM station, and being well acquainted with the genre by that time, was able for the first time to see their connection to our situation. One was PEG O'MY HEART, and the other AIN'T MISBEHAVIN'. My reaction was to say aloud "Why, those bastards!" before breaking into laughter.)

Six months later, Joe and I were sleeping together—a 'forties euphemism more gracious, if less accurate, than today's terminology. We would meet a couple of times a week, sometimes by design, sometimes by accident (my voice teacher's studio was a block south of Joe's room), stroll through a museum, go for a walk in Central Park or see a foreign movie, mostly at the Apollo on Forty-second Street. Then we would breathlessly climb the five flights of stairs to his tiny room near Central Park West and make love. Our affair was strongly sexual, though without the nuances that experience and a predilection for sensuality bring. I was overwhelmingly in love, not only with Joe, but with the new and wonderful sensations my body was discovering.

I was so distracted that I barely managed to maintain a low C average during my last year in college. I was so distracted that almost every minute I spent practicing the piano or my vocal exercises was wasted. I was so distracted that when Aunt Evelyn, my voice teacher, asked me point blank if I was having an affair, I was so amazed she'd guessed that I admitted it.

Only once, half way into our two-year affair, did I ask Joe if he was still in touch with Peggy. He said they wrote, but offered nothing more. I didn't pursue it. Lois, my pipeline to Joe's life away from me, had already told my mother that they were still corresponding regularly, and I had hoped he would be more forthcoming. But it wouldn't have made any difference; by that time I was so besotted that I couldn't have walked away either on principle or for the sake of my self-respect. It would take a good deal more than that.

Early one Saturday morning, my mother knocked on the door to my room, sat down on my bed and told me that Lois had just called to report that the day before, Joe had posted the bond required to bring Peggy here. Lois was devastated. She swore that if she'd known it was that serious, she would never have introduced us. Joe, singularly undemonstrative and very private, had never completely revealed his feelings to her. In fact, I don't believe he'd thought it through himself until a decision had to be made, making his behavior less deceit than denial. There is no doubt that he loved me after a fashion, just not quite enough. I was, after all, smart enough to be interesting, lively enough to be amusing and bosomy enough to warrant the attention of passing truck drivers, the litmus test of the 'forties. In addition, I was very much in love with him and made no demands; I'd simply played the waiting game without thinking about how I would feel if I lost.

I got dressed in a fury and took the subway to Manhattan. Forty-five minutes later, my anger at full throttle, I stormed into his room and shook him awake. I raged at him for twenty minutes. He should have told me he was sending for Peggy, I sobbed, and not waited until I found out from someone else. He sat mute with shame during the entire diatribe, offering no defense; he had simply been postponing the inevitable, hoping it would all go away. His not having told me himself was the only thing I could fault him for. I had known about Peggy from the beginning, and he'd admitted that they were still in touch. If I had asked the right questions, he would have told me the truth—lying wasn't in his character. But I hadn't asked, because I couldn't bear to know.

I left him sitting on his bed with his head in his hands. He had said not a single word. Half-blinded by tears, I stumbled back down the stairs. My heart, as I should have anticipated all along, was broken into small, bleeding bits.

Deja Vue

At precisely six-thirty PM, November 6th, 1995, one day before what would have been Ralph's and my forty-seventh anniversary, the doorbell rang. I took a deep breath and opened the door. There, holding a bottle of wine in one hand, a bouquet of tulips in the other, and wearing an expression as miserable as the one I'd lately been seeing reflected in my mirror, stood a total stranger. He looked far older than the seventy-two years I knew him to be, his jaw almost invisible under the dewlaps that age invariably brings, and a swath of scalp where wiry bronze hair used to grow. My young lover was nowhere to be seen. We stared at each other for some time. He was probably thinking the same thing about me. I must be demented for having agreed to see him, I thought. What could we possibly have in common after all this time?

The first half hour was as awkward as I'd feared. I asked if he'd like something to drink.

"Yes, thanks," he said. "A beer if you have any."

I didn't. He settled for club soda. I suggested we open the wine he'd brought.

"Not right now," he said. "I'll have some with dinner."

We sat for a while, saying little. I didn't have a clue as to how we could span the nearly fifty years between this meeting and our last.

The silence was getting to me. "It's rough, isn't it?" I said.

Some icebreaker, I berated myself, remembering how reticent he'd been about expressing feelings in the old days.

He nodded and looked down at the floor. We'll never make it through dinner, I thought desperately. I searched for something to say.

"Thanks for the tulips. They're lovely." It was all I could think of.

He nodded again. "You're welcome."

"Maybe we should eat," I said, and escaped into the kitchen.

I set the table and called him in. The soup was under-seasoned, the salmon was dry, and the orzo was well past al dente. I'd forgotten how to cook. But it hardly mattered; neither of us was hungry. Thankfully, our common lack of appetite gave us something to talk about while we picked at our food.

By the time dinner was over, we'd shared a little about our lives. Joe had lived in one apartment in Jackson Heights for the past forty-five years, while I had moved a total of seven times, from Brooklyn to Manhattan to New Rochelle and back to Manhattan. He had taught science in the same secondary school in Queens for all of those years, while I'd had seven successive careers—as a folk-singer, piano teacher, speech pathologist, college teacher, co-founder of a bed and breakfast agency, and writer. Joe's social life centered around the activities of three British expatriate organizations, one of which was founded by his wife, while mine was built around seeing other couples, and consisted mostly of concerts, theatre and dinner parties. Joe was a golfer, a bicyclist and a bird-watcher, I was a dedicated couch yam. He saw very few movies; I saw almost every one made. He'd gone to nearly every musical on Broadway; I saw mostly serious plays, and went to the theatre less often. He favored symphonic works—mostly Brahms, the French composers, Celtic music, marches, Gilbert and Sullivan and pop singers like Tony Bennett and Nat King Cole; I liked chamber music, lieder, jazz and Big Band. We both read voluminously, but his tastes ran to science, history and biography, mine to fiction and memoirs. I was impressed (and in some ways dismayed) by the different directions our lives had taken, including the apparent fact that Joe had no interest in how he looked: his clothes were ill matched and obviously untouched by an iron, while I always dressed with an eye for color and style, and ironed absolutely everything. In short, he was lamb shanks and I had pretensions to galantine.

When we were done with the facts, we entered the realm of feelings. Joe had been delighted with every aspect of his life; he'd awakened each morning asking himself what he'd done to warrant such luck. He adored his wife, was enamored of his children, and was loved by each of them in return. With the exception of one son's diagnosis of cancer in 1981—by coincidence the same year Paul was diagnosed with a sarcoma, both successfully treated—and, of course, his wife's death, his life had been remarkably happy and free of trauma.

It sounded like science fiction to me. As I described the kind of man my husband had been, the ever-present tension in our lives and the medical problems both children had in infancy and early childhood (both had celiac disease and were severely allergic) I could sense his amazement; in his well-ordered and sheltered universe, almost nothing went wrong.

We spent a few minutes talking about the different perceptions we had of our now ancient affair. There was one odd moment when he described an incident that had happened some months before we technically became lovers.

By his account, my parents had gone out for the evening and we were alone in the house.

"Wait for me here," he remembers me saying, "I'll be back in a minute."

At that, I disappeared into another room, to emerge a moment later entirely naked.

"Look," he recalled my crying out in unselfconscious pride, as I turned in a pirouette to reveal the lines of my firm nineteen-year-old body. "Isn't it beautiful?"

He never forgot that moment, he said. I didn't remember it at all. But it was strange and wonderful being reintroduced to that ebullient young woman, aware for the first time of how lovely her body was, and wanting to share her delight.

He admitted to having thought about me once in a while, but not in the way I had thought of him: his feelings were mainly of guilt for not having told me immediately about his decision to send for Peggy. Having failed to do so, he said, was the only dishonest thing he'd ever done. I told him we were even: in trying to replace Peggy in his affections, I'd racked up a little guilt myself.

We finally come to the thing we had most in common: the loss of our partners, alternately reminiscing and weeping as we spoke of their last months. We were like two toddlers who play side by side but not together: each of us had a story and we told it, but essentially to ourselves, waiting through the other's recitation until it was our turn again.

Joe was in even worse shape than I. The manner of Ralph's death had been a blessing, though it hadn't seemed so at the time. Peggy, on the other hand, had been ill for a year and a half. He had refused to let anyone help, caring for her entirely by himself, despite her being paralyzed and wheelchair bound during the last six months. His sons were attentive and concerned, but only Seth, their youngest, lived close enough to visit frequently. His eldest son, Robert, made the trip to from Virginia to New York every weekend, while John, a geologist who lived in Alaska, could make only infrequent visits. Until days before Peggy died, no one in the family had faced up to how ill she really was; no one was prepared for her death, though the increasing seriousness of her condition had been recognized months before. More than two months after her death, Joe was still in shock.

We talked for hours, and were thoroughly drained. In all that time, I had no sense of the person Joe had become, or whether any part of the wit and the intellect that once had me in thrall had survived the years. His air of hopelessness was pervasive, and masked everything else, if indeed anything remained.

I looked at my watch and was startled to find that it was past midnight. Joe stood up.

"I'd like to borrow a copy of your book," he said. My first memoir had been published sixteen years before, and I'd mentioned it during our catch-up earlier that evening.

I took his request to indicate that he wanted to see me again. To be honest, I wasn't at all sure if I wanted to see him, having no idea of what he was like behind the scrim of his depression. Given the range and tenor of our conversation, this one evening seemed closure enough. It was therefore with some reluctance that I gave him the book. We walked to the door. I was eager for him to leave, wanting nothing more than to sleep.

Standing against the half-open door, he put one arm around my shoulder and gave me the trace of a hug. I reached up to reciprocate. Then, the most astonishing thing happened: that small gesture grew into a full body hug that lasted several minutes and brought with it a deep exchange of feeling. All of our separate pain was melded and subsumed into that extraordinarily tender embrace. As we released one another, he bent and kissed me gently on the mouth. There was a faint suggestion of tongue. Hesitantly, I met his with the tip of my own and felt a surge of feeling in my groin.

"Oh, dear God!" I said to myself despairingly. "Not again!"

He left without a word.

I couldn't sleep despite my fatigue. My grief for Ralph and that goodbye hug were fighting for equal time, making for the worst interior battle of my life. Ralph's absence was palpable, and his death not yet entirely assimilated. Along with this was my growing sense of excitement over the prospect of being able to live only for myself. Now I was faced with the reappearance of someone with whom I'd once had a passionate affair. My barely nascent independence was being threatened. I wanted no involvements, no matter how carefully contained; in ways both positive and otherwise, my relationship with Ralph had been quite enough for one lifetime. Now my emerging future was being threatened by a hug. The worst of it was that despite being at war with myself over this new complication—or perhaps because of it—I was aware of feeling alive for the first time in months. At the same time, I resented the fact that it had taken a brush with my past to accomplish this; I wanted to have done it myself. I fervently hoped that Joe would hate the book, be turned off by the memory of the overcooked salmon and never call back.

On the morning of the second day, he phoned. "I owe you a book and a dinner," he said without preamble. "When are you free?"

I toyed with saying 'Never', but I was curious to know what he thought about my memoir; a writer's ego is not a sometime thing, and no one had asked to read it in years. I checked the calendar. Every day that week was full; my friends were taking good care of me.

"Nothing 'til next Friday, I'm afraid."

"What about today?" he asked. There was an urgency in his tone I hadn't heard even in the old days.

"Well, I'm going to a screening later, and the friend I was supposed to go with has a cold. You're welcome to come if you can tolerate a double feature."

Having been told two nights before that he disliked most contemporary American movies, I was surprised when he accepted.

"What time?" he asked.

"One-thirty," I said, and gave him the address. On reflection, I decided that seeing a double feature was probably a good idea. After the marathon talk we'd had the other night, I wasn't sure we had anything more to say.

We both arrived at the theater a half-hour early. I had to smile, watching him walk up the street: he was wearing a ghastly green tweed suit, a memento, no doubt, of his years of summers in England visiting Peggy's family. With time to kill, we decided to walk to Central Park and back. I noticed the change in him immediately: he looked years younger, and was lively, cheerful and amusing. His depression had largely disappeared. I asked him what had happened in the past forty-eight hours to have effected such a dramatic change.

"The hug," he said. I knew at once what he meant. I had felt the same healing force, and notwithstanding my ambivalence about seeing him again, I'd already noticed its positive affect on my mood.

He said that he was unaccustomed to hugging of any sort, much less the all-enveloping kind we'd exchanged two nights before. Hugs hadn't been in Peggy's repertory, as they hadn't been in Ralph's. I, on the other hand, was addicted to them, having had a mother who handed them out like tootsie rolls. I hugged my children, my friends and Ralph (though he was the least receptive) whenever I was moved to do so. Hugging, for me, was more expressive of feelings than words, and much more necessary. The embrace that Joe and I shared had been the equivalent of a therapeutic touch. It had dulled the edges of our pain and opened us to feelings we would not have given ourselves permission to feel towards anyone else. Our shared history had inspired the hug, which had in turn inspired the dramatic change in Joe's mood.

We entered the theatre and took our seats just as the lights dimmed. By the beginning of the second feature, a creeping anxiety had overtaken me, all but blotting out what was happening on the screen. During our walk, everything I had once found irresistible about Joe had again become manifest—his sweetness, his intelligence, his command of arcane bits of information relevant to practically any subject, and his wry apprehension of the world. A lifetime had passed since our halcyon days; he walked a bit stiffly as if touched by arthritis, and dressed in the manner of an English gentleman fallen on hard times, the result, I surmised, of having hung out with expatriate Brits for most of the intervening years. And I'd never had a relationship with male-pattern baldness before; throughout his life, Ralph's hair had remained as thick as when we'd met. Every physical vestige of the boy that had been Joe, with the exception of his voice and his disappearing eyes, was gone; I was sitting in that darkened theatre with an old man. But oddly, none of that mattered. He had made a tentative bid to become part of my life again, and before we knew if this second coming would lead to anything, some landmark events had to be gotten through, most disturbing of which was bed. Granted, it might not happen right away, but it was definitely in the cards. And I was having a problem with that.

I, too, had changed. My body now bore the stigmata of fifty years of aging, stretch marks from two pregnancies and a hysterectomy scar the least of them. With a sinking heart, I did a quick inventory of every one of my bodily defects, certain that they would be an immediate turn-off for anyone who hadn't experienced their accretion gradually. When I finished contemplating my own fleshly shortcomings, I tried to visualize Joe's. The prospect of having to deal with a body that might be in comparable shape, even if I had known it intimately a half century before, was less than beguiling. Besides, it occurred to me that he might no longer be sexually viable—my impression, garnered mostly from the pages of the New York Times Science section, was that most men in their seventies weren't. And even though at our age it might not matter one way or the other, the process of discovery was unimaginable.

My sense of discomfort grew. I was beginning to anticipate the inevitable denouement the way a gladiator might have anticipated his encounter with a lion. When it would come to pass was the big question; I couldn't imagine Joe making the first move. But given that it had to happen, the thought of having to live even one more day with the anxiety I was experiencing was becoming unendurable. There was no sexual component to the anxiety; going to bed with Joe in his present form was simply one more Herculean task to be gotten through, like Ralph's memorial.

By the time the movie ended, I was ready to suggest that we forget about dinner, go back to our respective apartments and never see each other again. But oblivious to my distraught state, he cheerfully suggested that we return to my neighborhood and eat at a Thai restaurant he'd passed on the night of his visit.

We couldn't find an empty cab—it was the height of rush hour—so we walked to the bus stop at the corner of Sixth Avenue to pick up the M5 bus. While we waited, we talked about the movies we'd just seen, though I could barely concentrate on the conversation, after which he said that having shared one of my interests, he would like me to share one of his. Would I care to visit a wildlife preserve in Queens and watch birds that coming weekend, or perhaps go cycling in Riverside Park? This last prompted, as a therapist of mine once termed it, a sudden rush of shit to the heart. I hadn't ridden a bicycle since my teens, wasn't good at it then, and suspected that if I tried again, I'd break a hip.

I was crazed. Here was Joe, laying himself out for me like a picnic lunch, and all I could think about was that sooner or later I would have to face bed. Between waves of panic over its inevitability and the need to keep up my end of the conversation, I considered the possibilities. On the one hand, he might run screaming from the room at the sight of me in my flowered flannel—the only nightgown I possessed. On the other hand, *I* might run screaming from the room at my first sight of him in whatever mode of dress he considered appropriate for a first encounter. And even if we could tolerate the sight of each other, we might not be moved to do anything more than—literally—sleep together. In light of our youthful passion, I found this scenario the most depressing of all.

Suddenly, with the bus less than a block away, I turned to face him. My next words came as a complete surprise—to me, as they no doubt were to Joe.

"You'll be staying over tonight," I heard myself say in an incongruously conversational tone. "Should we pick up some bagels for breakfast?"

I stood there frozen, aghast at my audacity. I was hardly a shrinking violet, but still, I'd never propositioned a man before.

Joe looked at me thoughtfully for a long moment.

"Bagels would be nice," he said.

The ride uptown was interminable. Not a word was said. Dinner was no better—just one more agonizing delay before the moment of truth. We bought some bagels on the way to my apartment, and I nearly groaned aloud when Joe expressed a preference for poppy seed. By unhappy coincidence they'd been Ralph's favorite as well. I'd always hated them: I was still finding months-old poppy seeds tamped into the grouting of the kitchen tiles. The bagel transaction concluded, we headed home. By then, it was almost nine. Like someone who is facing major surgery and is unable to picture anything beyond the incision, I couldn't imagine anything beyond putting my key in the lock.

I managed to kill five minutes by completely rearranging the closet as I hung up our coats. I killed another five moving the bagels with exaggerated care into poppy-seed-proof plastic bags. It was now eleven minutes after nine. There was nothing left to do but make a pot of coffee; bedtime at nine-eleven is for impatient lovers, and I was certainly not that. Neither, from the look of it, was Joe. He was sipping his coffee slowly, with no indication in his demeanor that his evening's companion had just made an outrageous proposal. In our day, nice girls don't go to bed on the first date, even the second. Not in the 'forties.

Time passed in excruciating increments. I kept looking at my watch, hoping both that the hands wouldn't move and that they would move faster so we could get it over with. Joe seemed unnaturally calm. After several centuries, the foyer clock struck twelve. The next move would have to be mine, it appeared, as Joe seemed perfectly content to sit and chat all night. I stood up.

"Well," I said in a voice more suitable to an execution than a seduction, "I guess it's time."

My flowered flannel was hanging on the back of the bathroom door. For a minute I considered getting under the covers in the altogether rather than put it on, but that, I felt, would be giving myself an unnecessary handicap. Better to wear the flannel with its pink peonies and red cabbage roses and take my chances. I am by character more flannel than silk, and on flannel would my future rest. Shivering, I slid the nightgown over my head, got into bed and pulled the covers up to my neck.

"Ok," I called weakly, and placed my fate in the hands of the gods.

There will be no description here, elliptical or otherwise, of what ensued. I am of the wrong generation for that. Suffice it to say that yes, he could, and our lovemaking was as delicious, intoxicating and graceful as it had ever been in our youth. There was not one moment of awkwardness; however altered, our bodies were merely the conduits of our mutual need and our joy in having rediscovered each other.

Later, I asked him playfully why none of the women he'd known for years, most of them now widows, had snapped him up. He thought for a moment.

"I'm an acquired taste," he said, smiling that remembered smile. His eyes narrowed, then disappeared.

With his arms around me, I settled into sleep. He was indeed an acquired taste, and it looked as if I was in the process of acquiring it once again. I silently begged forgiveness of Ralph, and fell asleep.

FLAB

Joe went back to his apartment to change his clothes—he would return that evening. I wandered from room to room in a daze of confusion about what I had wrought. What had happened the night before would never have taken place without my blatant invitation; Joe was not the sort to have initiated it himself, at least not for a while.

When I thought about it rationally, I was appalled: I had taken a lover a little more than two months after the death of my husband. It was not only unfathomable, it was, in my overwrought mind, grounds for excommunication from the human race. How could I have let such a thing happen, I asked myself, realizing immediately that the premise of my question was incorrect. I hadn't *let* it happen, I'd *made* it happen. I might better have stated it: How could such an upstanding citizen, who'd been to bed with only two men in her entire life, have made such a precipitous move? There had been Joe before my marriage and then Ralph, both for love. Irrationally, for a lifelong irreligious, I believed in the sanctity of marriage, and unless my friends were fantasizing or downright lying, I was the only woman in my circle who had remained faithful to her husband. True, I was guilty of having had what could be interpreted as adulterous fantasies about Joe through the years, but they had been a safety valve for what might otherwise have been untenable circumstances; I never thought about him when things were going well. In that way, he may well have saved my marriage.

Nevertheless, what I'd done was not only out of character, it affronted my sense of decorum and my image of who I was. Grieving such as I'd experienced over the last two months was incompatible with the ease with which I'd extended my impetuous invitation of the night before.

I tried to put a spin on it that would make it seem less arbitrary and reestablish my good sense of myself. To begin with, I argued, Joe had been a presence in my life since 1945—a literal presence for the first two years, and because of the nature of my marriage, a phantasmic one for the last forty-seven. Second, I had been very much in love with him, at times desperately. These two facts made him more than an acquaintance with whom I'd hopped into bed at the first opportunity. I was sure that had we met as strangers even a year later, this never would have happened; by then, I'd have been settled more or less happily into my independent state, his age would have put me off, and so would his natural reticence, which precluded easy intimacy.

But enough with the conjecture, I scolded myself; the deed was done. And despite having spent less than twenty-four hours together, it was clear that we were on again. By all the evidence, Joe felt the same; we'd discussed plans far into the future, pretending that the future stretched out as far as it once had. I was aware that the prevailing wisdom is not to jump into anything new for at least a year after the death of a spouse, but except for the difficulty I had simply believing that Joe and I were together again after all these years, it felt natural, inevitable and right. What didn't feel right was the fact that it was happening so soon after Ralph's and Peggy's deaths, and that we'd fallen so easily into a physical relationship again. Besides the speed at which it had happened, we were *old*!

In an attempt to reinstate reality, I stepped out of my clothes and stood in front of the full-length mirror on my closet door. I had already come to terms with the surface changes accruing to my aging flesh; it was its flaccidity that I minded. Still, I'd long ago rejected the idea of having any plastic surgery. I have always held in mild contempt, masked as amusement, those of my contemporaries who do to their bodies what, if anyone else did by force, would be grounds for an appeal to Amnesty International. Face lifts, nose jobs, breast augmentations, chin reductions, butt implants—all these have seemed to me capitulations to the unrealistic standards arbitrarily set by an ageist society.

I reminded myself that despite all the signs of age, I had just been found desireable by someone to whom I was similarly attracted, reason enough not to consider performing any of the atrocities on my flesh that modern medicine has made possible. Modern medicine had already made its mark on my flesh; when putting me back together after a hysterectomy, the surgeon had sewn my previously symmetrical belly-button into a narrow diagonal slit, leaving my abdomen with not only the usual scar, but also a look of mild inebriation. I could have complained to the surgeon, of course, and gone to the trouble of having my old belly-button restored, but it didn't seem worth it; there were too many other problem areas that would remain the same.

Well, I thought, looking hard at my face, it doesn't hurt to dream. With thumb and pinky, I stretched my skin into a reasonable facsimile of a facelift. Even though it did impart a more youthful look, it did nothing for my naturally receding chin and short neck, so I couldn't see the point of going through all that pain. Besides, even if I could get my face to look forty again, my hands were clearly thirty years older, something beyond the ability of the most skilled plastic surgeon to change. Still, the manual manipulations did temporarily eliminate my jowls, so it was with some regret that I let them drop back into place.

I took a last look at my body, reminding myself of the events of the night before as an antidote. Considering how many areas of the human form are subject to the malevolent forces of gravity, I found myself admiring the courage of those very motivated women, like Cher for example, who redo not only their faces, but the whole package. It must hurt a lot.

Pondering gravity, I ran a bath and lowered myself into the tub. I lay back with eyes closed, trying to forget the flesh that seemed so mismatched to the spirit that animated it. Then I squinted down at my body, trying to pretend that it looked no different from when it was young.

Suddenly, out of the corner of one eye, I glimpsed a sparkle. At first I thought it might be a mote of dust catching the sunlight, but the sun hadn't yet risen to the height of the bathroom window. I raised one arm and again caught that burst of luminosity. Looking closer, I saw that my skin was shooting off miniscule spears of light, much as a piece of mica will refract light, or certain kinds of asphalt glint in the sun. Puzzled, I turned my arms this way and that to catch the diminutive flashes, as hundreds of tiny facets reflected and re-reflected the overhead light. I felt marginally disoriented; it was like nothing I had experienced before. A moment earlier, I'd been glumly contemplating the deterioration of my body; only seconds later, my skin was studded with diamonds.

I stepped out of the tub, reached for a towel, and dried my arms to see if the jewel-like flashes would disappear, but dry, I sparkled even more. My puzzlement turned quickly to delight, the mild depression brought on by the inventory I'd taken before my bath obliterated completely. Who needed a face lift? Until further notice, I was sheathed in diamonds, and I blazed.

Moving Right Along

Over the next few days, Joe practically moved in, while I went through the motions of honoring arrangements I'd previously made with friends. After spending the evening out, I would hurry home, where Joe awaited my return. (It was unthinkable that I break any of those appointments; it had been a point of honor since my teens never to cancel plans with a girlfriend to accommodate the current boy of my dreams, even if they were for a Saturday night.)

I was in a disturbed and disturbing state of sexual and emotional tumescence, feeling once again all the heady and disorienting sensations of adolescent passion, this time without the pit-of-the-stomach ache that accompanies love unattainable. The emotions thus aroused were expansive and joyous, but they were competing with feelings of desolation that would overcome me several times a day whenever a familiar sight or sound evoked a particular memory of Ralph. My moods were like a yoyo, racing up and down from misery to delight and back again. Each state bumped up against the other, causing such turbulence that I questioned whether the exhilaration of the moment was worth the emotional vertigo I was suffering in its wake.

I had told only one friend about Joe. She encouraged me to continue seeing him, but warned me about getting in too deep too soon. There was no way I could make her understand that I had no choice; the decision had been made for me half a century before. In my current state of emotional lability, I didn't have the strength to go against either my instinct or my fate—however one interpreted it—regardless of the trouble they were causing.

When the week of seeing friends was over, I begged off other invitations to free myself for Joe. If anything, this made life even more difficult: the present pleasures and my unabated longing for Ralph battled ceaselessly for my attention. It was like having two serious medical conditions that both needed immediate surgery, and trying to stay alive while one of them was put on hold. But which one? A system of triage was desperately needed. I tried not seeing Joe for a few days, but this only made things worse; now a third ingredient—missing Joe—was added to the mix. There seemed no way out, so I gave up the struggle and went back to seeing him full time.

It wasn't long before Emily sensed that something was going on. To begin with, I was seldom home: Joe and I would take long walks in Central Park, drive to the nearby countryside, walk deserted beaches looking for small treasures at surf's edge, go to morning brunches, afternoon movies and evening concerts. She began to ask pointed questions, and expressed doubt over my evasive answers. She claimed there was an indefinable change in my voice that aroused her suspicions, but she didn't know of what. She feared I was ill and wasn't telling her, making me report my weight on a daily basis (I was now down twenty-five pounds, which hardly reassured her). Her concern, coupled with the increasing need for me to lie, caused me such distress that after a few weeks I decided to tell her the truth. As casually as I could, I mentioned that I was seeing someone. The pause that followed was so pregnant it almost went into labor. Then the questions really started.

"Are you sure it's a good idea?"

"Why not? It's nice to have company."

"Who is he?"

"Someone I knew before I married your father."

Another pause; she was processing this information, which goes against every child's assumption that her parents didn't exist before she was born.

"What's his name?"

"Joe."

"How old is he?"

"Seventy-two."

"Where does he live?"

"Queens."

That precipitated another moment's silence. Emily felt about Queens the way I did.

"What's he like?"

"Pleasant to spend time with. Relaxing."

I suddenly remembered that my mother had asked me those same questions, with the addition of "What does his father do?" and "Is he Jewish?. So too, had I asked them of Emily. We were three generations of worried women linked together in a daisy chain of love, suspicion and over-protectiveness.

For the moment, I'd managed to ease her fears. It took a while before she figured it out.

"You're having an affair!" she announced some two weeks later, sounding a lot like my old voice teacher: triumphant and slightly scandalized.

I felt guilty as hell. All I could think of to say was "I am?"

"Why didn't you tell me right away?"

"Stupid question, Em," I retorted, thinking it might be helpful to go on the offensive. But not liking the sound of it, I retreated. "I was worried it might upset you."

"It does, a little, but I think it's terrific!" she said. "Were you lovers back then?"

I sighed a mighty sigh. My daughter was finally catching up on my life. "Of course we were. Do you think I'd go to bed with a total stranger?"

She laughed. "Funny, Mom!" she said.

I told her about my fifty-year-old love affair and the way it had ended.

"Do you know how lucky you are," she asked, sounding both astounded and shaken, "having a chance to finish unfinished business?"

"Yes," I said, knowing better than she how really lucky I was.

"Call Paul. He's really worried about you, and he hasn't a clue."

"I'd rather wait."

"Why? He needs to know eventually."

"Because I'm not sure how he'll take it. He's having an even harder time over losing Dad than I am. Believe me, next month would be better."]

"Look, Mom, he's on the phone every night telling me how worried he is. He says you're as thin as a string and he thinks you're having a nervous breakdown. He'd feel a lot better if you told him."

I thought about it. "Give me two weeks."

"If you don't tell him by the weekend, I will." She meant it.

"That's blackmail," I said resignedly. "OK, but it'll be your job to deal with him if he freaks out."

I hung up and dialed Paul's number.

"I have something to tell you," I said, wondering exactly how to put it.

I could hear him catch his breath.

Direct is best, I thought, steeling myself. Don't fudge.

"I'm seeing someone. Somebody I knew fifty years ago."

He breathed out. "Why didn't you tell me sooner?"

"I was afraid it would upset you."

"Upset me? I think it's great! If I'd known you were having an affair, I wouldn't have worried."

"Hold on there, Bub. Who said anything about an affair?"

"At your age, you'd be a fool not to. Then I'd *really* worry."

I love my kids.

*   *   *

One of our excursions was to New Rochelle, the town where I'd lived for eighteen years and where my children spent most of their lives before leaving for college. I showed Joe the two houses I'd lived in, the second of which, Moorish sired by Tudor out of Colonial overlooked a picture postcard lake. I had given it up with great reluctance, having made a deal with Ralph that when Paul went off to college we would move back to New York, which he hadn't wanted to leave in the first place. I hadn't seen the house for more than twenty years. In my memory, it was quite grand; now it looked smaller and much more modest than I remembered. While I sat there toying with this mnemonic oddity, Joe suddenly said: "Let's go to Scarsdale."

We got back in the car and drove halfway across Westchester, where we parked behind a small playground across the street from a school. We got out and walked towards a sandbox where two very young children sat, determinedly filling plastic pails with sand. The young au pair standing over them recognized Joe and greeted him with a wave.

"My grandchildren," he said as we approached.

I looked at him in alarm. "Aren't you taking a big chance?"

"We'll tell the au-pair not to say anything."

I gave him a skeptical look. "The only way she won't is if she doesn't speak English."

"You're close," he said. "She's German."

It was the week before Thanksgiving. Joe had decided not to tell his sons about us until Christmas, believing that the later they found out, the more accepting they would be. I welcomed the breathing space, uneasy about meeting them. My own children's reactions, I knew, were atypical: Paul had already met Joe, and though he admitted that it was hard seeing another man in his father's place, he'd seemed comfortable with him after the first few minutes; Emily hadn't met him yet, but she'd spoken to him over the phone. She liked his voice.

"Are you sure you want to do this? Suppose your daughter-in-law comes by?"

"She won't."

He introduced me to the au pair, and then to his grandchildren. Charlie was three and a half and Lulu, short for Lucinda, was a sprite two years younger. At least *they* won't say anything, I thought gratefully. I wasn't so sure about the au pair.

We had been playing with the children for a few minutes when I spotted two women walking in our direction. It was Joe's daughter-in-law and her mother. Joe introduced me, but offered no explanation for my presence. We said awkward hellos, and after chatting for a few minutes, even more awkward goodbyes.

I expected that questions would be asked of Joe over the next few weeks, but his family was so, well, not Jewish, that not a word was said, either during their numerous phone conversations or at his regular Sunday visits, about the mysterious woman in the playground. I was in a frenzy about Christmas Eve, when most of his family would gather at Seth's house and I would have to meet them all. My presence would mark the seriousness of our involvement; their holidays were strictly family affairs. Not only was I unaccustomed to Christmas festivities, I had never before been in a situation where I would be introduced to the adult sons and daughters-in-law of a new/old lover who had lost his wife a scandalously short time before. That's a pretty exclusive category to be in, and I'd rather have been somewhere else.

Thanksgiving came and went. I spent mine with Emily and Paul at Em's and Mike's house north of Boston, while Joe spent his in Scarsdale. Still no questions were asked, not even when I called—I had left him with a bad case of bronchitis, and wanted to see how he was. Seth answered the phone, but passed it to Joe without asking who was calling.

The next month saw the end of Joe's bronchitis—which in my doomsday mode I'd imagined was TB—and the strengthening of our bond. The pleasure I took in his company was in direct proportion to the difficulty I was having over my faithlessness to my late husband. Although I never had any sense of Ralph's incorporeal presence, I imagined him somehow knowing what was going on and being furious about it. Joe seemed not to have the same problem. It was clear that we missed our former mates equally—we talked about them a great deal—and it was hard to square this with the way we felt about each other. Since both of us were having similar feelings, I figured it was probably a normal reaction, though I couldn't imagine that enough people shared our particular circumstances to be able to determine what is normal and what isn't.

The day before Christmas Eve, Robert, Joe's oldest son, drove up from Washington and stayed overnight with Joe in Queens. (His middle son, John, was still in Alaska and didn't have to be reckoned with, at least for a while.) The next morning, I met Robert when he and Joe picked me up for the drive to Scarsdale. I was wearing my most conservative dress, and only the subtlest makeup. I said a polite 'Hello", and got an equally polite one back. He shook my hand reluctantly and wouldn't look me in the eye. I doubt he could have described any portion of me to the police if I'd been kidnapped.

'Tense' is too mild a word to describe the mood in the car. Robert's attitude was eminently correct, but he spoke to me only when I addressed him directly, a tactic I soon abandoned. He spent the trip alternating between silence and intense dialogues with his father on an amazing variety of subjects. His erudition stunned me. Joe tried to draw me into the conversation once or twice, but I was too uncomfortable to join in. In addition, I had nowhere near their depth of knowledge. Among other things, they discussed the judicial process, military history, aviation and Bach. I did manage to engage Robert (he is definitely not a 'Bob') in a conversation about the aesthetic justification, or lack thereof, for transcribing original works for other instruments than the composer intended, but he was way ahead of me in his knowledge of the subject, so I thought it more politic just to listen.

My strategy for the afternoon was to sit back and observe, to make only the most neutral statements, and to appear more dignified than I am: no making a fuss over the children, no Yiddish expressions, no irreverent comments and no affectionate gestures toward Joe. In short, I tried to behave more like my idea of, say, a Presbyterian.

It worked well; I hardly recognized myself. Instead of laughing aloud, only the barest of smiles crossed my lips. Since no one asked me anything about myself, I remained the figure of mystery I started out as. There was an air of studied politeness on everyone's part, spiked by a faint aura of contained anger on Robert's. I was aware of having thoroughly ruined their Christmas, for which I felt vaguely guilty. But I didn't take their air of unmistakably strained civility personally. Ordinarily I'd have been wounded, having always been over-sensitive to people's reactions. But a little empathy goes a long way; I needed to remind myself only once that my presence underscored the fact that their mother wasn't there, and conversely, if a bit irrationally, if I hadn't been there, Peggy would have been. I was both a reminder and a curse.

The good-byes were cool; we touched cheeks and air-kissed, and at last the ordeal was over. It was obvious that they all loved Joe very much, and for that reason they had been, if not exactly welcoming, courteous to a fault. They'd even bought me a Christmas present, placing it under the tree along with those of the family. I had no complaints; they had behaved as well as could be expected, and, in fact, better than I might have in their place. It couldn't possibly be as difficult the next time. Maybe then I could allow a little more of the real me to show.

Eye Of The Beholder

It quickly became obvious that Joe and I, while differing greatly in temperament, were in one way alike: neither of us could remember anything that happened as recently as the day before. Not that it was ever much better. All my adult life, I have put things away for safekeeping and lost them for years. I've read the front page of newspapers with deep concentration, only to forget the lead story within minutes. In literary discussions, I invariably match authors with another writer's work, and have been able to memorize only two poems in my entire life, both eight lines long. I am sometimes unable to introduce my closest friends at parties because I have momentarily forgotten their names. And most exasperating, I have tried in vain to remember if ontogeny recapitulates phylogeny or if phylogeny recapitulates ontogeny, or if two other ogenies are involved altogether. Joe knew that one, but only because he taught science.

If anything, Joe's memory was worse. There wasn't a single appointment, whether medical or social that I didn't have to remind him about repeatedly, right up to the moment he had to leave. He always had more trouble coming up with names than I did, unless they were kings of England. And if I asked him to pick up even one grocery item, he had to make a list. But there were two areas in which his memory proved to be as keen as when he was young. One was for the fables of La Fontaine in the original French, which never failed to turn me to mush, and the other is for the lyrics of old songs.

We had been having a bantering disagreement about physical beauty, with Joe maintaining that there is no such thing as an ugly woman. Every woman has at least one mitigating quality, he stated categorically: a nice smile, the graceful curve of a cheek or interesting eyes. He was much nicer than I am.

Refusing to give up, I continued the cruel game, and from time to time pointed out women so homely that I was sure he'd have to admit defeat. One day, as we rode the subway towards home, I spotted someone who seemed to me the quintessence of ugliness. With a nudge and a faint nod, I called his attention to a woman sitting directly opposite, holding the arm of a small, nondescript man. She looked to be in her middle or late sixties.

I pointed her out as unobtrusively as I could, convinced that I had come up with an unchallengeable example. And indeed, she seemed a perfect candidate: above a sour expression, her hair was sparse and badly hennaed, revealing scabby, irregular patches of scalp. Her skin was scarred and wrinkled, her left eye was noticeably lower than the right, her front teeth protruded, her nose was misshapen, and to cap it all, she was seriously obese. Joe was silent for a moment.

I've got him, I thought gleefully.

He gave me a reproving look. "She's not ugly, she's a dear ruin."

"What's a 'dear ruin'?" I asked.

Then, over the ear-piercing, window-rattling din of the Seventh Avenue IRT, Joe began to sing. His high, sweet tenor rose above the sound of the metal wheels, attracting the amused attention of the passengers on either side. Throughout his rendition, he remained oblivious to their stares. This is what he sang:

> "Believe me, if all those endearing young charms
> That I gaze on so fondly today,
> Were to change by tomorrow and fleet in my arms
> Like fairy gifts fading away,
>
> Thou would'st still be adored as this moment thou art,
> Let thy loveliness fade as it will.
> And around the dear ruin, each wish of my heart
> Would entwine itself verdantly still."

Needless to say, he won. I never played that cruel game again.

Compromises

Harry, a former colleague and longtime friend of Joe's now living in San Francisco, had made Joe promise that he would come out for a week's visit at the beginning of January. As the date drew closer, Joe became more and more ambivalent about leaving. One day he would announce definitely that he was going, and the next, announce just as firmly that he wasn't. I was reminded of the rhythmic opening of one of Jimmy Durante's comic routines: "Didja ever get the feeling that you wanted to go, and then you got the feeling that you wanted to stay?" I could hear its jazzy beat in my mind's ear every time the subject came up. I didn't want him to leave, but at the same time I thought it would be a bad idea to cancel. Our growing interdependency, fed by the freedom we had to spend all our time together, was beginning to worry me. While I was upset about having to be without him for more than a week, it seemed important that we demonstrate some measure of autonomy.

Harry was calling every few days, urging Joe to come. Perversely, I was both pleased and hurt that Joe hadn't asked me to come along: pleased that he wasn't all *that* dependent on me, and hurt for exactly the same reason. Even if he'd suggested it, I wouldn't have accepted, but all the same, I'd have liked to be asked. I became aware of a growing uneasiness on my part: I was afraid that Joe wouldn't miss me, or worse, discover that he preferred being without me. It was also possible, I worried, that Harry, who had no obligation to honor my prior claim, would introduce him to some younger, ravishingly attractive widow and he'd be gone forever for the second time. In my more rational moments, I was disgusted with myself; I had abandoned adulthood and was headed right back into adolescence.

In the end, he went. I called him twice, but he sounded as remote emotionally as he was in miles. The attractive widow theory began to seem less and less theoretical. His absence caused me an almost physical ache in the vicinity of my heart, making it easy to understand why the ancients decided on that organ as the site of emotion. So yet another item had joined the growing concatination: I was not only mourning Ralph, adjusting to my new state of widowhood, battling the specter of insolvency and missing Joe, now I was worried about losing him.

The ten days dragged on little sloth's feet. I fretted constantly about the neutral tone of our conversations. Though he did phone me once near the end of his stay, he sounded no less removed. He described some of the sights he'd seen, but nothing remotely personal was said. I told myself that this is who he is, that compared to Ralph or any of my friends, he was unreadable, and I shouldn't try to interpret his words or his tone of voice, especially from a distance of three thousand miles.

There was another issue yet to be decided. I was committed to spending the summer months in Maine, and had already described the Workshops to Joe, stressing the informal campus-like atmosphere and the wonderfully polyglot student body. A couple of weeks earlier, I'd invited him to come with me. He had refused pointblank. We were both grownups, he said, and would survive the separation. ("Two *months*?" I'd shrieked, sounding little like the grownup he imagined me to be.)

"Why," I asked. "Does it sound like too much togetherness?"

"Not at all; we've been doing fine in that department since November."

"Is it because I'd be working and you wouldn't?"

"Silly question. There are always books, and I'm lazy by nature." (He's right; he could read without changing position for hours on end.)

"Why then?"

"Well, it was Ralph's turf, and I'd be an interloper. I'd also feel like your consort, which I don't think I'd like."

"So what will you do all summer?"

"The same thing I've done every summer since my retirement—read under an umbrella at Rockaway Beach."

"All by yourself?"

He smiled. "No, with a book."

"What about the weekends?"

"I'd be at Seth's. We've already discussed it."

I was getting nowhere; apparently his mind was made up.

I had thought a lot about the upcoming summer during the time he was away. I didn't want to be without him for two whole months; our respective ages mitigated against our having many more years together, and two months seemed like too big a chunk of what was left. At the same time, I didn't want to give up the opportunity David had offered me. There was also the matter of Ralph's ashes: there was to be a memorial service in Rockport for the purpose of laying them to rest, and David had suggested planting a sugar maple to mark his grave; maples did well in that climate, he said.

After much agonizing, I came up with a plan. I would spend one month at the Workshops to attend the memorial and get started on his book, then return to New York to finish it, keeping in touch with David by phone, fax and E-mail. It seemed a good middle course; I didn't want to be—or be seen—as a dilettante, willing to sacrifice her professional needs to a man. To this end, I composed a letter to David that outlined my proposal, making it clear that despite my new relationship, my commitment to do his book was primary. But before I sent it, I wanted Joe to look it over. He had shown me some of the letters he'd written to John and to his English sister-in-law, in which he'd shown himself to be a writer of elegance and tact; I wanted his help to assure that my letter be phrased delicately enough not to cause David to withdraw his offer.

Like any insecure seventeen-year-old in the throes of a new passion, I was a wreck waiting for Joe's return from San Francisco. During our last phone conversation, he'd asked me not to pick him up at the airport, as he wanted to spend his first night in Queens, unpacking and going through his mail. He would join me at my apartment the next day.

Despite, or perhaps because of the delay, our reunion was all I could have desired: it felt as if I had finally exhaled after holding my breath for a very long time. We clung to each other a full five minutes, unable to get close enough; if I'd held him any tighter I'd have come out the other side.

After we'd recovered from our greeting, I told him about the letter to David, and asked him to critique it.

"Not necessary," he said.

"Why not?"

"Because I've decided to go with you."

I was astonished. He'd been quite adamant before the trip. "What made you change your mind?" I asked.

"I didn't think I'd miss you as much as I did."

It was an answer with a double edge. I wasn't sure whether to be insulted or reassured, but after a moment's thought, I went with the latter.

"So how do you explain those phone calls? The man who recites the winning lottery numbers on TV sounds friendlier than you did."

"I've told you before that I only use the phone to make appointments and complain about overcharges. Anyway, Harry was always in the room."

It was settled, then: Joe and I would spend the summer in Maine. Not that his decision eliminated my concerns about how he would fit in; he knew nothing about filmmaking, and the people he would meet there were different from any he'd ever known. They were obsessive about their craft, making lunch and dinner under the dining tent one intense, non-stop seminar. Also, Joe's personality practically guaranteed that he would reveal little of himself and appear to have no identity of his own. I had already noticed his withdrawal into silence when in the company of the glib and/or eloquent, words that accurately described David as well as almost everyone who studied or taught at the Workshops. I also wondered how Joe would be perceived, and whether he would be uncomfortable. Selfishly, I wondered how *I* would be perceived, following such an overtly class act as Ralph with someone whose equally estimable attributes were not as easily discerned. I disliked myself for caring, as well as for the degree to which I'd depended on Ralph's charisma for my identity.

We visited Seth and his family every other week or so, and over the months that followed, I came to be accepted as inevitable. Their reserve slowly thawed, and as a consequence, I felt freer to be myself. Now it was "Say 'Hi' to Granddad and Davida" instead of to Granddad alone. Their greetings became more cordial and I began to feel, if not exactly part of the family, acknowledged as having a permanent role in Joe's, and therefore their, life.

* * *

Joe's trip to San Francisco came at a time when I was starting to look for a smaller apartment. The rent on the six-room behemoth Ralph and I had shared was far too high for my present circumstances. My accountant agreed. But everyone—including my accountant—advised me not to make any major decisions just yet; I could afford to remain in my present quarters for at least a year. At that time, I'd be in a better position to make changes. But just as I donated all of Ralph's clothing to a thrift shop within weeks of his death because I couldn't pass his closet without almost collapsing in paroxysms of grief, I couldn't wait for what other people considered the proper time to start looking for a new apartment. Something new and frightening had begun to happen: I was beginning to have terrifying flashbacks to the night of Ralph's death, reliving each time every detail of my efforts to resuscitate him. I needed desperately to leave.

This time, moving would be an absolute horror. I'd had experience with both up- and downsizing, first from a one bedroom just after my marriage to a five room apartment when Emily was about to be born, then to an eight room house with finished basement in New Rochelle, to another, larger house in the same suburb, back to a five room apartment in New York, up again to four floors of a brownstone (two rooms of which Ralph used as cutting rooms) then to the apartment in which I presently lived. Downsizing was worse. I was accustomed to moving—my parents had relocated every year during my childhood and adolescence. But for whatever reason, moving for Ralph was always a disorienting and exhausting experience even though it was his professional needs that were responsible for at least half our moves. But for me, the pain of relocating, like childbirth, was quickly forgotten. I would undertake the next move with the same feeling of positive expectation as the last, forgetting how truly horrific each one was.

If I wanted to remain on the Upper West side of Manhattan, and I did, I could afford only a one-bedroom apartment, and a small one at that. In earlier moves to smaller quarters, it was only furniture I had to jettison. Now I would have to part with art works, linens, clothing, kitchenware, and above all, books—in short, the treasured accumulation of forty-seven years of acquisitiveness. No area of my household would escape a major paring down. Most of Ralph's constructions and the hundreds of unrelated *tchotchkes* he'd collected for future projects, all the lovely old pieces I'd culled from boxes of contents over the years, all the photographs, reels of film, videotapes and personal artifacts from Ralph's fifty years in the film business, all the picture albums of our family I would have no room to store, all the rugs that wouldn't fit in smaller spaces—everything would have to be sold, given away or stored in Emily's basement, which was already packed with the remnants of her own moves. The sheer number of objects whose disposition would have to be considered was more daunting than the move itself.

Joe and I were not formally living together at the time, and I didn't anticipate that we ever would, although we spent most of every week together. He had proposed that I move to his apartment in Queens to save on rent, but for many reasons—its run-down state being one and lack of easy access to my beloved Upper West Side being another, I refused categorically. Underlying everything was my desire to remain independent.

I had looked at twenty apartments, some while Joe was away, becoming more and more discouraged with each one. All were tiny or dark or almost as expensive as the one I was living in, sometimes all three. But shortly after Joe's return from San Francisco, I answered one more classified ad in The NY Times real-estate section, and hit pay dirt.

It was for a moderate-sized one-bedroom in an old West End Avenue building on a high floor, with a small but relatively new kitchen, high ceilings and a bathroom with a line of old blue tiles running above the tub. The rent was a little more than I'd hoped to pay, but still considerably less than I was paying. More important, it had a foyer with a wall long enough to accommodate about two thirds of my bookcases; none of the other apartments I'd seen had possessed more than a whisper of a foyer. It was that plus the blue bathroom tiles that clinched it. The next day, I presented the landlord with a certified check for what seemed like the major part of my savings and signed the lease. I would take possession in six weeks. (I realized later that Joe's apartment and mine shared the same street number, two boroughs apart. It's enough to make one believe in fairies.)

Making arrangements to get rid of my possessions by sale, largesse and desperation was as traumatic as I'd imagined. Some of Ralph's students from Columbia had kept in close touch and offered to help me pack. At any given point there might be six or seven people including Paul, Joe and myself, emptying shelves and cabinets and packing what I'd decided to keep, neighbors rummaging by invitation through my discards, the used-book buyer from Shakespeare & Co. boxing the fifteen hundred books it was necessary to sell, and someone from the Workshops packing Ralph's collection of film books, which I had donated to their library. I interviewed six carpenters before choosing one I trusted to build additional kitchen cabinets for the new apartment and dismantle and reconfigure the bookcases. The doorbell rang incessantly in response to a notice I'd placed in the elevator that my dining room table and chairs were for sale, as well as several other pieces of furniture I'd never wanted to part with. Bedlam was quieter.

And through it all was Joe's unflappable presence. Having lived in the same apartment for more than forty years, he had no idea what he'd be in for. Still, he remained the sanest among us. Joe was my strength when I thought I'd collapse and my solace when I despaired of getting through another day. Without him beside me to provide stability when everything around me was in chaos, I might have left everything behind and gone to live on the streets.

It all got done, of course. By the beginning of March, I was in the new apartment, with four whole months to get everything in order before leaving for Maine. Somehow, during the process of getting settled, I discovered that very quietly and without any conscious decision made on either of our parts, Joe had moved in completely. It was a surprisingly easy adjustment, except for the one bathroom: I hadn't shared a bathroom since the early days of my marriage. But despite his laissez-faire attitude about housekeeping in general, his quiet presence, spirit of accommodation and ability to disappear entirely even when taking up the better part of a couch, made living with Joe in a one-bedroom apartment easier than living with Ralph, all sharp angles and contention, in a ten-room house. Whatever size, it was mine and I reveled in it, fiercely insisting for the first two years on paying for it myself, to maintain the illusion of independence. By the third year it didn't seem to matter so much, and I finally capitulated to Joe's insistence on equity.

At Easter, I got to meet John, who with his family was enroute from Alaska to a three-year assignment in England. By that time, Joe and I had been together long enough for there to be less strain with John than there'd been with his other sons. Just before he left for England, I thanked him for having been so accepting of me, and said that I realized how hard it must be for him to see his father with someone else so soon after his mother's death. He responded by telling us something even Joe hadn't known.

A few days before Peggy's death, she had called all of her sons together.

"After I'm gone," she'd said, her tone allowing no false remonstrance of hope, "your father will find someone else. I don't want you to be mean to her."

It brought us both to tears.

*   *   *

Came summer, and with trepidation on both our parts, we set out for Maine. I could sense Joe's discomfort. He really didn't want to go, but because we were now committed to each other and I to David's project, there was no turning back. Neither of us knew what to expect, and it didn't help that as an employee, instead of my former role as the wife of the Artist-in-Residence, I was assigned accommodations far less luxurious than those I'd enjoyed during previous summers. Joe, having sometimes lived in far humbler circumstances during the many summer institutes he'd attended during his teaching days, was perfectly content. But for me, going from that beautifully appointed private house with a big porch and a view of the ocean to a tiny box-like apartment with discount house furniture and a lawn the size of a box of Cheerios, took some getting used to. I hadn't been a proletariat since my early twenties.

Our first meal under the tent was traumatic. All my old friends on the faculty gathered around me with hugs and expressions of condolence, glancing sideways at Joe, who sat mute and ill at ease, wondering, no doubt, how he was going to get through the summer. No one chose to eat with us that night. It could only get better.

The memorial was set for the following afternoon. Chairs were set up a few feet from the small sugar maple, its roots carefully burlapped, that David had chosen the day before. Old friends and former students began to arrive from Boston and points beyond, as students and faculty members drifted over and waited quietly for the ceremony to begin.

When the eulogies had all been spoken—I gave essentially the same one I'd had to record nine months before—Ralph's ashes and the maple tree were placed in the ground and everyone tossed shovelsful of earth into the hole that had been dug that morning. Then each of us took turns watering it until the ground was saturated. The spirit of renewal was both moving and uplifting; leaving the grave site, I felt Ralph's presence for the first time since his death.

Joe had insisted on attending the ceremony. While I appreciated the gesture, I was concerned that it might increase his sense of alienation; Ralph had been lionized at the Workshops, becoming, since his death, a figure of mythical proportions. But Joe made good use of his outsider status, videotaping the proceedings from beginning to end, thus providing me with a permanent record. If his presence as unofficial photographer seemed odd to my friends, the strangeness of attending my late husband's memorial with my present lover prevented me from thinking about anyone else's opinions; I had enough unsettling thoughts of my own to keep me occupied.

In the end, the summer was a positive experience for both of us, but not in the way I'd expected. David proved reluctant to part with any of his essays, insisting that every time he started to print something out, he felt compelled to revise it immediately. Somehow, I managed to cajole enough material out of him to structure, rewrite and edit about seventy pages. I was pleased with the results, and so, for a while, was David. In fact, after reading it, his first delighted words were: "My God, it looks like a *book*!!" In the end though, he set it aside to put his creative efforts into a new relationship and first-time fatherhood. As far as I know, he hasn't worked on it since. For my part, I decided that I much preferred spending time on my own work than on someone else's.

As for Joe, shortly after our arrival he was asked to act in three short student films that required an elderly leading man. The most notable was about an old army veteran of World War I. The action takes place on the fourth of July, at which time he reverently takes out his old uniform, attends the holiday parade and visits the town monument to pay tribute to his fallen comrades. It became a source of much amusement to Joe, as well as later to his sons, who know about such things, that the uniform supplied by a Belfast, Maine surplus store was that of a Marine gunnery sergeant from World War II, and the monument in front of which he stood, presumably overcome by emotion for friends and comrades lost in battle, had been erected to commemorate veterans of the Civil War.

While the demands of three shooting schedules cut down considerably on his reading, it gave him a cockier affect, many young admirers, and a host of good stories with which to entertain friends. He could now chat knowledgeably about Steadicams, gaffers, dolly shots and back stories, and came to consider himself a veteran not only of the Second World War, but of the movie business as well.

The Literary Life

My first published work was a family memoir written twenty-five years ago. Far from being accepted with open arms by the reading public, it was never reviewed and sold only three hundred copies. Since then I'd written a novel, four novellas, many poems, a play, three movie scripts and a book of essays, none of which ever saw the light of day.

During my first months with Joe, I would find myself doodling at the computer keyboard. I'd been suffering what is commonly called writer's block for some time, but in my case it was less block than plain discouragement; the rejections I'd been collecting all those years had finally gotten to me. But now I felt something gestating, though after several weeks of false starts, nothing had yet taken shape.

One day, I reread a long sentence I'd just written in an idle frame of mind, very like the one that opens this section of the book. It was the most promising line I'd produced in months, and over the next year it grew to be an article that related the story of my reconnection with Joe and our first night together. When it was finished, I put it in a drawer and forgot about it; I had no magazine connections, and was too jaded to think it had even one chance in a million of being rescued from a slush pile, to which I suspected it would be relegated.

I was looking for something in my file cabinet some time later, when I came across the article and read it again. For the first time, it struck me as something that might be relevant to the lives of other women of my age and circumstances, and I began to think seriously about who among my acquaintances might be able to funnel it to the right publication. I came up with Patricia Bosworth, a biographer and friend of many years who had always been supportive of my work and who, two years before, had generously given me the names of some magazine editors she felt might be receptive to my essays. In the end, none were published. But because Patty had not only allowed me to use her name, but had called the editors herself to pave the way, their replies had been both prompt and personal. I wondered why I hadn't thought of her before. Her response was immediate. She liked the article, considered it publishable, and gave me the names of three editors to send it to; she would alert them to its arrival. I submitted it to each editor in succession.

The first two sent me highly laudatory letters in which they lamented the fact that my piece didn't suit the needs of their publications. The third was from Steven Dubner, then editor of the New York Times Sunday Magazine, who apologized for having let my article languish on his desk for three weeks, as it would have been perfect for their issue on aging, which had closed only days before. However, if I were willing to cut it down to a thousand words (it was more than twice that length) I might try contacting the editor of LIVES, the personal essay column that appeared each week on the last page of the Sunday Magazine, and see if he could use it. I sighed in resignation; there was no way I could cut it by half, and rejection in any form was still rejection. Sadly, I placed the article, along with its complimentary comments, in the same bottom drawer that held so many other failed projects. To hell with writing, I thought. Who needs it? My life is full enough.

The following morning, I received an excited call from a man who identified himself as James Atlas, editor of LIVES. My essay had been making the rounds of the office, everyone loved it, and he definitely wanted to buy it. I was thrilled but defensive. I told him I'd love to have him publish it, but under no circumstances would I cut it by half. Although LIVES articles had always been confined to a single page, he said he was planning to run mine on two. It would appear at the end of June, and require virtually no cuts.

Joe and I danced around the apartment like two four-year-olds before we began to wonder how his sons would take it. My relationship with them was still a long way from solid, and I worried that they might be offended by my going public about their father's love life. Considered that way, they most certainly would be.

I asked Joe if he'd thought about the consequences.

"No," he replied, "not until you brought it up."

My heart in my mouth, I offered to withdraw the article if he thought it would erase the gains I'd made with his family over the last year and a half.

He was all for going ahead. His sons were grown, he said, and would have to deal with any feelings the article aroused. Whatever their reactions, it would ultimately work out. Anyway, didn't I think they would be pleased to know that their father was still sexually active at seventy-four?

"No," I said, "I don't think so. But if you're really OK with it, we'll let it rip."

I let it rip, and it was the beginning of an exhilarating and revelatory summer. As for Joe's sons, neither Seth nor Robert mentioned it, even to comment on its literary merits, while John's wife later reported that John had made a face after reading it and said there were some things he'd rather not have known.

Joe and I were in Massachusetts—another Rockport, this time the one on Cape Ann—when the article came out, and we celebrated at a festive brunch with some new friends we'd met through Emily. That afternoon, the phone started to ring, and it didn't stop for a week. Everyone I'd ever met called to congratulate me. This included several long-lost friends from as far back as my early twenties, a cousin visiting in Los Angeles, (where the article was apparently the talk of the town) and whom I hadn't seen since Ralph's death, three agents who wanted to represent me, two movie company representatives who wanted to discuss an option, total strangers (one a well-known Broadway actress whose name I failed to recognize, which is probably why she never called me back) who wanted me to be their mentor as they reluctantly approached old age, other strangers—mostly older widows—who said I'd given them hope for the future, my former agent, who three years previous had given me up as a client after having been unable to sell any of my work, and most startling of all, two people from Joe's Bronx crowd of fifty and more years ago, who recognized our story even though I'd given Joe a pseudonym. One of them was Jerry, the pianist who'd played Peg o' My Heart and Ain't Misbehavin' so mercilessly, and the other was Lee, who subsequently arranged a reunion of the old bunch, and has since become a friend.

A slew of mostly favorable letters-to-the-editor was printed over the next three weeks. Of these, some were openly envious, others applauded the coming out of the closet of geriatric sex, still others reminisced about their own past love affairs, and two spoke of their fear of disillusionment if they were to look up their old lovers, preferring to keep their memories intact. I was curious about those letters that hadn't been chosen, and called The Times to ask if I could see them. About twenty-five letters arrived some weeks later, most of them similar to those already printed. One, however, was from a self-identified teenager who castigated me for having out-of-wedlock sex, warning that fornication was a sin against God, and therefore wrong at any age. It was so intelligently phrased and well thought out that despite its tone of severe disapproval, I was filled with admiration. And then there was a letter from a distant relative of Ralph's, who had known us many years before, who wondered in a cramped handwriting how Ralph, having been so extraordinarily good-looking, could have been attracted to anyone as homely as I was. Now, I never thought I was a beauty, but 'homely' was a word I never would have used to describe myself, especially as a young woman. I must admit that her comments gave me a jolt: by intimating that I didn't deserve Ralph, she was suggesting that I probably didn't deserve Joe, either. I couldn't believe that she expected it to be published, being completely beside the point.

In the meantime, I was interviewed long distance by the Irish branch of the BBC, and more exciting, the article was purchased by the London Observer. They were so taken with it that they went to the trouble of hiring an American photographer to get some shots of Joe and me together. Joe was adamant about not wanting to be photographed, but the photographer wouldn't give up. In the end, they reached a compromise: he posed us sitting on a bench and holding hands, and took the photograph from behind.

The Observer printed the article verbatim, but placed a teaser of their own on the first page of the Entertainment (!) section. THEY HADN'T SLEPT TOGETHER FOR FIFTY YEARS, it blared, AND WHEN THEY DID, THE EARTH MOVED—AGAIN! For weeks we lived in fear that Joe's very proper English sister-in-law might see it, but fortunately, her taste in newspapers was as proper as she was.

The entire experience was a gas, if a painful education on newspaper spin. At the age of seventy, and for the first time in three years, I had an agent and a possible future as a writer. Life looked very good.

When we returned to New York at the end of August, I met Phillipa Brophy, my new agent, for the first time. I was instantly impressed by her no-nonsense manner; she came across as a benign drill sergeant. Our meeting lasted ten minutes, during which not a superfluous word was spoken. There was a book in the article, she said, but she didn't quite know what it was; fashioning books was not her forte. She would discuss it with a couple of editor friends and get back to me.

A week later, she called to say that one of the editors she'd spoken to had an idea for a book and wanted to meet me. She worked at a venerable publishing house and had read RELATIVES and my unpublished book of essays, both of which Flip had asked her to look at. On the basis of my writings, the editor had cleared her idea with her board, and there was every likelihood that we could have a deal.

"Tell me the idea," I said, suspiciously, already anticipating what it might be.

"Roughly, your last year with your husband and your first year with Joe." I'd guessed right.

"I'm afraid I can't," I responded almost before she'd finished.

I explained that I valued honesty in writing, and would have to tell it like it was. If I undertook such a project I would be revealing intimate details about my marriage that were nobody's business but mine. My children would be devastated.

"Isn't the article full of intimate details?" asked Flip, the next day.

"Yes, but it described only one incident and was written out of the sheer joy of the moment. What you're asking is that I write intimately about my two love relationships purely for gain. I can't do that."

I apologized for my intransigence, realizing that I might be depriving her of a commission. She had taken me on as a client because she thought I had a book in me, and here I was refusing to listen to an offer other writers of scant success would kill for. She must have thought I was crazy for rejecting it, but she had the grace not to say so. At her urging, I agreed to meet the editor before I made my decision final.

The meeting was both enjoyable and ego-enhancing. I found the editor to be intelligent, enthusiastic and sympathetic, and someone I would have enjoyed working with. She was also very persuasive, but I had made up my mind. It was with regret that I turned her down, knowing that this might well be my last chance to be published. Still, I was sure I'd done the right thing.

It was two years before the book I'd sent to an early grave came back to haunt my nights and insist on being written. You are reading it now.

Into Each Life

Behind me on the subway steps, I could hear Joe's labored breathing. When I turned to see what was the matter, he smiled with obvious effort.

"You go on ahead. I'm OK."

When he reached the top of the stairs, he leaned against the nearest wall to catch his breath. Knowing him as an intrepid bicyclist and someone who didn't mind walking a mile in sub-freezing weather from the subway to his Queens apartment burdened with a shoulder bag that weighed at least twenty pounds, I was immediately concerned.

"What else do you feel?" It was a question I'd asked Ralph many times in the days after his heart attack, and which I heard myself ask Joe with a sinking heart.

"A little light-headed, that's all. It'll pass."

"How do you know?"

"Because it's happened a few times before, and it always goes away."

"A few times when?"

"Over the past week or two. I haven't wanted to worry you."

I frowned. What is it with men? Anyone who's reached the middle of his eighth decade should have given up the macho thing years ago.

"It's doctor time," I said grimly. "You're seeing him this week."

"Why? I'm sure it's nothing."

I sighed. "I'd rather someone with a medical degree verifies your diagnosis."

Joe reluctantly made an appointment with Dr. C., his primary HMO physician, whom he hadn't seen for eighteen years. He didn't believe in doctors, he told me, and cited never having been ill in his entire life as proof that avoiding them was good for one's health. I didn't know at the time that during those rare occasions when for one reason or another he had to visit one, he would speak only when spoken to and offer nothing in the way of symptoms unless the doctor was trained in getting blood from a stone.

This particular MD, by unfortunate happenstance, asked few questions and gave his medical opinions in an almost unintelligible Chinese accent. By mutual agreement, they colluded in his diagnosis of a virus. Joe left his office with a prescription for some penicillin, which, had it actually been a virus, would have been the wrong medication anyway.

When he wasn't any better a week later, I insisted that he call the doctor again. We were about to leave for England the next week to visit John and his family, after which we would be touring Italy for ten days, I wanted to be sure that it was all right for Joe to travel. Because of my experience with Ralph, I wondered if it might be his heart. Joe had suffered a bout of rheumatic fever as a teenager, so it wasn't unlikely.

I happened to pick up the phone when Dr. C. called back. At first I couldn't make out who was calling because of the opacity of his accent. He advised Joe to renew the prescription. At my urging, Joe asked if there was any reason he shouldn't make the trip. None at all, Dr. C. assured him, the penicillin should do the trick. I marveled at Joe's ability to translate.

On the day after our arrival in England and in the middle of a visit to Hampton Court Palace, Joe collapsed. I alerted a guard, who helped me half-walk, half-carry him to the caretaker's office. As soon as we got there, he declared himself much better and ready to continue. My response—"You're out of your mind!"—must have shocked the very reserved caretaker, who offered to call an ambulance. Joe insisted that he was fine. I didn't believe him. We took a taxi back to John's, and called him at work. He was home ten minutes later.

John phoned his physician at the National Health Service, and to his amazement—he was accustomed to waiting days or weeks for an appointment—was told to bring his father down immediately. Joe was feeling so much stronger by then that he balked at seeing the doctor at all. We pulled and pushed him into the car, while he protested that he'd never felt better in his life.

Bypassing a full waiting room, all three of us were ushered into Dr. M's office the moment we arrived. She asked many pointed questions to which Joe gave only the most cursory answers. It was my first exposure to his 'patient' style, which was minimalist. The doctor then asked him to remove his shirt and placed a stethescope to his chest. She listened for longer than I thought usual.

"There's fluid on the right lung," she said. "Was an X-ray taken in New York?"

"No."

Her frown deepening, she asked if the symptoms of breathlessness and lightheadedness had been the same then.

"Yes," he replied, "but not as severe."

She made an immediate appointment with a pulmonary specialist at another center, giving us just enough time to drive there. We barreled through the narrow roads of Surrey and arrived in record time, to be greeted personally by a Dr. B., who with his effervescent manner, impressed me as being uncharacteristically perky for a Brit. Again we were led past a full room of waiting patients. After all the negative things we'd heard about the inefficiency of English medical care, we were amazed at the service a visiting American was receiving. We attributed the bad press to the grumblings of a few Tory malcontents, and thanked Dr. B. for seeing us so promptly. He asked only a few questions—apparently, his colleague had filled him in on Joe's history—and ordered an X-ray.

Ten minutes later we were shown a picture of Joe's chest cavity. His left lung was of normal size, cozily enclosed in its air-filled pleural cavity. But his right lung was a shocker: it was compressed to the size of a fist, pushed upward and almost to his shoulder by what the doctor identified as some kind of fluid. The first step, he said ebulliently—his style was unsettling in its excessive cheeriness—was to drain it off by means of a needle inserted into the pleurum, a procedure he made sound like a trip to an amusement park, and the second was to ascertain the nature of the fluid, which would determine the diagnosis. Blood would be drawn, and another X-ray and a CT scan taken. The X-ray would show if the lung had returned to its normal size; the scan would pick up any tumor that might be impinging on a neighboring structure, or a problem with the lung itself.

Joe was taken into another room to have the fluid drained, while John and I, who had up to now seen each other only twice—the year before at Seth's Easter party, and the night before, after our arrival—now found ourselves discussing the most private of family matters as if we'd been intimates for years.

Two hours later, we left with the following information: first, the lung had descended to its customary position, though it was likely to be compressed upward again as more fluid accumulated, until whatever caused the buildup was identified and corrected, and second, the CT scan revealed nothing abnormal; there was no tumor. This last was good news, but it wasn't enough to rule out other potentially serious conditions. The blood and fluid analyses would take a few days, sparkled Dr. B., and in the meantime, have a good weekend.

I don't remember what we did for the next three days. I did spend an inordinate amount of time on the phone being transferred from one extension to another as I canceled our plane, train and hotel reservations for what had been a much anticipated tour of Italy. Joe's symptoms were beginning to return.

On Tuesday, while Joe was in the shower and everyone else at work or in school, the phone rang. I picked it up. It was Dr. B., sounding like a newly opened bottle of seltzer.

"Good news!" he bubbled cheerily.

"That's wonderful," I said in relief. "What is it?"

"Lymphoma!" he said triumphantly, as if he were presenting me with the news that we'd just won the Irish Sweepstakes.

My heart sank. Unless the New York Times Science section, where I pick up most of my medical information, had misled me, he was talking about cancer of the lymph nodes. It is the second leading cause of death in the Times obituaries, which I have read every day without fail since my sixtieth birthday to be sure I'm not in them.

"That's good news? What's good about it?"

"It could have been something much worse."

The fluid he'd drawn contained immature lymphocytes, an almost certain indication of lymphoma. Though he'd found no grossly abnormal lymph nodes in his physical examination, and no tumor was evident in the CT scan, he was certain of his diagnosis, a type of lymphoma treatable by means of a particular regimen of chemotherapy. When it recurred, and it almost always did, it could be treated again and again. In other words, a piece of cake. In the meantime, we'd best get back to the States and start treatment. And by the way, when will you be paying your bill?

"Bill?" I said, surprised. "I thought medical care was free here."

"Only for citizens. Sorry, I thought you knew."

That explained the VIP treatment. It wasn't triage or courtesy, it was the color of our money. It came to fifteen hundred pounds, the equivalent of twenty-five hundred American dollars, which would later be reimbursed by his HMO.

John went to the nearest bank to exchange some dollars for pounds, and Joe paid the bill. I don't think we'd have gotten out of the country if he hadn't.

That night while everyone was asleep, I made my way to the bathroom, and in a barely audible voice, railed at God, asking bitterly why he had sent Joe back to me, if he was only planning to take him away again. Was I being punished for having behaved in such an unseemly fashion so soon after Ralph's and Peggy's deaths? What would become of me if I were alone again; could I survive a second loss? And surely Joe, as the more passive participant in the reactivation of our affair, deserved something less than a fatal disease. For half an hour, I wallowed in self-pity. As someone who believes neither in God nor in Karmic punishment, it was an unlikely scene. It would have given my maternal step-grandfather—a cantor—and my father, a Rosicrucian, equal satisfaction. As I listened to myself whine to God, I realized that the prospect of losing Joe was bringing out the worst in me: I was focusing on my pain instead of on Joe's.

This upset me enough to rid me of my self-pity, and I didn't indulge it again. This ability came as a surprise: I'm as self-protective as the next person. What inspired it, I think, was the sudden realization that with a different toss of the dice, it might have been me with the potentially fatal disease. And there was no doubt in my mind that had the roles been reversed, Joe would have cared for me as selflessly as he had Peggy.

*   *   *

We arrived at Kennedy twenty-four hours later and fell into bed without unpacking. The next morning I was galvanized. Not only did Joe have no idea how to navigate the system, but after two years together, I knew his pace: he was a tortoise. I, on the other hand, was the proverbial hare. But unlike the protagonists in the popular fable, Joe was likely to expire before he'd had a chance to win the race, and I'd had experience in a marathon. Ralph's seven-year illness had taught me a lot, and I was in a fighting mode.

To begin with, I thought he should sue Dr. C. for negligence. True to character, he was reluctant to hurt the doctor's feelings. Yes, he admitted, a chest X-ray should have been done, but the man had done the best he knew how; his incompetence wasn't deliberate. We should drop it and move on. I couldn't believe what I was hearing; there's a limit to saintliness, and Joe had just exceeded it.

OK, we'd forget about suing. But someone had to manage his managed care, and I volunteered for the job. Unnerved to the point of paralysis by the unexpected turn his life had taken, he agreed, relieved to put himself into someone else's hands.

He was still enrolled at the HMO's Queens center, more than an hour's subway ride from our apartment. If he remained registered there, he would be at the mercy of doctors and hospitals I already thought of as inferior on the basis both of Joe's recent experience and what I'd learned in bits and pieces about Peggy's treatment. I called the Manhattan center, convinced the only family physician on duty that day to see Joe as an emergency patient, dug the CT scan and the X-ray out of the still untouched luggage and set out to bring the medical establishment to its knees. I was so single-minded, it's amazing that I remembered to bring Joe along; he was still in shock from the diagnosis. Feeling weak again from a new buildup of fluid, he had reverted to the passivity of a child whose mother was ready to take on the world in his defense.

Dr. L. examined Joe briefly, and made a referral to an oncologist in a center across town. I disliked Dr. L. from the first moment, put off by his failure to offer any words of sympathy or encouragement. He probably didn't like me either, because I'd argued so aggressively for him to see Joe as an emergency that same day. I was prepared also to dislike the oncologist, having avoided joining a managed care plan myself, precisely because I am so fiercely committed to choosing my own physicians. And between the original Dr. C. and that day's Dr. L, my decision had been amply validated.

I had confidence in Dr. Ross, though, from the minute he ushered us into his office. Scottish by birth, and with the residue of an accent to document it, his manner was open and straightforward without being brusque, and with just the right combination of professionalism and empathy to invite confidence. He answered my flurry of anxiety-driven questions, many unnecessary, with patience and without condescension, gave us a run-down of the many possible treatments and prognoses, and seemed to understand that we were not fully ourselves: Joe was uncharacteristically catatonic and I was immoderately crazed. We gave him the X-rays, the CT scan and the letter from Dr. B. that contained the outcome of all the tests done in England as well as his impressions. Dr. Ross agreed with the general diagnosis, but said that more rigorous tests and a biopsy had to be done before he would know exactly which of the several different types of lymphoma Joe had. This would entail locating and doing a biopsy of any affected tissue. In the meantime, he would take some bone marrow to see if any cancer cells could be detected, and since there appeared to be a new buildup of fluid, he would send us to Beth Israel Hospital to have it drained. Joe's problem was now being well managed, but it seemed that we were back at square one. He extracted some marrow, got on the phone to the lab at Beth Israel to be sure someone would be there when we arrived, and sent us on our way. For the first time, I could have kissed the feet of a living human being.

When we called the next day to get the test results, he reported that happily there were no cancer cells in the bone marrow, but his guess was that something was impinging on the pleurum, which would explain the continued buildup of fluid. He suspected a tumor, but since the British radiologist had seen nothing on the CT scan—he had not himself looked at it—Joe would have to enter the hospital for more tests and another scan. He'd already spoken to Dr. K., a crackerjack thoracic surgeon, with whom he would collaborate.

And so the journey began.

Breaking Eggs
to Make an Omelet

Non-Hodgkins lymphoma is a type of systemic cancer that affects the blood and the lymphatic tissues, and is the sixth most prevalent cancer in the United States. It is also the second fastest growing in mortality. Jordan's King Hussein and Jackie Kennedy are two of its more prominent victims. No one knows why it has proliferated at such a rapid rate; there were, in 2001, more than three hundred thousand people nationwide so afflicted, with more than fifty-five thousand new cases diagnosed every year. It consists of over twenty different subtypes, some of which are quickly lethal, and others of which respond in one degree or another to a variety and/or combination of therapies. These include surgery, radiation, chemotherapy and more recently, the delivery of antibodies specific to the particular malignancy. Each subtype calls for different combinations of procedures and/or drugs. The next phase of Joe's saga would determine his treatment and his prognosis.

We arrived at Beth Israel at eight AM. Joe changed into a hospital gown and was taken to the nether regions of the hospital for his scan. Moments after his return, he was set upon by four white-garbed Harpies, who managed to get his gown down around his hips and his right side betadined before I could ask what was happening.

"Chest tube," one answered crisply, as she took me by the arm and began to usher me from the room.

Dr. Ross had told us that he'd persuaded the surgeon to hold off on a chest tube until after the CT scan results were known. If surgery was indicated, he said, a chest tube would no longer be a matter of choice. It was not a pleasant procedure, and he wanted to spare Joe as much discomfort as possible.

I pulled my arm from her grasp. "I was told no chest tube until after the new scan is read."

"The order just came down from Dr. K. He's in charge of this case, and he wants it done."

It was the word 'case' that did it.

"Sorry", I said, not sorry at all, "But until I can speak to Dr. Ross, I suggest you go punctuate somebody else."

The head Harpy, a striking-looking Eurasian, gave me a long look, which had she been human, might have expressed anger at being thwarted. But her expression remained blank. She looked a bit like a blood relative of Mr. Spock.

She shrugged. "Call him, then."

Gathering up their paraphernalia, which included yards of wicked-looking tubing, piles of gauze pads, many rolls of adhesive and a number of cutting instruments, they disappeared down the corridor.

I called Dr. Ross at his office and left a message.

"I'm afraid he's right," was the discouraging news when he called back. "I hoped we could spare him this, but K. knows his business, so I think we ought to go ahead. It isn't always good medicine to make decisions out of compassion alone."

Oh well, Joe had been given an hour's respite, and Dr. Ross had earned points: he wasn't dogmatic and could be persuaded by a good argument. I was only sorry it had to be at the expense of Joe's comfort.

The Harpies returned. This time, I didn't wait to be ushered out; I can handle most things medical, but watching needles being given or incisions being made are beyond my tolerance. I waited in the corridor, pacing up and down in front of Joe's room with my heart beating as fast and hard as if I, not he, was the patient.

The procedure lasted more than half an hour. The Harpies, otherwise known as Dr. K.'s surgical team—residents in training as thoracic surgeons—marched resolutely out of Joe's room to their next assignment. I entered the room hesitantly, afraid of what I might find. Remnants of tubing, bloodied bandages, adhesive and other detritus littered the floor. The nurse on duty followed me in and shook her head when she saw the mess.

"Surgeons!" she said, her lips set in disapproval. "They're all alike. And these aren't even certified yet!"

Joe was on his back in his hospital bed, which had been raised to a half-sitting position. A tube about three-quarters of an inch in diameter emerged from his right side and ended in a large plastic receptacle set on the floor, which already contained an inch of viscous yellow fluid. His face was completely drained of color.

I took his hand. "Was it bad?"

"Very bad", he said. "They came in without a word, told me to turn on my left side, and then they jammed the damn thing in. It hurt like hell." It was the first time I'd heard him complain.

Furious, I went to the nurse's station and demanded to speak to Dr. K. They paged him; he was in surgery. This was true for the rest of Joe's stay. Every time I called K.'s office, he was in surgery. By the third day, I couldn't understand why he needed an office; the man lived in the OR. I never did get to talk to him about his team's bedside manner, though I continued trying to reach him every few hours.

Until the next development, Joe would be tethered to the bed. As I had with Ralph after his heart attack, I set up housekeeping in his room. Hospital patients, I knew from experience, need full-time advocates. Although the nurse to patient ratio was higher in Oncology than in other departments, the nurses, like nurses everywhere, were in constant demand. And at night, with fewer on duty, they always seemed to be in another wing. During the day, the interns were our most frequent contact, along with the kitchen aides who delivered the bouillon, jello, apple juice and tea that constituted Joe's diet.

If the site of the intravenous needle began to look inflamed, if his lunch or dinner hadn't arrived, if his blood pressure hadn't been checked at regular intervals (hypertension had been diagnosed by Dr. C. just before our trip to England), if the pouch of nutrients hadn't been replaced more than half an hour after being consumed, if the container of lymphatic fluid became full, if he required a bedpan or needed one to be emptied, and if, as happened more often than not, the call button failed to prompt a response, I would leave his side to chase after a nurse. They didn't like me much, but they came.

Nothing more would happen until word came down from radiology. The scan had been done on Wednesday. By Friday, there was still no word. The interns, concerned over the delay, were checking with Radiology every couple of hours. By six o'clock, it became evident that the scan wouldn't be read until Monday. I had still not resigned myself to the slow pace of hospitals. Only the chest tube had been placed expeditiously; everything else had taken place in slow motion. The tortoises reigned. True, Joe was not the only patient, as I was constantly being reminded by the nurses, but it seemed to me that if *somebody's* X-rays were being read, they might as well be Joe's. Still, neither my pleas nor my complaints had any effect. Another weekend would pass without answers.

Since the first day of Joe's confinement—internment was more like it—Seth had been coming to the hospital twice a day, bearing overstuffed sandwiches, fruit and containers of yoghurt that he'd cadged from his firm's commissary. He arrived at lunch-time and after work, staying well into the evening hours and returning to his office at the end of visiting hours to make up the lost time. I would bring him up to date on the latest medical developments, while his calm presence helped neutralize my all but unbearable anxiety. He provided relief for Joe from my unceasingly vigilant attitude, which allowed for little in the way of relaxed humor or discussion of anything unrelated to his illness, but which Seth brought in abundance to Joe's bedside. He was a tonic; I came to depend on his visits like an addict. The fact that he trusted me with his father's care was reassuring and augured well, I thought, for my eventual acceptance as an extralegal member of the family, especially after his and his brothers' studied non-recognition of my Times article.

Dr. Ross arrived every morning to check on his patient's patience as well as his state of health. As far as patience was concerned, Joe wasn't the problem; I was. On the verge of nervous prostration myself, I wondered why he wasn't railing against fate or at least sick with worry. But Joe was being as consistent to his character as I was being to mine. He had resigned himself to waiting as long as necessary, both for the results of the tests and a battle plan. His being such a paragon of endurance was driving me to a frenzy. I wanted company.

On Monday morning, most of the test results came in, but not a word from Radiology. All the other tests were negative; they'd even tested him for TB.

"What about the scan?" I asked the intern who'd brought the news.

"It hasn't been read yet. Maybe later this afternoon."

"Does that damn radiologist have any idea what it's like to wait this long with a chest tube stuck in your side? Where is the man's heart?"

The intern said she didn't think radiologists had hearts, and promised to call again and see if she could hurry him along. Just as I'd given up hope, she returned.

"They found it!" she said triumphantly.

"Found what?"

"The tumor. Everybody on the floor was betting there'd be one."

I hadn't realized that Joe's case had been such an anomaly or that the medical equivalent of OTB had been set up in Oncology. Almost certainly lymphoma, there had to be either a tumor or enlarged lymph nodes, but until now, neither had been found.

The mass was between Joe's spinal column and his esophagus. It was the size of an adult's hand. Pressed against the lymphatic duct that abutted the right pleurum, it was preventing drainage of the lymph fluid that normally coursed through it, forcing it instead into the pleural cavity where it was exerting upward pressure on the lung.

"How could it have gotten that huge in such a short time?" I asked, reeling from the effort of having to integrate an actual tumor into the reality of Joe's illness. "It wasn't there when they did the scan in England, and that was only two weeks ago!"

"If you have those pictures, I'd like to see them," she said. "It's got to be there. They must have missed it."

An anglophile by marriage—Ralph, like Joe, had loved everything about the English—I bristled.

"I can't believe that. They were terrific!"

The next day, when I brought in the films, the tumor was there, plain as day. It was hard to miss once you knew where to look.

As the intern and I talked, the phone rang. It was Dr. Ross.

"I just heard, and I've spoken to Dr. K. He'll be going in to get a piece of it later today."

There were three possible ways to go, he continued. The first was a needle biopsy, which he doubted would work because of the tumor's inaccessibility. The second was a forty-five minute procedure called a thorachoscopy, in which an instrument would be inserted through the opening previously made for the chest tube, and a sample of the tumor taken. If this wasn't successful, something called a thorachotomy would have to be done. This was major chest surgery, and would take between two and three hours. No attempt would be made to remove the entire tumor mass, only a sample; not only was it dangerously close to the spinal column, but if it was a lymphoma as he expected, its removal would be fruitless; lymphoma is a disease that affects the entire lymphatic system.

The exploratory was scheduled for later that evening. Now, finally, we were on the fast track. We still hadn't met Dr. K., and I had a thousand questions, none of which would affect the outcome, but might have relieved me of the iron weight of my ignorance, and therefore of some of my anxiety.

Joe's passivity continued to bother me. "Don't you have any questions at all?" I asked him.

His answer was maddeningly logical.

"I don't know the slightest thing about all this, and there's no time to do any research beyond what you and John found on the Internet. I've never heard of a thorachotomy, so I wouldn't know what to ask. I trust Dr. Ross, and if he says this is the way to go, this is what we'll do. I don't see the problem."

Such rational thinking drives those of us who operate almost purely on emotion to distraction. And the idea of doing major surgery to take a tiny piece of tissue from a malignant tumor without cutting it all out seemed irrational. Abandoning my usual optimism, I felt in my bones that the more invasive surgery was inevitable. Whatever else Joe might have to endure as the situation unfolded, I suspected that he would also be dealing with a massive assault to his body.

In the waiting room next to the OR, I waited. Forty-five minutes passed, and still no word. I waited some more. One hour, an hour and a half, two hours. Now I was sure that they'd had to do the most extreme procedure. For the second time in two years, I found myself unable to read. I thumbed through the magazines piled on the small table beside my chair without registering a word. I paced. Finally, I was reduced to reciting under my breath the only two poems I'd committed to memory, and singing, sotto voce, a few of the songs I'd learned in my late teens during my aborted career as a folk-singer. When I'd run through as many as I could remember, a slight, youngish man, his surgical mask hanging below his chin, approached.

Tentatively, I said: "Dr. K.?"

He nodded.

"Your husband is fine. They'll be bringing him into Recovery in a few minutes."

I wondered if I'd have been given this information if my marital status hadn't been assumed.

"Did you get what you needed?" I asked.

"Oh yes. It's been sent to pathology. Unfortunately, the first two procedures weren't productive, so we had to go ahead and do the thorachotomy. But he won't be accumulating fluid anymore; while I was in there, I took out the pleural membrane."

I was still angry about his not having seen Joe before the operation and for tolerating such an unfeeling attitude on the part of his assistants. But he looked so exhausted and I was so relieved that Joe had come through the surgery and that we would soon know what had to be done, that I decided to let it go. This experience must be humbling me, I remember thinking; I had seldom let things go before.

Joe awoke the next morning in the surgical wing after a heavily sedated night. He would spend the next week there, tended by, I was assured, specially trained nurses, quick to respond to the call button. One of them, Joe's nurse, unfortunately, was the exception.

When I first realized what she was like, I tried to worm my way into her good graces by sympathizing loudly when she complained about her swollen feet, agreeing with her (while mentally crossing my fingers) about some really bad movies she thought were brilliant, offering her fresh fruit from a lavish basket Seth had sent Joe, and complimenting her hairdo, which was, in truth, grotesque. All this because she approached her duties with the slowest walk I had ever seen in a nurse.

She daydreamed when she checked Joe's blood pressure, her eyes focused on some far away scene that could not possibly have any connection with a sphygmomanometer. She walked her regal, slow-motion walk to and from visits to her assigned rooms, oblivious to the impatience fulminating around her, as patients clamored for medications and fresh IV bags. God forbid if one of her assignees required emergency attention: her movements were so deliberate that anyone might bleed to death before being attended to. Nothing deflected her from her languid pace—she was like a seaworthy ship, plowing stalwartly ahead, oblivious to the twenty-foot waves. Somehow Joe survived, probably because she was off for the last three days of his stay.

The morning after his surgery, Dr. Ross called with news. The tumor was an indolent B-cell lymphoma, requiring a specific chemotherapy. The tumor would shrink substantially after the first couple of treatments, and a partial or complete remission of symptoms could be expected after four months. Joe's type of tumor often returned within two or three years, at which time it could be treated again, hopefully with the same result. There was no cure, but people lived comfortably for years with this disease. Chemo would be started in the hospital, and would continue at Dr. Ross' office after his discharge. The worst was over, he said. He made it sound easy.

We were relieved. It wasn't the best prognosis, but it wasn't the worst either. Everything was under control. Everyone breathed a sigh of relief.

Onward and Upward

Joe was home and, we hoped, healing. His first two chemo treatments had, as promised, effected a dramatic shrinkage in the tumor, but a new problem was emerging: he had become sluggish and was unmotivated to move. It wasn't an ordinary fatigue; it seemed more a failure of will. Though no longer in pain, it took major cajoling on my part to get him to go for walks, a necessary part of his recuperation. I was growing impatient with what I saw as an exaggeration of his customary lassitude, and I gave him pep talks, worthy of a losing football coach, to get him going. After breakfast, I would clean and dress his incision and help him get dressed. Then, if my efforts at motivation had been successful, we would embark on our daily walk.

His first goal was to get to the corner and back. Mission accomplished within a week, but he wasn't progressing any further. The visiting nurse, who arrived every afternoon to take his blood pressure and check the incision, which was slow to heal, began to express concern about his lack of progress. Even Dr. Ross was at a loss to explain it; at this stage, fatigue due to chemo wasn't sufficient explanation. He concluded that Joe's age was probably a factor, and that it was only a matter of time before he would begin to pick up.

We were having our morning walk when Joe suddenly slumped against the side of the building. Alarmed, I asked what was wrong.

For a moment he couldn't speak.

"There's a burning pain across my back," he said, when he could catch his breath.

My heart dropped to its knees. Noticing my expression, he tried to reassure me. "It's fading already. It'll be gone in a minute."

"Is it the incision or something else?" I demanded.

"It's not the incision, it's nearer my shoulders. The same thing happened a couple of times last week, but it wasn't as strong."

"Damn it, why didn't you tell me?"

"I didn't think it was important. Anyhow, it's almost gone."

We waited until he could walk, and we slowly made our way back into the lobby; fortunately we were only a few steps away. The possibility of angina had occurred to me, but I rejected it because the pain hadn't been in his chest. As soon as we got to the apartment, I called Dr. Ross.

He questioned me closely as to the nature and location of the pain and when it had occurred. He hadn't asked for Joe, having learned that I was the better informant. There was a long silence; I could hear the wheels turning.

"It sounds like an unstable angina to me, and I don't think we should take any chances. Get him to the emergency room at Beth Israel and we'll see what's going on."

One thalium stress test and an echocardiogram later, blockages in two of Joe's main coronary arteries were diagnosed. An angiogram was scheduled for the next day to pinpoint their exact location and severity, and determine what treatment was indicated. Two of his three major arteries were ninety-five percent blocked, and either one could have closed up at any moment. At six that evening, Joe underwent two angioplasties. Both arteries were thoroughly reamed out, and five stents inserted to keep them open. Awake throughout the entire procedure, he described the sound as being similar to a dental drill and at least as noisy.

In the middle of the second reaming, he told me later, the telephone rang. The anesthesiologist handed Joe the phone.

"It's for you," he said casually, as if everyone received personal calls while undergoing a life-saving procedure just inches from his heart. Only Joe seemed to find it surreal.

It was his friend Harry, who never takes no for an answer, calling from San Francisco. It was his regular Friday call, and he was not to be thwarted. Angioplasty notwithstanding, he'd insisted that the hospital locate Joe and put him through.

Thirty-six hours after having been admitted to the hospital, Joe was discharged. From that moment on, his recovery accelerated: within two weeks his incision had healed and he was walking almost a mile a day.

At the same time, his hair abdicated. It had started to fall out after the third installment of chemo, but now the loss was complete. Because of his size and bulk, still considerable despite the inevitable loss in weight, he looked like a combination Golem and Frankenstein's monster. But because of his expression of pure goodness, which throughout the entire ordeal had never left him, he looked most like Daddy Warbucks. (I so liked the look, in fact, that I begged him to shave his head when his hair started coming in, but he had missed his monk's fringe, and refused.)

By the next-to-last chemo, Joe was suffering extreme fatigue. As his doctor explained, this was due mainly to a reduction in the number of red and white blood cells. To combat the anemia, Dr. Ross prescribed injections of two new medications. The injections would be given by the Visiting Nurse, who was still seeing Joe daily.

A week later, the nurse announced that Medicare was pressuring the service, which was in turn pressuring her, to file a report stating that daily visits were no longer necessary. And it was true, she confided. There was no need for her to come that often, were it not for the injections. She asked if I was willing to learn how to do them.

"Good God, no," I said panicking. "I can't stick a needle into a *pincushion!*"

My stomach was churning just thinking about it; I get nauseous watching simulated injections on television hospital shows.

She turned to Joe. "Do you think you could do it yourself?"

"I could do the injection," he replied. "But I'd never be able to remember all the steps involved in filling the syringe."

The solution came to me in a flash of inspiration. Our angel of mercy would teach me the first part, with special attention to ridding the syringe of air bubbles (killing patients by embolism was not in the protocol), and Joe would do the actual injection—after giving me time to leave the room. It was a perfect solution and the ultimate collaboration, as befits two people joined by circumstance at the proverbial hip.

Two months later, Joe's cancer went into remission. The six-month checkup showed no change. It wasn't until a year later that the lymphoma returned. By that time a new treatment, which carries with it none of the pernicious side effects of chemotherapy, had been approved by the FDA. Four infusions one week apart, and the cancer was back in remission.

In the three and a half years after the initial diagnosis, Joe had three remissions and three recurrences. When one treatment didn't work, another would. For a while we were able to think of his lymphoma as a chronic condition, much like diabetes or hypertension, something that needed vigilance and an occasional tune-up to keep under control. In the meantime, we tried not to notice that the intervals between recurrences were becoming shorter.

This made every day, no matter how we chose to spend it, a gift. We would chat happily over morning bagels—he never lost his preference for poppy seed, take long afternoon walks, and at night I would lie spoon-fashion against his large, comfortable body. And if on occasion I chafed that yesterday's socks lay where he'd abandoned them until I picked them up, or that he left the Arts section of the Times in a shambles before I had a chance to read it, or that he couldn't seem to internalize the cosmic truth that toothpaste is best squeezed from the bottom, I thanked my lucky stars to have him there to share the toothpaste with. Age and illness became part of the backdrop of our lives, like the muted grief we continued to feel for our lost companions. For us the circle had closed, and with love, gratitude and mutual delight, we were in it together.

The End, Again

For nearly four years, we lived as if Joe's cancer was a footnote. We took two trips a year (paid for six months in advance to take advantage of discounts), traveling on our own to England and Italy, on tours to middle-Europe, and taking cruises when Joe wasn't up to the rigors of touring. We even did a helmet dive in Bermuda to see underwater corals and be bitten (me) by what had been advertised as a friendly moray eel. We spent every summer on Cape Ann so that I could be near Emily and Mike, even the summer when Joe needed chemo; I called every hospital within thirty miles until I found one willing to coordinate with Joe's health plan, and we worked around the inevitable nausea and fatigue.

During a particularly lamblike March, we went to Spain on an art tour, where we were dazzled by Gaudí in Barcelona, the Prado in Madrid, and the new Guggenheim in Bilbao. We left thinking Joe was in remission. But two weeks later, we were brought up short by the results of a new CT scan.

The tumor had returned. This time it was growing ominously towards his spine. Fearing paralysis, Dr. Ross arranged for radiation. It was almost certain, he said, to shrink the tumor quickly and short-circuit this latest threat. Joe was told to expect external and internal burns as well as difficulty swallowing, but was assured that these side effects would resolve themselves in a matter of weeks. They did not. Instead, they continued to increase to the point where he could neither swallow without severe pain nor hold anything down. His weight loss was alarming and he had developed a mysterious rash over his entire body.

Now hospitalized, a series of tests revealed both a life-threatening virus and an equally serious skin syndrome. Initially, the doctors were, as the saying goes, cautiously optimistic. But after two weeks of a continuing worsening of his condition, despite aggressive treatment, and with his blood and platelet counts sinking daily, his recovery became more and more unlikely.

Joe died on July 7th, 2001. His deterioration during the two weeks before was rapid, and excruciating to watch. He was struggling to breathe, his skin was peeling off in sheets, and swallowing had become so painful that he could no longer eat or drink. Despite attempts to feed and hydrate him by IV, he had become too weak even to shift himself in bed. Finally the ICU doctor and Dr. Ross called his sons and me together and told us what had been apparent to me for days: that despite heroic efforts, there was virtually no hope. But his sons, clinging to the word 'virtually', were convinced that their father still had a chance of winning this battle as he had won it many times before. This time, however, he had no resources with which to fight off the infections. The massive doses of radiation had killed not only his tumor, but his immune system as well.

Two days before the end, as I sat in the waiting room of the ICU with Joe's youngest son, I cautiously raised the subject of hospice. Having become reconciled to the realities of Joe's condition, I wanted only to have his suffering eased. Seth's response was volcanic. He wanted to keep his father alive, he said angrily, not kill him. Stunned by the heat of his response and wounded by its inference, I backed off.

In the end, Joe's ICU doctor managed to satisfy us both. She continued treatment, even to transfusing platelets within hours of his death, but also started a morphine drip at Joe's request to ease his tortured breathing; he had earlier and unmistakably refused a ventilator. He soon slipped into a coma and died peacefully.

*   *   *

My friends had been uniformly delighted for me when I first met Joe. But upon meeting him, some of them, perhaps out of a sense of loyalty, compared him unfavorably to Ralph. They mistook his serenity for complacence, his store of knowledge for pedantry, his reserve for blandness, his gentleness for weakness and his tolerance for lack of discrimination. He was, as he had always been, slow to reveal himself. But as they came to know him, they began to see and to value the qualities I had grasped intuitively half a century ago: his sweetness, his laid-back humor and his quirky, wide-ranging intelligence. While he couldn't critique movies like a film buff, or delve into the subtexts of plays like a dramaturge, or say anything more about a piece of art than that he liked it or he didn't, these are not, I have discovered, essential skills for happiness. As an analyst once told a friend of mine who complained that her otherwise perfectly satisfactory mate wasn't intellectually stimulating enough, "You want stimulation? Go to a lecture".

I got from Joe something far more important than discussions about aesthetics: a mixture of kindness, consideration and unwavering respect. I had received these only sporadically from Ralph. Alternating between anger and admiration, Ralph would punish me for pursuing goals at the expense of some aspect of his comfort, and then shower me with praise once I had achieved them. This made what should have been triumphs equivocal and exhausting experiences. But our marriage also had its glory days. Ralph's extremes, as only one aspect of an otherwise fulfilling relationship, forced me to develop the strength I needed to persevere in the face of discouragement and to realize a vision of myself that incorporated more than that of wife and mother. It enabled me to become, finally, the person that Joe later freed me to be. On Joe's watch, I emerged as a strong, capable woman, able to acknowledge and build on my talents and to feel worthy of the unconditional love he so freely dispensed. The paradox is that given the insecurity and self-doubt of my younger years, both men in aggregate proved to be exactly what I needed.

*   *   *

After Joe's death, a widowed friend asked whether I regretted having made a commitment to someone who became ill two years into what was to be only a six-year relationship. My answer: Not for one minute. Not even during the final wrenching chapter of his illness, when his suffering was so intense that I dreaded going to the hospital every day. She suggested that our story was enough to discourage any older person from establishing a new relationship after the death of a spouse. On the contrary, the years we had together—in sickness and in health—gave me a store of happiness, serenity and love to bank as security against being alone in the years that lay ahead. However much time I have left will be filled with memories of the countless restorative moments I would have missed had we not seized the day.

As a couple, Joe and I had a beginning and an end, but no middle. Those six years, interrupted but never compromised by the illness that ultimately took him, were among my happiest. And I will remember for the rest of my life the moment, two days before he died, when he reached for my hand, locked his eyes onto mine and held my gaze for what seemed like minutes, in an unspoken declaration of love.

At Joe's request, his ashes were divided three ways. Some were interred beside the wife he had adored for forty-seven years, some were scattered into the ocean at Rockaway Beach, where he had spent so many idyllic summer days with his young family, and a small portion was given to me.

Almost every evening for five summers, Joe and I would spend an hour sitting on a rock overlooking the large quarry that forms the nucleus of Halibut State Park on Cape Ann. A dirt and gravel trail follows it at a distance of several feet, with short, widely spaced detours leading to its edge. Each vista is unique. Joe's favorite was one that directly faces the ocean that laps, or in inclement weather crashes, against the massive chunks of granite that form the park's western border. From there, one can look across the still, fresh water of the quarry to the roiling waters of the Atlantic that lie just beyond. The sunsets are spectacular.

On a cool August evening, six weeks after Joe's death, I pocketed the pouch that held my share of his ashes, and entered the park. As I walked the trail, I allowed bits of ash to trickle through my fingers in much the same way that Hansel and Gretel dropped breadcrumbs in the forest. Each time I reached the end of one of the byroads that lead to the edge of the quarry, I would gently toss a handful of ash into the glistening pool. Then I sat on our rock and watched the sunset.

I will miss him always. My first love and my last, he was the bookends to my life.

Observations From
Over The Hill

The Colors of Home

The forlorn little dwelling cowering in the autumn chill was a sorry sight from the top of its stone foundation to its chipped brick chimney. The roof slates, not quite plumb, were a tired gray. The exterior shingles, a sickly yellow-beige, were pitted and peeling. Equally shabby and of the same flat color were the window and door trim. With expectations that the interior would be no different, I opened the front door and walked in.

I was not looking to buy; I was simply role-playing to help one of my friends, a newly licensed real-estate broker, acquire experience in showing houses and dealing with sellers' agents. During that summer, my tenth as a summer renter on the north shore of Massachusetts, we had already visited several properties to that end. This particular house was described as an "Arts and Crafts Bungalow in Move-in Condition". As a lover of both arts and crafts, I was curious to see what a house of that style would look like. Since I had no intention of moving in, its move-in condition was irrelevant.

As I crossed the threshold, I gasped. Oh, the color! Before me was a large, sun-filled living room painted a deep colonial red, its seven tall windows trimmed in white. One wall was bisected by what had to be the original fireplace. The kitchen, which could be seen through a doorway at the far end, was papered in pale-yellow flowers and leaves of spring-green tumbling on a claret background above white wainscoting. The large bathroom had a big, old porcelain tub, and was newly tiled in black and white. Its wallpaper was forsythia-yellow with a faint scallop design in a lighter shade. Every room was perfection. The owner, I learned, had redone the entire interior just two years before, having apparently decided to leave the outside to the elements, as had its previous owners. She had even refinished the floors. It was indeed in move-in condition. I wanted to move in.

It didn't matter that five minutes earlier I'd had no intention of leaving Manhattan, where I lived nine months of the year, and which had nourished me for most of my life. It didn't matter that a house that old (built in 1928, and thus one year younger than I was) might have serious problems, that the wiring and plumbing might be as old as the house and need extensive, expensive repair, or that there was no dining room, entrance hallway or coat closet to accommodate visitors. It didn't matter that a majority of the shingles edging the detached garage roof had slid past the roof's edge like a passel of Dali's melting watches, or that the lawn was brown and spotty, with sparse plantings that drooped like drunken derelicts. It didn't matter that I could have bought any house, if indeed I had wanted to buy one at all, and painted the living room the same luscious red. All I knew was that I didn't want to leave that lovely carmine space with its original fireplace and its seven white-framed living room windows. I made a bid. To my horror, it was immediately accepted.

*   *   *

My moods have always been strongly influenced by color. Where choices are permitted, I usually choose bold colors not always appropriate to the function of the object in question, at least in the eyes of others. My first car, for instance, was a lobster bisque Chevy with cream trim, at a time when most cars were black or gray. Seeing that car every morning with the sun bouncing off its brilliant surface always raised my spirits. It looked even brighter at night.

The colors of my living spaces are especially important to me. As a newlywed decorating my first apartment, I chose a deep forest green for the living room, and for the bedroom, terracotta. They were popular colors in the late forties, especially in Greenwich Village, where they could be glimpsed through the windows of under-furnished, street-level Village apartments, inhabited by couples I imagined to be living in sin. At the time, Ralph was more malleable than he proved to be later, and willingly went along with my choices. He, too, had walked the streets of Greenwich Village.

Soon after we moved in to our freshly painted apartment, I came to realize that dark colors are not the best choice for rooms that look directly onto a brick wall. All of ours did. The kitchen gave no relief; I had made it a deep chocolate brown. I would retreat to the bathroom periodically for a breath of daylight. Fortunately I'd had it painted robin's-egg blue, which at the time I considered a regrettable lack of imagination.

Ralph, in an understandable reaction to the excesses of our first apartment, insisted that we paint every room white in the next one. I was unable to talk him into anything else, even a pastel. Until I hit on the solution of covering the walls with museum posters, we might as well have lived on a hospital ward.

The sad little house on which I made that impulsive bid would be, in essence, my first. The two I had owned with Ralph decades before had essentially been his, my decorative instincts having been quashed under the weight of his Depression mentality. The stark white walls already gracing the Tudor we ultimately bought, would have to serve. It wasn't that he didn't trust that my aesthetic sense had matured—he did—but spending money unnecessarily was anathema to him. He budgeted compulsively. Though also a child of the Great Depression, I had somehow come out of it with a boundless faith in the bounty of America and my husband's future earning power. These, plus the salary I earned as a part-time public school speech pathologist gave me a sense of security that he did not share. I would have had no hesitation doing whatever was necessary to make that classic house into the image I had of it. That I had the same plans for Ralph was a reflection of my naiveté, and in particular, my youthful ignorance of the immutability of character.

*   *   *

Now, in possession of the modest nest egg that existed only because of my husband's foresight, I had the wherewithal to create my own personal vision within the thousand square feet of living space of which I had become so suddenly enamored. The impulsiveness of my behavior had frightened me. For the next few days, I seriously considered canceling the sale. But as I carefully considered my options, moving to Massachusetts made more and more sense. I had been twice widowed and was now, I shuddered to think, only two years short of eighty. Though in relatively good health, with only the usual arthritic pains to remind me of my age, I knew that realistically I could anticipate increasing frailty. Emily and Mike lived only five minutes from the colonial red living room, and their proximity as the years went by might keep me out of a nursing home, barring a serious health crisis. In fact, they had both been urging me to move to their area ever since Joe's death four years earlier. Moreover, we actually got along. In truth, I wasn't particularly attached to the apartment I occupied in Manhattan. For one thing, the walls couldn't be painted anything but white; it was a clause in my lease. Furthermore, like my first apartment, most of the windows looked out onto a brick wall. I'd had no choice; it was soon after Ralph's death, and relatively inexpensive one-bedroom apartments with ample light were simply not available at the time. I found some small solace in the fact that it was larger than any others I'd seen in my search. Fortuitously, my lease was about to expire. Rather than sign another, I decided to go through with buying the house in Beverly. The timing was such that it seemed preordained.

*   *   *

The first time I walked through the kitchen, it was obvious that the owner didn't cook. All four stove burners were covered with delicately patterned Limoge salad plates, a dead giveaway. The refrigerator had nothing in it except a can of coffee and a small container of half-and-half. I learned later that both the stove and the fridge were nineteen years old. There wasn't a scratch on either of them. The oven, apparently never used, gleamed like those in Easy-Off commercials.

I also learned that my seller's predecessor had hardly used the kitchen either. He was a man in his seventies, I was told, who ate out of cans. He also owned two free-range Corgis, which explained the permanent, amoebic black stains on the otherwise pristine wood floors. I hadn't noticed those marks on my first visit; I'd been too bowled over by that glorious living room. I had loved the kitchen wallpaper at first sight, and expected us to be thoroughly compatible. But after I moved in, the optically challenging dance movements of the large floral pattern on a cranberry field became intolerable. It had been beautiful before all of the small appliances, cooking utensils, cleaning aids, dishtowels and other essentials of a working kitchen were added. But once I'd set my dozens of culinary imperatives on the counters, migraines abounded. Besides, the deep claret of the wallpaper's background made the room too dark to work in comfortably, even with sunlight streaming in.

Something draconian had to be done. On the day that I could take no more, I decided that the wallpaper had to go. I abandoned the brisket I was preparing and drove to the nearest paint store, where I bought a color fan from a nice young man behind the counter. After flipping through it, I decided on something in the yellow family. Ah, but which yellow? There were dozens. I returned to the kitchen and spread the fan on the floor, which was surfaced with not very attractive quarry tiles in mottled beige. But because they were in too good condition to replace, they had to be factored in.

But oh dear, all those yellows! Pale Ale, perhaps? No, not enough contrast. Yellow Submarine? Too much, and of the wrong kind. Yoseminite Yellow? Too light. Hathaway Gold? Too dark. Happy Valley? A little too happy. I found three that were possibilities and went back to the paint store for samples. Returning home, I painted a large swath of each, and continued preparing the brisket, my back to the wall. Fifteen minutes later, I looked. Wrong, wrong and wrong. I didn't stop to analyze why. I went to the basement, where there were a few extra floor tiles, put one in the car and drove off to the paint store again. There, after listening to my dilemma, noting my emotional state and examining the tile, the nice young man behind the counter quietly suggested a color called Powell Buff. I looked at it.

"It's not yellow", I said.

The nice young man smiled. "It will be."

I was so addled by then that I forced a suspension of disbelief, bought a gallon of Powell Buff on faith, and drove back. I made yet another swipe at the wall and cut some onions, my back to the swath as it dried. Finally, I turned around. Miracle of miracles, it was yellow. The yellow I'd dreamed of, a warm, beigy yellow. Perfect with the tiles. Not too dark, not too light, not too happy.

* * *

As winter gave way to spring, there was a much bigger decision to be made. The garage roof had been replaced, the wiring and the plumbing brought up to code, the central air-conditioning installed and the furnace repaired. The scrubby lawn that abutted the side of the house had been leveled and a large stone patio built and enclosed by a stockade fence. Round dowels topped the vertical poles that joined the sections, and the entire enclosure was stained a warm honey tone. I had selected patio stones of grayish-beige shot through with tan flecks, hardly dramatic, but in keeping with my plan. Even my new car, a PT Cruiser in a not-very sexy almond color, was selected with forethought. All this because from the beginning, I had known exactly what color my house must be.

A charming Colonial in Salem had caught my eye the summer before. It was painted a kind of pumpkin color. Well, not really pumpkin and not exactly ginger, not as dark as burnt orange and much lighter than terracotta. I had never seen that color on a house before. Actually, I hadn't seen it on a pumpkin either. A few weeks earlier, I had asked the owner of the Salem house for a small piece of peeling paint, and compared it to similar samples in the color fan. I couldn't find a match, so it had to be specially mixed. I called the owner and asked if he could remember the ingredients. No, he said apologetically, it was too long ago and he no longer had the can.

Convinced more than ever that only that color would do, I again went to see the nice young man at the paint store. He looked at the fragile paint sample that I had carefully wrapped in aluminum foil, and disappeared around the back. Ten minutes later, he emerged with a quart can and a mixing stick covered with—the exact match! I raced home, found a fresh brush and covered a few square feet of shingles with the new paint. Twenty minutes later, I went outside to see the result. It was by far the ugliest color I had ever seen. It was so aggressive that my eyes began to tear. Squinting, I reached for the original. It was the same, but then again, it wasn't.

My son-in-law, Mike, who can do anything, had prepped the exterior of my house some weeks before, with the help of Ed, a painter friend of his. Had I been able to afford it, I would have had all the old shingles replaced with new ones. But the cost would have been astronomical, and my nest egg had recently developed a crack. Instead, I'd settled for a heat-gun, a scraping, a sandpapering, a primer coat and an assurance by Ed that the house was at least tight, if not restored to its original state. The shingles were still pitted, some few even more so than before the prep. The paint color I had chosen was calling attention to every irregularity, and sunlight magnified them even more.

I went back to the nice young man at the paint store. I was beginning to think of him as a close friend.

"Did the Salem house have shingles or clapboard?" he asked.

"Clapboard," I said, though not entirely sure.

"Does it get a lot of sun?"

"No, it's shaded, I think."

"That could be your problem," he said. "Clapboard is smooth, so it takes color differently. Old shingles look better with dull colors, especially if the house gets a lot of sun."

I drove back past the Salem house to check. There it stood, sheathed in clapboard and surrounded by several majestic maples. It was obvious that my house could never be pumpkin. I would have to activate Plan B. I didn't much like Plan B; pumpkin had been my dream and Plan B merely a fallback position. I sighed and opened the color fan to Plan B.

Great Barrington Green is a soft mossy color without much character, which has the single virtue of blending in with the surrounding greenery, just beginning to emerge after a long winter. When I tried a sample on the house, it did indeed camouflage most of the irregularities. The shingles looked reasonably smooth, even in bright sunlight. But it wasn't pumpkin, and I knew that it would be a long time before I became reconciled. I chose off-white for the trim, not wanting to take any chances.

So here I am, a feisty Manhattan woman used to making statements, and wanting my house to do the same. Instead, it sits there, speechless. To be honest though, the house looks quite comfortable in its new identity. Passing neighbors interrupt my feeble attempts at gardening with compliments. Maybe they saw the original pumpkin sample and are relieved that I changed my mind.

My cats, Ben and Charlie, go well with the colonial red living room, even though, by coincidence, both their coats are pumpkin. With them in mind, I bought a mustard yellow couch, armchairs in a red, pumpkin and mustard plaid, and pillows in—you guessed it—pumpkin. Finding pillows that color wasn't easy, but it was worth the search; they work beautifully. The living room has become the cats' favorite play area. They particularly enjoy destroying the pillows, the roughness of the corduroy being exactly the texture they like to claw. I will have to replace the pillows eventually, but maybe by that time, I'll have a wider choice of fabric.

Even after three years, I love my home as passionately. But I have never completely reconciled to Great Barrington Green. It's not bad, but it will never make a statement. Still, I'm not ready to think about a replacement. I need more time to cleanse my palette.

Getting Used To

My Aunt Fanny always said that life was a matter of getting used to, and the sooner you do it, the better off you'll be. It didn't occur to me until much later that she had never gotten used to anything, railing loudly against every aspect of her life until she died of a stroke shouting at her second husband. Nevertheless, I have always tried to do what she said rather than what she did, and I've found that it was good advice. I'm still getting used to my new home, a new space in a new city that provides shelter not only for me but everything that I've brought with me: things inanimate like the furniture, the paintings, the kitchenware and linens; living things like my plants and my cats; plus those intangibles that are as much a part of my life as everything else: memories of my life in all its aspects, and especially of my two men.

As I have done often since finding myself alone after fifty-three consecutive years of couplehood, I talk to everything except the furniture: I praise my plants, telling them how beautiful they are; I talk to the cats about pretty much the same thing, along with baby talk I'd be ashamed for anyone to overhear; I talk to Ralph and Joe, telling them I miss them and reminiscing about the good times. I scold Ralph for his rages and his casual infidelities, and Joe, who in our first incarnation was less than honest with himself and with me about his feelings for the woman he ultimately married. Sometimes I apologize to both of them for my having sweated so much of the small stuff, not then understanding the unimportance of the small stuff or the permanence of loss. It takes some getting used to, talking aloud to my ghosts and my cats and my plants in this new space, so much bigger and airier than my previous digs.

I have also had to get used to the openness of this house. Because I can be seen through most of the fourteen windows that make of it one large sunroom, I keep the blinds up and my clothes on. I dislike slatted blinds, but they came with the house, and it would be too expensive to replace them. Those blinds were something else I had to get used to. In the mornings, when I look like the Wicked Witch of the West without the hat, I keep all the lights off on the theory that if the outside is brighter than the inside, anyone outside can't see in. I hope I'm right.

There is only one blind that I close at night: the one in the bedroom that looks out onto my neighbor's front door from a distance of twenty feet. The window in the bathroom is similarly situated, but I have solved that problem by placing in the window a large, whimsical collage by Enrico Baj of Lord Nelson, instead of closing the blind. I prefer having Lord Nelson observe my ablutions to my neighbors doing the same.

All the windows in my living room and one in the kitchen look out on the street, where passersby can be spied on, and if lighting conditions are right, they can spy on me. Despite all this visibility, I feel completely safe and private, security always having been, for me, a state of mind.

I write on a laptop that sits on Ralph's old six-foot long rosewood desk, one I had always coveted. I still haven't gotten used to the idea that it is now mine. His desk is in my study, the smaller of the two bedrooms, which holds much of the rest of what makes up my life: the radio, CD and DVD players, a CD rack, an old television set and my books. Once the children left for college, Ralph and I sold the house in New Rochelle, the suburb we'd moved to when the kids were small, and returned to Manhattan, where we lived in a succession of large rental apartments. Ralph would set up his office in the otherwise unused second bedroom, while I used a corner of the dining room or the foyer, whichever could accommodate my miniscule computer desk and a file cabinet. It was one of the few 'small stuffs' I didn't sweat. Perhaps it's because we had a friend, a successful biographer, who wrote in a corner of her dining room, while her husband, a failed writer, used the second bedroom. I figured that if she didn't mind, I shouldn't. Getting used to having my own study hasn't been easy. It got easier once I got over the feeling that I should keep the desk available for Ralph.

I've also had to get used to taking the garbage cans and the recyclables to the curb once a week, where city garbage trucks pick them up before 7 A.M., which to me is the middle of the night. Half the time I forget to put them out the night before, leaving me with a smelly garage and a car that smells a lot like my garbage. I've been planning to ask my doctor if there's anything I can do about my failing memory, but I keep forgetting.

I had never shoveled snow, even when we lived in New Rochelle. We'd always hired someone to do it. Here, having moved in the middle of winter and knowing that the snow season was far from over. I bought myself an ergonomic shovel. A couple of days later it snowed. I put on my winter gear, which included thigh-high Wellingtons bought one summer afternoon in Venice to walk the flooded streets, and pushing against a strong wind, I opened the storm door and started down the side steps. The steps were unexpectedly slippery (anyone more sensible would have expected them to be) causing me to bounce down each one of the four steps on my tailbone, which was fortunately protected by a down coat. Unhurt, I picked myself up, vowing in the future to keep the shovel near the door so that I could do the steps first.

Feeling very much like a pioneer woman, I ignored both my age and the fact that I never exercise. I eased the shovel under the snow, feeling more competent than I'd felt in years. I did it again. And again. My shoulder, the one I'd broken five years before, sliding along the marble floor of a hotel in Rome, started to ache. So did my wrists. I'd forgotten I have arthritis. Something gave in my back, but I tried to work through the pain. Two more shovelsful were all I could manage. Ergonomic, my ass, I thought, and gave up. I went inside and decided to let my fingers do the walking, knowing that shoveling snow was something I would *never* get used to. I made a call, and two hours later a pickup truck with a plow attached pulled up and did the job in five minutes.

It took me a couple of weeks to get my back back. I suspect that ten years from now, the snow shovel will be as pristine as when I bought it. What I got used to as a result of that episode was the idea that there are some things I shouldn't attempt, a list that has come to include putting in and taking out storm windows, lifting anything heavier than ten pounds and getting on my knees for anything at all.

When I was still in New York, I'd been brooding a lot, missing Ralph and Joe in turn, depressed and lonely in a city of millions. I was still living in the apartment where Joe and I had spent our six years together, within three blocks of the building where Ralph had died. Though I hoped that in Beverly my life would be more relaxed and less prone to unhappy memories,

I never dreamed that only weeks after moving here, I would be feeling a kind of muted elation in which the deep satisfaction of an earned solitude was at its base. So I've also had to get used to being happy.

It is rare that I have needed to accommodate so many changes in so short a period, especially at a time in my life when I no longer expected any changes except the ultimate one. But I've gotten used to it, even though all that getting used to has taken some getting used to.

Bathtubs I Have Known

The size of the bathtub was one of the most important criteria for any apartment I ever considered renting. It could be clawfooted or no-footed, porcelain-coated or plastic, but what it could not be was short. In search of the model bathtub, I have given up spiral staircases, French windows, dropped living rooms, doormen and killer views. But it was absolutely necessary that almost all five-foot four of me, from my ankles to my neck, be underwater when I bathed.

When I am asked if I am happy here by people who are astounded by my move from Manhattan to a suburb of Boston, I say "Oh, yes, very," hesitant to add any of the adjectives that would express the extent of my happiness, which sometimes feels as strong as euphoria and hardly appropriate to some of the things that contribute to it, like the size of my bathtub.

The first time I entered my Beverly house, I made sure, of course, to check out the tub. It was old and huge: porcelain-coated steel, with high sides, and even longer than the one in my New York apartment. I couldn't wait to luxuriate in its sybaritic concavity.

Moving was not, initially, an easy decision. But having spent many summers on Cape Ann, about half an hour northeast of where I now live, I had built up a cadre of friends who'd been begging me for years to live in Massachusetts year round. Added to this were the pleas of Emily and Mike, long-time Beverly residents, who'd been pressing me to move here since

Ralph's death nine years before. Emily insisted that she wanted to be able to take care of me as I got older. The thought of not being able to care for myself was unthinkable. I was touched, but unconvinced. But then I fell in love with this semi-wreck of a 1928 Arts and Crafts bungalow with the big bathtub, and made the decision to spend my remaining years in Massachusetts. I looked forward to relearning my daughter and son-in-law after twenty-five years of too-short summers and unsatisfactory long-distance winter phone calls. The fact that my body was reminding me more and more frequently of my advancing age, coupled with those rich red walls, are what gave me the final push.

*   *   *

It was the morning after my move. Emily arrived early, bearing breakfast. Along with hundreds of other artifacts amassed during a long acquisitive marriage, I had packed, but not yet unpacked, a rubber bathmat with suction cups designed to prevent any tub from morphing into an ice rink. Not sure that I could manage without a mat, I asked my daughter if she would wait to have breakfast until I had taken my bath. To justify why I couldn't eat breakfast first, throw on some clothes, drive to the nearest hardware store to pick up a bathmat and THEN have a bath, it is necessary to explain what a morning bath means to me.

In addition to being an indispensable substitute for meditation, which I am otherwise too jumpy to employ, I suffer from arthritis, and for boring medical reasons am forbidden to take anti-inflammatories. My morning bath enables me to straighten up from a C-shape and walk, with minimal pain, like a relatively normal person. For me, it's like taking a daily trip to Lourdes. Lowering my aching body into the steaming hot water gives me a delicious jolt that both wakes me up and loosens my joints. I then lie there for a few minutes in a cloud of physical and spiritual nirvana. Actually, I couldn't survive without my morning bath, and to have its full effect, it must be taken before I do anything else, including breakfast and the New York Times.

And so I lay in my big new/old bathtub for the first time, blissfully osmosing the healing warmth, until the cooling water suggested that it was time for me to get out. I set my right elbow into the upper right corner of the bathtub, gripping the other side of the tub with my left hand, planted my feet firmly on the bottom and tried to lift myself. This had always worked in Manhattan. But my feet slid on the floor of the bathtub as if it had been coated with vaseline. Next, I grabbed the faucet with both hands and tried to grip the porcelain with my toes. I managed to raise myself a few inches, but gravity won and I fell back into the water, raising a spray that soaked the tiled floor. I feared that if I ever did manage to stand upright, the wet tiles would present yet another challenge. I tried again, this time grasping the side of the tub with both hands and twisting my body towards my hands, but this time my feet slid out from under me with such force that I sustained a bruised tailbone that remained with me for several days.

Hearing the unmistakable sounds of a body repeatedly falling against water, Emily naturally knocked on the door and inquired if I was all right.

"Not exactly," I said. "I'm afraid I'm going to need your help to get out of this bloody bathtub."

After a long silence, the door opened.

Though my daughter is a small woman, she is an avid exerciser, unlike any of her ancestors living or dead, and she had no difficulty lifting me into a standing position. I thanked her profusely and got dressed. I was aware of a slight uneasiness between us during breakfast, but ascribed it to the fact that we had to eat standing up and with our hands, as Emily had neglected to bring silverware.

For a few days, our conversations, mostly on the phone, continued to be strained. It was obvious that something was wrong between us. In such circumstances, I have learned to wait; if I ask questions too early, I get stonewalled. But sooner or later—mostly sooner, she will tell me what is on her mind. Neither of my children has ever kept any of their grievances a secret for long. Not that I wasn't discomfited by Emily's aloofness, especially as she and Mike were among the main reasons I had moved. There is always the possibility of an estrangement with one's offspring, and I couldn't help wondering if the move had been a mistake. Whatever the frustrations of communion by long-distance, there is less of an opportunity to get into trouble when two people talk to each other only a couple of hours a week.

Her call came a few days later.

"Hi, Em," I said hopefully. "How are things?"

She did not disappoint. With a rush of relief, I heard the words I had been hoping to hear all week. "Mom, we have to talk."

She drove over a few minutes later.

"I think you know I haven't been myself."

"So?" I said gratefully. "Who were you?"

"That bathroom scene the other day really upset me."

"I don't blame you," I said. "Seeing myself naked upsets me too."

"That wasn't it. I guess I didn't think I'd have to take care of you so soon."

"Come on, Em", I said. "We discussed this ad nauseum before I agreed to move up. You kept saying you *want* to take care of me."

"I do", she replied. "I just didn't expect it to start the day after you moved in."

Her expectation, she explained, logical or not, was that I would be able to manage by myself well into my nineties, after which she and Mike would happily do whatever was necessary to help me remain in my own home.

"By then," she said, "We'd be retired and we'd have all the time in the world to help."

She then described the fantasy she had carefully constructed. At my inevitable demise, she said, all my friends and relatives would be standing around my bed (in size places? I irreverently asked) to watch me die gracefully and without pain. There would be, of course, the second movement of Schubert's Piano Trio in E flat playing softly in the background, as per my request. The probability of these events actually occurring on her timetable had been rudely put into question by the episode of the bathtub.

But I wondered whether that was the whole story. Perhaps facing her mother's seventy-eight-year-old body might also have played a part. I don't much like looking at it myself, and I live there. Wallace Stegner, in a novel about a couple in their ninth decade, rhapsodizes about the incredible smoothness of old skin. I assume that he couldn't find any other positive comments to make about aging. It must have been quite a jolt for my daughter, younger than me by twenty-five years, to face the effects of surgeries, normal wear and tear, gravity, culinary over-indulgence and too much early sun exposure in that one shocking instant, possibly presaging her own fate.

Shortly after, I worked out a modus operandi that precludes her ever having to attend me during my baths. All it took was a magic (waterproof) pendant, which, when activated, summons a trained EMS worker in case the suction cups under my now cracked and elderly bathmat happen to fail. They will also respond for less urgent reasons, such as a stroke or a heart attack.

My bathtub continues to delight me. It took a couple of weeks for me to hit upon the right combination of hot and cold water to prevent either a third degree burn or a fatal chill, and I soon mastered the art of getting out of the tub safely in less than five seconds. I haven't fallen yet. I still have hopes that if I lose another inch or two in height, my toes will be able to join the rest of me underwater. In the meantime, I soak blissfully every morning in my venerable tub, cocooned in soothing heat from ankle to neck, secure in the knowledge that at least in this one area I have finally found perfection.

Gardening

On that late September day in 2004 when I first saw my house, the lawn looked like fodder for horses: the grass was long, yellow, and the texture of straw. The path from the sidewalk to the front steps might have been laid by the Crooked Man of nursery rhyme fame. It cried out to be replaced with something less dangerous than the few jagged flagstones that threatened to trip unwary, possibly litigious, guests. I didn't have the courage to think about what it would cost to make the outside as beautiful as I hoped to make the inside. If I had, I'm not sure I'd have closed on the house.

I had been feeling impoverished after I moved in and considered the cost of landscaping. After what I'd already spent on the house, I began to wonder if I had made a mistake. Months later, I was still wondering. I would add up my assets daily, calculating how long they would last if I lived to be a hundred. I would just begin to think that I might squeak by, but then my alter ego would appear, bent on keeping me feeling poor and on the brink of financial disaster.

"I'm already seventy-eight," I would argue. "I probably won't live another twenty years."

"*But what if you do,*" it would insist.

"Not likely," I'd reply. "Longevity doesn't run in my family." But I wasn't convinced.

When spring arrived, little green things began to sprout all around my property. Everything was so fresh and beautiful that I forgot what it had looked like barely six months before. With the proprietary feelings of a new mother, I watched each promising sprig become a plant. Perhaps, I thought hopefully, I can avoid all the work I dreaded having to pay for. But as they grew, it became apparent that my garden was still a crazy quilt of randomly growing plants and an expensive intervention seemed unavoidable. The building of the patio created more problems: forty linear feet of new beds, quickly filling up with weeds. It took a couple of weeks of observing with growing dismay the disaster overtaking my yard to decide to begin the landscaping. To assuage my panic, I planned to do it over three summers and pray for a bull market. This modest schedule, I hoped, would mollify my alter ego, which was still muttering in the background. The patio borders seemed a good place to start.

Having made my decision, I called my friend Leslie, who as a house gift had offered me as many plants as I needed from her colorful, if overgrown garden in Rockport. The next morning, I drove up to make my choices.

Leslie's garden was in full flower. It was hard to choose, but I decided on several varieties to start with, among them sedum, hostas, orange poppies, daylilies and several other plants whose names I forgot as soon as she identified them. Leslie and my neighbor, Lila, who had come with me to help, started to dig. One after another, small blobs of living matter were placed on the ground, already wilting in the ninety-degree heat. Uprooted from their previous housings they looked puny and unhappy.

"Don't worry," chirped the perennially cheerful Leslie. "They'll look great by midsummer."

My God, I thought, will it take that long? I gazed ruefully at the twenty or so plants lying listlessly on the pavement and wondered what I'd gotten myself into. Lila assured me that they would be fine. We wrapped the plants in wet paper and put them in the back of my car. I sped home, fearing they would die before we got there. We made it in record time, but I noted that Lila was a little green as she exited the car.

I had planned to work along with her, but each thrust and lift of the spade evoked a lightening strike of joint and back pain. Since it was clear that I could no more be a laborer than a shoveler of snow, I promoted myself to supervisor.

I called Mike, who agreed to help. He and Lila placed the now moribund perennials along the borders, leaving a lot of space between them. Aloud, I wondered why, as there were still more plants waiting to be set in the ground, the beds looked so sparse. Mike explained that they would grow into the space, and would probably fill it by September.

"Slow down," Mike admonished me when I complained. "Enjoy the process. It's not instant pudding."

This was not what I'd anticipated: I had expected my garden to emerge fully grown, like Athena springing from the head of Zeus. Oh, well, I consoled myself, this will teach me patience, a virtue not in my repertory.

Some hours later, after the addition of some mulch, which set off the plants nicely, the job was done. By then, the patio borders were looking neat, but only partially dressed, like a woman still in her underwear.

By the end of July, the plants looked healthy and upstanding. By August the beds were glorious. Sedum, sprouting tiny reddish flowers lined up with giant daylilies, which abutted a bearded iris, which stood next to a small quince tree, and further down, a white rose bush, just starting to bud. There were other colorful flowers in these narrow borders, but their names are forever lost in the folds of my aging temporal lobe.

Unfortunately, they made everything else on my property look like impoverished relatives. I argued with myself for three days, and then called Dave Phillips, a weekend gardener who had created a delightful garden for my next door neighbors, and who'd been tending my lawn and hanging around, awaiting orders he knew would come eventually. Fearlessly, I asked him to draw up plans for everything that still needed to be done.

"I want to be able to enjoy it before I have to look at it from a wheelchair." I said. It wasn't easy to ignore the voice in my head that accused me of frittering away savings that will have to last as long as I do.

"Why shouldn't I spend it?" I said defiantly to you know who. "There'll be plenty left; I've just been too chicken to use it."

"*But what if you live another twenty years?*" it countered, as usual.

"In twenty years, I won't know who I am," I said. "So to hell with process; what I want is results! And I want them NOW."

Alter ego slunk away. It knew I was a changed woman. Dave started working the next day, and the entire project was finished in a matter of weeks.

*   *   *

It is 8:30 A.M. on a mid-July morning, and I am standing at the back of my house admiring the newly planted strip of land that separates my backyard from that of my neighbor. The outdoor thermometer already reads eighty degrees. I am doing the first of the two daily waterings that were mandated by Dave. This six by fifteen foot strip, previously a haven for weeds, an old Michelin tire and several other memorabilia of my house's past, is now a quirky, lopsided marvel.

Several feet to the right of center there stands a small crabapple tree shaped like a pixilated candelabra, which Dave had wanted to take down. He'd conceived of a weeping Japanese maple, centered, as the crabapple is not, which would have made the design more symmetrical. My insistence on keeping the crabapple tree had forced him to rethink the entire project. He was not happy.

But I had already developed an attachment to that tree, partly because I like its odd shape, and partly because it is the offspring of a much larger crabapple tree standing majestically in the middle of my neighbor's yard, some twenty feet away. It seemed cruel to separate a child from its mother. I finally pulled rank, but offered a compromise: in exchange for leaving the tree, Dave could have carte blanche with everything else. Reluctantly, he'd accepted, then come through brilliantly after banishing me for most of two days so that I wouldn't be tempted to interfere.

Now I look at a combination of ornamental grasses, green and white hostas, day lilies, sedum, arborvitae, Mohawk daisies, moonbeam coreopsis, a Rose of Sharon with hundreds of tiny buds, and at least fifteen other varieties of perennials that will have to remain nameless. My little crabapple tree is standing in the midst of all this beauty, its own enhanced by its new surroundings.

I wrap the hose around its housing and walk slowly around the house. No longer a garden virgin, I have been deflowered—or rather flowered—over the course of less than one summer. I look carefully at the foundation plants along the front: rhododendrons, which only last fall looked tired and thin, seem much happier now after a deep root watering. What space remained between them has been filled with a gift from Dave of four giant hostas, the buds on their long stalks ready to pop into bloom. Most of the remaining bare spots have miraculously filled in with a carpet of lilies of the valley, none of which were evident the year before. Along the north side of the house, bushes that last fall had looked depressed and spindly have filled in, shot up, and now need pruning. The front lawn was seeded in early June, and with daily watering, is now definitely green. And in place of the few randomly placed flagstones leading from the street to my front steps, there now exists a stone path, designed and executed by Mike, which Dave has lined with six plump boxwoods.

I pull out a few tiny fronds of crabgrass that are peeking out from between the stones, and look critically at the walkway. Something is missing. Hmm, I think, a few low-lying annuals would look great in the spaces between the boxwoods. Yellow ones. Maybe orange.

I go inside and call Dave.

Neighbors

Before moving here, I lived in a series of old, well-kept apartment buildings on the Upper West Side of Manhattan. My life as a retiree was delightfully sybaritic. Days didn't start much before ten every morning, by which time most of my neighbors had already left for work. Those few that I did encounter were mostly stay-at-home mothers, nannies or the elderly, who emerged from their separate spaces at about the same time I did. We would eye each other furtively as we entered the elevator (the children would mostly make faces at me or cower in their carriages), or, less often, smile, and perhaps exchange a word or two about the dreadful or delightful or unseasonable weather awaiting us outside. But usually, we descended silently to our individual imperatives, and in the service of not having to make eye contact, would stare at the numbers on the lighted display of the floors we were passing as if they contained vital information. Once on the street, we would quickly put space between us, even if we were walking in the same direction.

I lived in my last apartment for eight years, and though I knew most of the tenants by sight, we almost never spoke. There was the young mother who glared at me as balefully as if I were planning to abduct her unpleasant eight-year-old twins, who regarded me with as much suspicion as did their mother. There was the older woman, who tottered on impossibly high heels, and whose brief statements consisted only of complaints about her feet. There was the psychologist who lived on the eighth floor and had an office off the lobby. He would bow stiffly (I pegged him as Old Europe), and always insisted that I leave the elevator before him, inspiring an 'After you, Alfonse' pantomime each time. Ultimately, I succumbed to his impeccable manners; tradition is a hard thing to fight.

Then I moved to Beverly and a whole new world. Joggers stopped to tell me how much they liked what I had done to my house, or how beautiful my new plantings were. People I had never seen before would say "Hello" as they walked by, sometimes stopping to critique the rain—too much or not enough—or discuss the latest local scandal as reported that day on the front page of the Salem News. Some asked me where I had moved from, which always evoked the same question: Don't you miss New York? Or its corollary: Isn't Beverly boring after you've lived in the Big City? The answers, no and no, never failed to amaze them.

With my move, I acquired my first friendly neighbors, people who indulge easily in what linguists call phatic speech: amiable, stereotypical exchanges consisting of sentences such as "How are you?" "Fine thanks. You?" "Nice weather, isn't it", and the like. I've always been envious of people who could do this easily, as it seemed so, well, sociable. But it was hard for me to get any practice, as New York is not a city that nourishes small talk. Things are different here.

At the top of the hill lives Moira, a 45-year-old woman and her elderly mother. Moira is the lone unmarried daughter in a Greek-Irish family of seven children, and therefore fated to be the caregiver. She is going slightly batty trying to balance her mother's tyrannical rule with her own independent spirit. One result is her daily early-morning motorcycle getaway or fast turns around the block on her racing bike. She is often angry at her mother, but wears a patina of forbearance that is very convincing until you get her in one of her rebellious moods. Though she looks androgynous and is difficult from a distance to distinguish from a young man—she has a rangy body, always wears blue jeans and sports a very short haircut—there are always men, often on motorcycles themselves, hanging around to flirt. Some years before, she'd had a love affair with an observant Jew, who died tragically after what she describes as six idyllic years together. Since his death, she has idealized him to such a point that no subsequent lover could possibly measure up. During my first week here, we would exchange friendly comments about the weather, and she would offer to help any way she could. Then she started bringing over portions of Greek delicacies, redolent of lemon, and would tell me all about her lost love, as well as the rest of her life. She would sit for an hour reciting her lover's hagiography and insisting, in classic denial, how she didn't resent taking care of her mother, who was not easy to deal with. As a result, much of my unpacking took a lot longer than it needed to. She kept apologizing for the state of the shingles on her house; they need a painting badly, as does the fence. Her mother will not allow it. She did, however, permit the replacement of the roof, formerly a sickly green with many tiles missing, which helps a little. Moira came over during a recent heat wave to see how the little old lady, as she calls me, was weathering the weather. She breathed my air-conditioned air gratefully, and then went out into the inferno again.

Coincidentally, Moira's sister was the seller's real estate agent for this house, and one of her brothers replaced the motor on my garage door when it refused to let my car out, so there is always someone waving at me from the top of the hill as they visit their mother. Sometimes they will walk over for a neighborly chat. Somehow I have become more adept at small talk in my new circumstances. While I like doing it, my skills are limited. I always get to a point where I feel the need to cut it short and get into something more meaty. My neighbors, on the other hand, seem to have an endless talent for that sort of *shmoozing*.

Next to my house, in a pale yellow colonial, lives a charming eight-year-old named Melody. Like her parents, she waves at me when she and her mother walk their dog. I bought 10 boxes of Girl Scout cookies from her last year, which I am still trying to palm off on guests. Even when my own children sold them, they were never as good as Nabisco. Her parents, Anne, a librarian and Ted, a salesmanager, are former New Yorkers and very active in the community. They let me know when important political meetings or rallies are about to take place, or hand me the petition *du jour* to sign. We're not exactly friends, just very friendly. They have several times reminded me that I can call on them for shopping or other help at any time. I suppose they are thinking of my vulnerability as an old lady, which is heartwarming, but makes me feel older than I am. I have offered to stay with Melody in an emergency, but so far neither of us has taken the other up on the offers.

The neighbors behind my garage are a young couple with a four-year-old son named Seth. We're not exactly friends, either, though we have done each other important favors: when they discovered that I'd been a speech pathologist in a former life, they asked for help in dealing with their son's prominent stutter. I assured them that it was a normal developmental stage, and gave them a few do's and don't's to avoid having him become self-conscious about it. I like to think that my advice was at least one factor in his stuttering having completely disappeared. On their part, they recently visited New York, and without my asking, brought back some authentic bagels. Good bagels and

Off-Broadway theater are about the only things I miss about New York. Besides that, we engage in the usual pleasantries. I inquire about their health, and they ask about mine.

I consider these three families my most immediate community, my closest non-intimate friends, and my insurance against feeling alone. Though none has offered to shovel snow or water my outdoor plantings—these are services that can be bought, after all—they do check up on me if they haven't seen me outside for a week or two or if I forget to pick my newspaper up off the front steps, ask if I need candles when the electricity goes out, and a year ago rang the bell to see if I needed help after an unexpected flood. None of this ever happened to me in New York. There, one has fellow apartment-dwellers, but no neighbors.

My neighbors will occasionally tell me how glad they are to have me living on their street. It may be my age: I provide a missing demographic link, as most of the homeowners in the immediate area are young couples who bought from people opting for retirement communities. Or maybe it's because I don't have any barking dogs or loud teenagers, and that I enjoy, as do they, the undemanding pleasures of phatic speech.

"How are you?" I hear, and my day is made.

My Relationship With Trains

Just before I made my decision to buy this house, which is a block away from a train station, I asked the broker if it wouldn't be noisy to live with railroad tracks only thirty feet away. She assured me that in winter, with the storm windows in, one could barely hear the train at all. I didn't ask about spring and summer, when storm windows hibernate in basements, because I didn't want to hear anything that might make me think twice about what I was about to do. I rationalized it thus: being able to walk to the station was a plus; being in a designated 'Quiet Zone', with only bells to announce the coming and going of the trains, was another; and fooling myself that the trees that hid the tracks from sight would muffle the sound in summer was a third. I was reassured when I moved in a couple of months later, one week after a blizzard had buried Beverly under several feet of snow, that only the slightest rumble from the passing trains could be heard from inside the house. The sound was almost romantic.

Came the middle of May, and off came the storm windows. I continued to sleep soundly. Perhaps my cats' nighttime positions—one pressed against each side of my head, helped minimize the train sounds. Besides, without my hearing aids, the world spins in relative quiet. But that summer I discovered, while chatting on the patio with a friend, that trying to communicate over the roar of a locomotive requires a strategy. I put a finger to my lips, indicating that talk should cease until the train passes and take those thirty seconds as an opportunity to rethink what I was about to say, and perhaps rephrase it more artfully.

When I am alone in my study reading, on a day when the central air-conditioning has kicked in, I don't hear the trains passing at all. But when the windows are open, which is most of the time, and I begin to hear what Wordsworth called the tintinnabulation of the bells, I put my book down and find myself thinking about other trains I have taken in earlier, more peripatetic times.

There was the trip Ralph and I took from Denver to Oakland in the sixties. We had bought the tickets very near the date of departure, and were too late to get a double roomette. Instead we were assigned two singles situated across the corridor from one another.

After dinner, we chatted for a while and then said goodnight. I was eager to explore the mechanism whereby pulling down the bed caused the chair and the sink to disappear and reduced the entire sitting room to a cozy bed. I performed the magic a couple of times, trying to figure it out, then settled in for the night. I had bought what promised to be a good mystery at the Denver station, snuggled into what I found to be a surprisingly comfortable bed, and began to read. Soon I became sleepy, but the sound and rhythm of the wheels beneath me were so delicious that I fought sleep until fatigue gently eased me into unconsciousness.

The next morning, I awakened early, feeling rested and happy. I dressed quickly, restored the bed to its original hiding place, and crossed the aisle to say good morning to Ralph.

"Come in", he said to my knock. His voice was oddly hollow.

I opened the door. There he sat, his clothes and hair disheveled, looking twenty years older than when I'd last seen him.

"My god, what happened?" I asked.

He then told me the story of his night, which bore no resemblance to mine. Like me, he had undressed, pulled down his bed and tried to sleep. He found the bed lumpy and hard and the rhythmic turning of the wheels intolerable. Getting out of bed, he put it up again, sat in the chair and tried to read. He found the closeness of the roomette unbearable, and for the first time experienced the suffocating claustrophobia that he suffered for the rest of his life. The entire night had been spent alternating between the bed and the chair. He had gotten no sleep at all.

Now that his door was open, he refused to close it. I went back to my own roomette and left mine open as well, hoping he would find this arrangement reassuring. But nothing would console him, and soon I could sense his growing anger. Here he was, having endured the worst night of his life, frightened and unable to lose himself in sleep, and there was his wife, looking kempt, cheerful and ready for her upcoming San Francisco adventure. Ralph was often infuriated by my perennially perky attitude. This was one of those times. As a result, he sulked for the rest of the trip. He never got over his fear of small, enclosed spaces, and it was a long time before he could see the humor in that night on the California Zephyr as it chugged its way to Oakland.

But the train trip that Ralph and I took from Frankfort to Wiesbaden in West Germany about fifteen years after the end of World War II remains my most powerful memory. Ralph had been invited by a German film club to do seminars on editing in a number of different cities. We were luxuriating in an impeccably clean, beautifully appointed train, when we passed several old boxcars standing on a siding. They were well out of sight before I made the connection. With a growing sense of horror, I realized that they might well have been some of the very same boxcars in which Jews had suffered, and died on their way to the camps. Like almost everyone in the world, I had been sickened by the still pictures and films that came out of the liberation of the concentration camps, but seeing those ancient boxcars on the tracks of that well-maintained, precisely on-time German railroad brought home to me in the most visceral and horrifying way, the unspeakable reality of the holocaust.

Then there was the summer, about ten years ago, when Joe and I took a train from Florence to Venice. We had arrived in Rome three days before, and on the second day I'd slipped on the marble floor in the lobby of the hotel in which we were staying, slid at what felt like fifty miles an hour over half the length of the lobby, and broken my shoulder against a pillar. A visit to a hospital in which nobody spoke more than a couple of words of English ('Broke' was one of them after the x-ray was read), earned me a body cast that produced unbearable itching from my neck to my waist and totally immobilized my left arm. Although Joe tried to talk me into flying back to New York, I refused to cut our vacation short. Joe finally gave in, because he could see that I wasn't going to. Florence was next on our itinerary. We traveled by air-conditioned bus, which soothed somewhat the ever-present itching and the pain.

The train to Venice was another story. We got to the station just in time to find it so over-booked that a compartment meant for six people was forced to hold eight. It was a hot, humid day. The temperature inside the train must have been over ninety degrees, but the other passengers insisted that the door remain closed, despite my visible body cast and wild-eyed, heat-struck panic. I sweated copiously under that fiendish cast, which only increased the itching. Squeezed between a soldier in full regalia and a very fat woman, the pain intensified until I came very close to fainting. I spent the last hour standing in the aisle with Joe near an open window that admitted only hot air and noxious fumes. At least there was a breeze.

One last train memory: It was 1943 and I was returning home on the subway on a sweltering June afternoon, after having given blood to the Red Cross for our soldiers fighting in Europe. Because my family and I were leaving for the country a few days later, I had decided to donate only six weeks after my previous donation instead of waiting the mandatory eight. I had obviously cut it too close. Unable to get a seat, I was standing between two cars, trying to capture a breeze. Suddenly I felt faint, and slowly crumpled onto the floor of the subway car. As I was helped up by a fellow standee, a voice behind me said disgustedly, "So young and already a drunk!" I was too woozy to express my indignation, but I remember thinking it was something my Aunt Fanny might have said. I got off at the next station and walked home in high dudgeon, trying to regain my self-respect.

*   *   *

I hadn't thought about those scenes in many years until one steamy July afternoon, as I weeded my garden and listening to the 4:20 pull into Monserrat Station. Sometimes, when a train is passing my house, one or another of those train memories rises to the surface of my consciousness. Because of this, the Rockport line is for me not just a commuter train that takes me south to Boston's museums or north to Cape Ann to visit friends, but a means by which I travel backwards in time and look again and again at the tapestry of my life.

Help

The renovation of my house and garden took the better part of the year. Once the house was capable of looking after itself, I found myself with time on my hands, and for the first time, began to fret about not being useful. I was also feeling a certain amount of ennui. Concerts and theater were less accessible than they had been in New York, and I was becoming increasingly disenchanted with films, mostly because of their increasing dependence on electronic wizardry and unnecessary depictions of violence. Partly out of boredom and partly out of guilt, I decided I must do something besides read, which, though my favorite activity, was useful only to me. True, I was spending a couple of hours a week assisting a visually impaired friend to navigate her life, but as she was a friend, it didn't count.

I had retired more than a decade before, having decided that I was done with helping. During thirty years as a speech pathologist, I had helped the unintelligible to speak more clearly, helped people with voice problems speak more mellifluously, helped non-fluent children speak with greater fluency and, as I did with my next door neighbor, helped their parents refrain from sabotaging the gains. Later, I helped acolytes entering the field become proficient in their own ability to help. I was done, I thought, with helping.

Volunteering offered a solution. I thought about offering my services to the local library, perhaps re-shelving books. But arthritis had already become a daily companion, and lifting books and pushing a cart would elicit those sharp pains I tried hard to avoid. Anyway, I feared that I would spend more time browsing in the books than shelving them. I also considered working at a soup kitchen, but that seemed too much like helping.

Then one day I noticed an ad in the local newspaper that a hospice in my area was offering training for would-be volunteers. My heart leapt in an unmistakable response, informing me in no uncertain terms that there was no escape from destiny. I was mildly amused that the only volunteer work that really grabbed me after wanting desperately to get away from helping, was visiting the moribund.

Hospice care is focused mainly on relieving pain in dying patients, rather than treating them for the terminal diseases that underlie their condition. Hospice also offers physical therapy, nursing, medical evaluations, household help, personal care, counseling for both patients and their families, and even bereavement services for the survivors. Volunteers supplement the other services by offering empathic listening and companionship, as well as short periods of respite for caregivers.

It occurred to me briefly that it might be difficult for dying patients to see someone older than many of them still bopping along like the Energizer bunny. But I decided to put my concerns aside, and hope it wouldn't be a problem. For myself, I didn't anticipate any difficulty in working with the dying. After a lifetime of losses, death wasn't frightening, only immeasurably sad. I had lost my parents, of course, as well as untold relatives, my husband, my partner and most of my contemporaries. All of these had taught me over time and not without struggle, that death, the last point on life's continuum, is as natural an occurrence in its own way as any other. Having accepted the inevitability of the progression had given me the ability, I hoped, to see and accept the end of life as being the equivalent of, say, the period at the end of a sentence, and often a welcome release from a life that has few, if any, pleasures left. Since I knew well what death looked like, with its preambles and remissions and inexorability, I hoped that I could be dispassionate enough, without being unfeeling, to be of use to the dying. I wanted to approach them with thoughtfulness, humor, kindness and empathy, and without fear or distaste. But I hadn't yet tested myself. I hoped it would have a transformative effect on me as I watched people of my own age, sometimes younger, finish their lives. Perhaps there were things for me to learn about my own dying that I hadn't yet imagined.

*   *   *

I stood nervously on the threshold of the nursing home where, as a new hospice volunteer, I was about to meet my first patient. A few weeks before, I had completed the course required of all volunteers, and was uncertain as to whether I could be the paragon of patience and empathy that I felt was required. Originally, I had asked to be paired with someone who was mentally alert and dying at home, but Jeanette, the patient to whom I'd been assigned, was an eighty-four year old nursing home resident with dementia. Sensing my discomfort, the volunteer coordinator urged me to meet with her at least once, assuring me that she was a delightful woman and that I would love her at first sight. I couldn't conceive of loving a stranger whose mind was no longer functioning, but I reluctantly agreed after the coordinator told me that most hospice patients these days suffer dementia of one sort or another, and relatively few die at home. My negative feelings around both nursing homes and dementia were based on a time, years before, when my mother-in-law had been a resident in a home that was sometimes hard to distinguish from a medium security prison. But I was in for a welcome surprise. This nursing home was clean, cheerful and quiet, with friendly nurses and aides who greeted me with a smile as I entered, and could be heard bantering lovingly with their patients.

As I walked past the rooms along the corridor, I could see that each was decorated with personal photographs, gifts, cards, sometimes even stuffed animals piled on windowsills and dressers. I learned later that call lights were answered promptly and patients' needs attended to with tact and concern. A far cry from my mother-in-law's 'home', where family members were well advised to visit daily to make sure that their relatives weren't being ignored, or worse, mistreated.

Jeanette was very frail, with hardly enough heft in her body to contour the blankets under which she lay. She had been in hospice care for about a year, confounding doctors who had certified her as likely to die within the expected six months. However, by the time I met her, she weighed a mere seventy pounds, and, as she was continuing to lose weight, remained eligible for hospice. Her arms and wrists were pencil-thin, her face drawn and similarly gaunt. Kathy, the volunteer who had been seeing Jeanette from the beginning of her life as a hospice patient, was waiting to introduce me. I was to supplement Kathy's visits, as she was unable to see Jeanette as often as needed.

Kathy had told me earlier that Jeanette's dementia consisted not of periods of fantasy, but of an almost complete loss of her short-term memory for even the most recent events. Though her memory problem was severe, she was very much in the moment, and could also remember things about her past life—World War II, for example—and corrected Kathy when she misnamed her husband's war service. "Seabees," she'd whispered sternly, when Kathy mentioned to me that he had been in the Navy.

I stood awkwardly alongside the reclining chair in which she lay, looking feeble and totally out of scale. "Hello, Jeanette," I said, "I'm Davida. It's good to meet you."

In response, she broke into the most dazzling smile I had ever seen. It was as if the sun had suddenly broken through clouds. No longer an emaciated, dying wraith, she had become, for a brief moment, a beautiful, vital woman.

Over the next weeks, our relationship grew. Every time I visited, I would be rewarded by the same brilliant smile. She was unable to speak more than a few syllables at a time because of weakness and the breathing problem, but responded with facial expressions, a few whispered words and a warm hand squeeze. At first it was hard for me to think of things to say, because having a dialogue was physically too difficult for her. I asked her daughter, who visited every morning, what might interest her. She loves jewelry, her daughter informed me, and indeed, Jeanette always wore a necklace or a pin, even earrings on days she'd had her hair done (the nursing home had a hair salon). She also wore her engagement and wedding rings; she had been married for over fifty years to her beloved John, who had died the year before.

At my next visit, I brought my entire collection of jewelry. It consisted mostly of silver and odd enameled pieces, bought for me over the years by Ralph, who had an eye for such things. She handled each piece carefully, trying on some of the rings and necklaces, and making expressions of appreciation. She laughed at some of the more whimsical pieces, especially a pendant of half a woman's face and one breast. "Naughty", she whispered, giggling voicelessly.

On two occasions, I brought art books for her to look at, counting on her appreciation of jewelry to carry over. But her aesthetic sense didn't extend to art, though she looked at the pictures and listened to my amateurish commentary with a polite smile. She did, however, ask about my family, and after telling her that I had recently moved to Beverly, asked me to describe my house. She seemed very curious about me, and so our visits became filled with anecdotes about my life, to which she listened with great interest, once patting my hand after a story about a minor disagreement I'd had with Emily with the words "Good Mommy!"

At the end of one visit, I hugged her gently, overcome by a strong surge of affection.

"Goodbye Jeanette," I whispered. "I love you, you know."

She pulled back a bit, looked at me intently, and took a deep breath.

"But you hardly know me." It was the longest sentence she had yet spoken.

"That's true," I replied. "But sometimes it isn't necessary to know someone a long time to love them, and I feel as if I know you very well."

She considered this for a moment before taking another deep breath. She smiled that dazzling smile.

"Then I guess I love you, too."

That night a poem wrote itself. I read it to her at my next visit.

> When Jeanette smiles, I grin inside.
> I need no further mood prescription.
> When Jeanette smiles, I feel a tide
> Of joy that beggars a description.
> When Jeanette smiles, the room turns bright
> No artificial lights are needed.
> When Jeanette smiles, my heart is light,
> The gardens of my soul are seeded
> When Jeanette smiles.

Jeanette died of pneumonia six weeks later. The poem was read at her memorial.

Soup Beautiful Soup

In the household I shared with Ralph, whoever got the urge first would make a soup. The ingredients for our soups were the equivalent of other people's compost heaps. Mine, like Ralph's, contained leftovers, but only the freshest, with a dominant vegetable bought fresh, as the spirit moved me. Unlike his, they always had a theme. I made broccoli soups, carrot soups, lentil soups, mushroom and barley soups, but one was hard put to identify Ralph's. He used anything he found in the refrigerator. This is because he was unconcerned about quality and proportion; whatever there was, even if poised on the cusp of inedibility, got thrown in. What resulted was usually quite tasty, if considerably shorter-lived than mine, as his soups began to go bad within two days. They also tended to taste alike, which in principle is similar to mixing colors: if you put enough of them together, the result is one or another shade of brown, or, as in the case of Ralph's soups, green. I usually enlivened my soups with a garnish of sour cream and scallion tops, a practice that Ralph scoffed at. He accused me of using them as a crutch.

We would fight for refrigerator space. I was often forced to make my next soup before we finished eating one of his, because if I waited too long, he would already have embarked on his next, preempting all of the leftovers I was depending on using. We would tilt over a half-dozen wilted spears of asparagus, a teaspoon of lemon juice, a slightly aged green pepper. Ralph would puree everything into slop until I suggested that he release the blender's

'On' button sooner. After that, his soups at least had a variety of different textures, if not different tastes, depending on the nature of the ingredients. My soups looked better and were less dense. His looked like excrement, but being thicker, were more appealing in a blizzard. Mine, being less scattershot, may have lacked the globally nutritional variety of his, but his were more nourishing—until they went bad, that is—as they contained at least one item from each of the major food groups.

We constantly had stand-offs about who would make the soup for guests. He considered mine too narrowly conceived, and I considered his too unpredictable. This remained a major bone of contention between us and made for some pretty tense pre-dinner party discussions. However, I had a reluctant admiration for Ralph's creativity. Who else would have been visionary enough to throw in, along with the usual onions, potatoes, carrots, celery and cooked leftovers, a few aging potato chips, a random mixture of leftover cereals, a couple of soggy saltines, a handful of wizened grapes, the scrapings of nearly empty jars of apple sauce, chutney and horseradish, the last dollop of ketchup from an encrusted bottle of same, some miscellaneous olives, six stale macadamia nuts, a handful of moist corn chips and half a brown banana, and still come up with something edible?

*   *   *

Today is definitely soup weather—slate gray, cold and wet. A storm has been predicted. More to give myself an excuse to stay out of the blow than to gratify any strong desire to cook, I decide to make a soup. But as Ralph is no longer here to urge me to put in the rest of the eggplant I didn't finish last night, and despite a vegetable compartment packed with a variety of greens in states ranging from farm-fresh to rotting, my soup will be a curried butternut squash and apple soup, exactly as prescribed by The Silver Palate Cookbook. (I bought the necessary ingredients yesterday in preparation for the expected storm.) This is the first time I have made a soup from a recipe. I find the prospect empowering: if it doesn't turn out well, I can blame it on the cookbook.

No need. This afternoon's labor has delivered me of a soup that I honestly admit is far better than any I have thrown together in the past. It is subtle, exotic and recognizably orange. Moreover, it is snowing hard, and a good hot soup is just what I need for supper in my warm kitchen. I am now done forever with soups consisting of leftovers, no matter how fresh, and will continue to put myself in the hands of the experts. I pledge henceforth to read M.F.K.

Fischer for the recipes as well as for the narrative. I will carefully peruse the N.Y. Times food section instead of discarding it unread, and finally, the soup pages of From Julia Child's Kitchen will no longer remain spotless, but will become as stained as the rest of the book.

Ralph was after me for years to loosen up in the soup department. He had it wrong. What I should have done is the opposite and worked only from recipes. But he never understood that loosening up isn't in my character. I'm too Capricorn.

The Beep

It wakes me from a delicious nap as I doze lightly on the recliner in my study: a short, assertive beep. I had fallen asleep over Hamlet, which I must finish for a class that meets tomorrow. Rising reluctantly, I drag myself into the kitchen, where the sound is coming from. There it is again. I decide to time them and find that they are occurring every thirty seconds. They seem to emanate from somewhere near the side door. For several minutes I stand there, trying vainly to pinpoint their exact place of origin, but since each beep lasts only a fraction of a second, it is gone before I can locate it. I examine the most likely spots. It is somewhat reminiscent of a smoke alarm, but I don't have one in the kitchen. I had removed it almost a year before, as it would start to wail every time I used the broiler. Too often I would find myself standing in the open doorway in winter, wildly flapping a dishtowel in the direction of the stove.

On a hunch, I open the door to the basement and put my ear close to the carbon dioxide detector, listening for the next beep. It arrives. No, it is definitely behind me, somewhere in the kitchen. I examine the walls: I see nothing but a few decorative items, making not a sound. I check all the electrical appliances, large and small. None are emitting so much as a cheep, while somewhere behind me that infernal beep continues to sound exactly twice a minute. I even dig my cell phone out of my purse to see if the battery is low: it is fully charged, and anyway, it never beeps. I go through all the drawers near the side door. The only possible culprits are two remotes: one for the garage door and the spare for the car. But they are lying there quietly next to the aluminum foil, silent as ever. I extend my search to the other drawers and the kitchen cabinets. Still the beep persists. I am stumped, I have run out of options.

"Listen, house," I say, barely suppressing my annoyance, "Except for the flood in May, you've behaved well. If I've insulted you somehow, I apologize. Now please do something about that goddamned beep!"

The next one comes on schedule. I put my hands on my hips and look squarely at the large ceiling light, where a spirit might hide.

"If there's a poltergeist in this room," I say, "please go away. I am not intimidated. If you stop that beeping and behave yourself you can stay, but otherwise, go away!" No wispy form materializes to apologize for the inconvenience.

As I've noted before, talking aloud is not a new development. In addition to Ralph and Joe, the cats and the plants, I also talk to my appliances when they sabotage my efforts to use them. I sometimes talk to myself to work out a personal problem or for the semblance of company, in which case, I take both parts. And now I have talked to a ceiling fixture.

I continue listening to the beep for half an hour, but I still cannot identify its source. Frustrated, I call my son-in-law, who is a trouble-shooter without peer.

"Hey Mike," I say. "I'm really sorry to bother you, but I've got a beep."

"A beep? What kind of beep?"

I describe the beep and the efforts I have made to find it.

"Hold the phone out so I can hear it."

I do so. A few seconds later, it obliges.

"Hmmm. That's a beep alright."

"It is, isn't it?" I say, hoping that he will offer to come over and help me track it down.

"Look, I'm in the middle of something right now. Could you call a neighbor?"

"Nobody's home. I checked."

"Can it wait until tonight?"

"Sure," I say brightly, not sure at all. How can I stand it for another few hours? It isn't very loud, but I can hear it from anywhere in the house. Not knowing what it is is what's driving me nuts.

There is a pause.

"I'll tell you what," he says. "I'm getting curious. I'll be right over"

I hang up blessing the day that Emily found him at a party in Greenwich Village thirty years before.

It will take him about seven minutes to get here. I pull out a chair and sit down. All of a sudden, the beep stops. I wait another minute to be sure. I furiously dial Mike's number to head him off, but there is no answer. He has already left, and Emily must be out. I remain in the kitchen disconsolate, as Mike appears at the door.

"The damn thing stopped," I say.

"Shit!" he says. He sits down and we chat a while, hoping for the beep to return. Our hopes are dashed. After a while, he gets up to leave. I give him two large portions of a soup I had made a few days earlier, so his trip won't have been entirely in vain. As soon as he leaves, I thank the house for having answered my earlier plea.

A few minutes after my statement of gratitude, the beep resumes. I am desolate: I have no Plan C. The phone rings. It is Emily.

"Hi, Mom," she says. "Mike told me about the beep. He said it stopped before he got there."

"Yeah," I say. "But it's back."

"Oh, good," she says. "I want to hear it. Hold the phone up."

I hold it up.

"That's no beep," she says. "It's a ting."

"Sounds to me like a beep."

"No, it's definitely a ting."

"OK, so it's a ting. Do you have any suggestions?"

"Do you want Mike to come over again?"

"No thanks. It'll probably stop as soon as he walks in."

"Can you call a neighbor?"

"Nobody's home."

"Then maybe you ought to call the police."

"For a beep?"

"It's not a beep, it's a ting!"

"OK, for a ting then."

"If you're not going to take my advice, why did you call?"

I sigh. "I didn't call. You called me."

"Oh."

I overhear a short discussion between her and Mike.

"Mike says to call him tomorrow morning if it's still there."

I go into the bedroom and dig out the earplugs I used to use when Ralph snored. I put them in. I can still hear the beep tinging faintly through the plastic. There seems to be no solution. I return to the recliner and pick up Hamlet. I come to his famous soliloquy, which I deliberately misread as "To beep or not to beep". I congratulate myself on the pun.

Five minutes later, the beep stops. It does not return. I call Mike the next morning and tell him he needn't come. He sounds disappointed.

*　　*　　*

Four days pass in glorious silence. The demise of the beep has restored my serenity, even though I am left with the mystery.

This afternoon, Em and Mike drop in for a short visit on their way to the supermarket. I am making a squash soup, because my appeasement gift to Mike the other day has left me soupless. I ask Emily if she will get out the large blue pot, which has migrated to the very back of the lowest kitchen cabinet nearest the door. I am grateful that she's here, because she can still kneel. I can't.

Emily gets down on her knees and pulls out the blue pot. From inside, comes a rattle. She reaches in and holds out something round.

"What the hell is this?" she asks.

I turn from the sink where I am dicing onions. Through onion tears, I see that it is a smoke alarm, the very one I had wrenched off the kitchen wall in a fit of pique the year before. I now remember that I had decided to keep it in case someone from the fire department decides to inspect the house.

"Isn't that the smoke alarm you used to have on the far wall?" Mike asks.

"Yes," I say.

"You'd better put it back. Your insurance company won't pay if you have a fire and there was no alarm up."

This had never occurred to me. I realize that I must resign myself to once again be buffeted by winter winds as I flap a dishtowel against the smoke in the open doorway.

Emily shakes it lightly; it produces a weak facsimile of the sound that had bedeviled me days before. She turns it over. There is some faded print on the back.

'When the battery is low,' she reads aloud, 'This instrument emits a loud chirp.'

We were all of us wrong: it was neither a ting nor a beep; it is a chirp.

For a moment we are silent.

"How about we call it a birp?" I suggest, spelling it.

We then have a discussion about naming sounds. Mike, a devotee of onomatopoeia, votes for 'birp'. I second. Em is silent. After a while, they get up to leave. We hug goodbye. Emily is halfway out the door when she turns.

"It's a ting", she says defiantly over her shoulder. Before I can reply, she is gone.

"It's a birp," I say to the onions, now sizzling in the bottom of the pot, and start peeling the squash.

We Gather Together

Ralph and I had always hosted Thanksgivings at our home. Except, that is, for the five consecutive years when one or another of us was either in the hospital or just out of one. This was beginning to feel like a tradition, until the sixth Thanksgiving, when the spell was broken.

To spare anyone from having to travel on the day itself, we celebrated it on Friday, the day after the traditional Thursday, which put us a bit out of step with the rest of the country. While America's fathers were, for better or worse, slicing into their turkeys, I was out buying yams for my perennial sweet potato 'pie'. By the evening of the official Thanksgiving Day, all my side dishes were finished, and the turkey was not yet done defrosting. The following day, everybody would travel to our home without having to go through several levels of hell to get there.

I remember—vividly—the Hospital Thanksgivings. Paul was hospitalized for two of them: once for an appendectomy, and two years later, when he was twenty-six, in the same Hartford hospital, for a misdiagnosed aneurism that turned out to be a sarcoma. This last was so unusual a specimen that it took Sloan Kettering, one of the primary cancer hospitals in the country, three weeks to identify it, only to tell us it that it was so rare that there were no statistics to assure us that it wouldn't return. Twenty-five years later, it hasn't. I remember Ralph and me making frantic love in the Hartford hotel room the night after Paul's surgery, less out of passion than desperation, as a way, I think, of reaffirming life in the face of what might be a death warrant. Coming out of the OR, the surgeon's only words to us had been: "Don't go back to New York yet. He's going to need you in the morning". He didn't speak the dread diagnosis; he didn't have to.

One year, Emily required a biopsy to check out the possibility of cervical cancer. She was twenty. After a harrowing week, the lab report came back negative.

The next year, I had an unnecessary hysterectomy courtesy of an hysterical gynecologist—no pun intended—who had a phobia about fibroids and ovarian cysts, and threatened me with cancer from before the surgery until the biopsy report came in—everything benign—ten days later.

Then Ralph had a near fatal heart attack, necessitating coronary by-pass surgery and a touch-and-go convalescence. When I look back, I shudder at the possible scenarios. But we all pulled through, even Ralph, who lived on for seven fruitful years.

On those awful days, we would leave the afflicted family member to the mercies of the hospital kitchen and go out for a dinner of fast food, which we ate with no appetite and as quickly as possible so as to get back to the ailing patient. I remember the horror of having to eat Thanksgiving dinners of over-battered chicken at KFC, a limp salad at McDonald's, and a fish sandwich at Burger King. When I was hospitalized, they ate at Jack and Jill's, a meal they all agree was the lowest point of any of the Hospital Thanksgivings. Even at airport layovers, I will not patronize those eateries for the memories they evoke.

I remember keenly the Thanksgiving of 1995, only a few months after Ralph's death. Paul and I drove to Beverly from New York to spend the weekend with Emily and Mike. By serendipity, I had just reconnected with Joe, and the few evenings we'd spent together the week before held the promise that I would not be alone for long. All that weekend, I suffered a combination of grief and giddiness overlaid with guilt. I had told my children about Joe, and though they appeared to be happy and excited for me, I suspected that they were dissembling for my sake. Like me, they were wondering how I could be seeing someone else so soon after losing Ralph.

After Joe died, I found myself grieving for both of them at the same time, not having given myself enough time to mourn Ralph before Joe re-entered my life. It was at that Thanksgiving that my children finally admitted to me their mixed feelings about Joe's appearance in my life so soon after their father's death. And I was able to admit to them the anguish I had suffered over the same issue. It was a devastating holiday, for more than one reason.

First, it was the year of 9/11. I was still living in Manhattan then, my move to Beverly not even imagined. For weeks afterwards I breathed in the acrid smoke, knowing that every breath was infused with the ashes of the dead. That grief became inseparable from my own mourning.

Of all the Thanksgivings I can recall, 1971 is the one I remember with the greatest pleasure. It was memorable because for the first time in years, both my brother and my mother attended—it would be her last Thanksgiving. Bo, having been mentally ill since adolescence, would disappear for months and years at a time. That particular Thanksgiving, I had been able to locate him, and asked him to join us. Nevertheless, I awaited his appearance with some trepidation—he was prone to mumble to himself, to claim to be Jesus, or conversely to say nothing at all, paralyzed by depression. In later years he was diagnosed as either bipolar with schizoid tendencies or schizophrenic with manic/depressive tendencies. To the last, he remained a psychiatric mystery.

But having Bo and my mother with us that year made my little family feel almost complete again (my father had died fifteen years before). I remember sitting at the table, leaning into the laughter and basking in the heady sense of family that friends, no matter how dear, can never provide in quite the same way.

Bo disappeared soon after that day, and I never saw him again. Once in a while, there would be a sighting by a relative, but he never revealed where he was living. I soon stopped trying to locate him, partly because my feelings about him had always been overlaid with fear, the cause of which my years of therapy have never revealed, and partly for selfish reasons. With my mother gone, I would have been his entire support system, and my life then was hectic in the extreme with two children, a job and a difficult marriage. I was exhausted and unhappy for years, until the children left for college and desperation led Ralph and me to go into therapy as a last resort. With effort, we were able to forge a number of happy years as a result.

After Ralph died, I tried to find Bo, but he had left no trail. The last I heard from the doorman at the small hotel where he had been living, was that he had suffered a severe mental breakdown some years before, and had been sent to one of the hundreds of small, poorly monitored homes for the mentally ill that exist in New York's outer boroughs. Because he had changed both his first and last name several times, and I didn't know his social security number, there was no way even to find out if he was still alive. In recent years, my guilt at having abandoned him has slowly worked its way underground, but it surfaces occasionally to stab me in the heart before I can push it back down again.

*   *   *

This last Thanksgiving, again held on a Friday, was a joyous one. This time I didn't have to drive more than five minutes from my Beverly home to get to Em's and Mike's. Again I made my side dish of yams with walnuts, nutmeg, orange juice and much too much butter, and again we sat at their long, festively decorated table and feasted on the usual array of goodies. This time, however, there was a new addition: Paul had married his Maria in February, and I now had a daughter-in-law. For the first time since the day so many years before that my mother and brother joined us at the Thanksgiving table, my family once again felt complete. Yes, Ralph is gone, as are Joe, my mother, my father and my brother, as well as all of the many friends with whom I shared Thanksgivings in the past. And yes, there was a hint of melancholy when we first sat at the table and acknowledged those who are no longer here. But our sadness soon dissipated. We, at least, were here, and the stuffing was superb.

The Sublime and the Ridiculous

I awoke this morning with these lines of Emily Dickinson's running through my mind:

Parting is all we know of Heaven
And all we need of Hell.

I wondered why those particular words had slipped into my semi-conscious, until an ache in the vicinity of my upper right molar cued me in: the tooth that once filled that space had been pulled the day before; its thirty-year-old crown had broken off, leaving too little tooth to build on. But what was the relevance of the quote?

Aha, I thought triumphantly through the throbbing that was making a tom-tom of my cranium, I have it! 'Parting' was the actual extraction, painless until the Novocain wore off. 'Heaven' is the knowledge that the tooth is now gone and will never bother me again. 'Hell' is the pain I am now suffering, due to my gum having to be cut and the tooth removed in several pieces. It hurts furiously, far beyond the power of Extra-Strength Tylenol to do more than mute it.

I do not mean to disrespect Miss Dickinson's poetry in misappropriating lines meant to refer to the irreplaceable loss of loved ones. As a matter of fact, that couplet comes from the poem of hers that I love the most. But in my half-asleep state I cannot be responsible for having assigned its meaning to something as trivial as a lost tooth. Nevertheless, it boosts my ego to know that I have made a literary allusion that elevates a toothache into a respectable metaphor. If it is poetry rather than prose, all the better. Prose is commendable, poetry is more so, but metaphor trumps all.

The Me in Art

"Something there is that does not love a wall," writes the poet Robert Frost. That 'something' is me. Walls, in my opinion, are aesthetic ciphers. They are there only to hold up ceilings, provide a backdrop for furniture and books—and, above all, to display art. In my previous homes, art works have always filled as much of the walls as their dimensions can handle. It was mostly Ralph who bought the art, but I had veto power. I also had the responsibility of hanging it, a task that Ralph came to regard as an art in itself. He had a mystical belief that I could always find space for a new piece, no matter how crowded the wall. He was right. Most surprising, each new arrangement, after some trial and error, looked as if it had always been that way.

Ralph's choices were eclectic. He favored no particular style or subject. If there was one underlying quality in the art he liked, it was whimsy, but the whimsy was always subordinate to the quality of the art. Fortunately, I shared his tastes, but I had never chosen a painting on my own.

One afternoon, some years after Ralph's death, I was brought by a friend to meet Christine Amarger, an artist whose work I had admired in my friend's apartment. Christine showed us a collection of her etchings, and enchanted by one in particular, I knew I had to own it. The one I chose was of a young woman in a yellow-orange dress sitting at a table. She is leaning on her left elbow, her hand supporting her head. On the table is a single piece of writing paper with the words "Mon Cheri" in script along the top. In her right hand, she holds a pen. Her perfectly round face is stylized, as is the shape of her body; her expression suggests that she is pondering what to write next. She is a quirky figure, but not at all a cartoon. The most striking thing about her is her hair. It surrounds her head like a cumulus cloud consisting of a host of scribbled French and English words. The angle of her bent head allows the edge of the cloud to touch the sheet of paper, as if poised to release onto it a torrent of words. I knew why I was so drawn to this particular litho: it was as if I was looking at myself. I was that writer, and her expression is mine as words begin to spill out of my head and onto paper. Never mind that she is writing a letter and not a memoir; I write letters, too. After several less appropriate placements, she now hangs over the desk in my study—my doppelganger, a mirror image of my writing life.

This was the first piece of art with which I so strongly identified. Well, almost—in my early teens I had hanging in my basement room, a cheap, badly framed print of a seated young woman in a billowy turn-of-the-century dress whom I liked to think I might someday come to resemble. I lost the painting during one of my many moves. It was, I think, by Pascin.

*   *   *

As mentioned earlier, Ralph had bought a metal weathervane in Maine a few days before his death. When it was standing in front of the gallery in Camden, it hadn't seemed especially large. However, now indoors, it seems very large indeed.

Above a red pyramidal base topped by a golden ball floats a horizontal lady with a Greek profile in a bright blue oblong dress studded with different colored button-like protuberances. Her legs, incongruously spindly in pink and green striped stockings, are stretched out in a straight line from her body. So are her arms, index fingers pointing bravely into the future. And her hair, five black, wavy strands of steel, flows behind her determined face as if she is bucking a stiff wind. One hand holds a wand, on top of which a small silver fish with a bright green nose faces into the breeze. The entire steel sculpture is surfaced in a coat of bright acrylic paint; the colors are dazzling. At two and a half feet in height and four feet in length, she weighs at least forty pounds. In short, a working weathervane for some country squire's slate roof, hardly appropriate for a New York apartment already filled with too much art or even an Arts and Crafts bungalow in the suburbs of Boston. But I had long since fallen in love with the Lady, and therefore she was one of the two items that would have to be accommodated wherever I made my home (the other was a headboard I couldn't live without). In New York, she had sat on the mantelpieces of two successive apartments. The Beverly house, too, had a fireplace mantel, where I planned to put her. There she would float, facing into the wind, until the day I left that house one way or another.

But alas, when set on that mantelpiece, she lost her authority. The dimensions were wrong. She needed to fly, but there, she seemed earthbound. I looked around the living room. There was no other space big enough for her. Then I thought of the long bedroom windowsill, the only other place with enough depth. The next day Mike came over and we set the Lady up on the bedroom sill. There was an immediate transformation: suddenly radiant, she soared. And though at that time I still had no inkling of her relationship to me, I loved to look at her.

The Lady was the first thing I saw in the morning and the last at night. When I awakened, I greeted her aloud. Her look of calm resolve spoke of purpose, and all those bright primary colors started my day with brio, even on dark winter mornings. Still, it was almost a year before I had my epiphany.

I am lying in bed, my back to the windows in front of which the Lady floats. I'm thinking about my life in relation to an article I'd read the night before, which lists a certain number of stress points related to various life crises. In this scheme, I seem to be off the charts. In the past twelve years I have weathered the loss of my husband and my partner. I have survived colon cancer and, at the advanced age of seventy-eight bought a house in an entirely new environment. As I look back, I realize that much of my past was a struggle as well: the economic poverty of my early years, surviving a driven, domineering father, going back to school for two advanced degrees despite my husband's attempts at sabotage, and trying, with some success, to balance my own needs with those of my family.

On this particular morning, I turn over in bed, and look for the thousandth time at the Lady in the blue dress, holding steady in the face of strong winds as she makes her bright, solitary way above the landscape. I suddenly see her as a symbol of my own life. In her I see a survivor, indefatigable, a second doppelganger to add to the writer with the cloud of words for hair.

In contrast to the biodegradable life I continue to live, she will last for decades, almost indestructible. So too, with a little care, will the litho. It is comforting to know that they will likely survive me. Meanwhile, I often wander from study to bedroom to see myself reflected in those two dissimilar figures. Seeing in them the essence of who I have become, I smile in recognition.

Yet Again

There is a red étagère in a corner of my bedroom. On the second shelf from the top, next to pictures of Ralph and Joe, with me looking up at each of them adoringly, are displayed three smaller snapshots. One is of Emily looking adoringly at Mike, another of Paul looking adoringly at Maria, and the third of me, sitting next to a balding, bearded man, both of us with hands folded, looking straight ahead at the camera, no adoration in sight. The man is Bert, my gentleman caller of the past five years.

Bert and I met at a concert at Town Hall in New York City a year after Joe's death. There was a perfectly normal-looking man sitting on my left, who hadn't said a word. No, it was the oddly dressed person on my right with the bald pate and the long, stringy fringe of gray hair, in bright red suspenders, disreputable denims and a hunter's cap, who started a conversation. Despite his unconventional looks, I found him interesting to talk to, and agreed to go out for coffee. Two concerts and his recitation of love poems by Pablo Neruda later, we bonded over a CD of Bach's Unaccompanied Cello Sonatas and became lovers. I have always been a sucker for intellectuals.

Embarking on an affair at the age of seventy-six was somewhat disconcerting. After a long marriage and a live-in relationship with two men I'd loved, I was now having a bona fide affair with a man I liked and admired, but definitely did not love. It was the first time I had broken my own mid-twentieth century moral code, based on the idea that one must love the man one beds with. But our liaison was a pleasant convenience for two lonely people with interests in common, respect for one another's intellects and initially, at least, enough of a sexual appetite remaining to make for an unexpected bonus.

Two years later, I moved to Massachusetts, and a year after that, Bert followed. He, like me, had lost many friends to death, and his only son, who lived in a New York suburb, traveled a lot. Bert moved into an assisted living community knowing that at some time in his life, he would need care.

After my move, and before his, he would visit me every couple of months. We still maintained all aspects of our previous relationship, but at some point we found ourselves rethinking the carnal part. We were both experiencing flagging libidos: sex was becoming more an obligation than a pleasure. And the fact that he needed to pack nearly two-dozen medications, including refrigerated insulin whenever he stayed the night was another consideration: due to his increasingly poor short-term memory, the contents of his backpack were becoming unpredictable. I gingerly introduced the subject of sex and discovered that we were both having the same thoughts. To my—and his—great relief, we agreed to dispense with that part of our relationship. It is still nice to have him stay over now and again: I would otherwise miss the cuddling and the pillow talk as we teetered on the edge of sleep.

As compensation for my having cut out most sleepovers, solitary breakfasts require less cleaning up; I never let him help, though he is more than willing. The tremor in his right hand has me holding my breath whenever he walks anything to the sink. I am very fond of Bert, but I also have a deep attachment to my fifty-five-year-old hand-painted Portuguese plates. I don't use my everyday dishes when he's here, because I am old-fashioned enough to feel that if one is providing a meal for a guest, even if it consists only of a bagel and cream cheese, the best china is called for, though my best china is actually earthenware.

Because we are both very much set in our ways, we were and are unwilling to share for more than an occasional night our respective living quarters. Besides, I find his low-level anxiety, his honesty-to-a-fault bordering on tactlessness, and more serious, a tendency toward depression (shades of Ralph!) to be traits I choose not to deal with on an everyday basis. Whatever he finds difficult about me is his business. Having this kind of semi-committed connection felt very modern and a little wicked before we went from being lovers to being close friends, as well as having added spice to our couplings.

Our discussions are lively and wide-ranging, from music to politics to books, though sometimes we find it difficult to hear each other; we both have a moderate hearing loss. I consider this the price we are paying for not having died earlier. It could even be looked upon as a plus: words heard inaccurately can take on an air of intellectual acumen that they may not actually possess.

The fact that Bert resembles a bearded Jewish prophet is a plus, but is of small importance. Still, my feelings about him have constantly wavered. When he has made a particularly witty remark, or comes up with a few lines from an obscure poem or song that are germane to the conversation, or when we are having a serious talk about something to which he brings his enviable erudition, I feel enormously drawn to him. He seems to know the answer to the most esoteric questions thrown at him. Once, early in our relationship, I wondered idly what the difference was between a squid and an octopus. With no hesitation, he enlightened me. I checked it later on the internet, and he was right on. And this is a man who can't remember what he had for breakfast an hour after he's had it. Besides, he was a statistician in his working life, which usually doesn't include the biology of cephalopods or an intricate knowledge of the Beethoven Piano Sonatas. Or, in fact, almost any other subject.

But when I pick him up for an evening at a friend's house and he is wearing ill-fitting trousers with those same red suspenders and a faded tee shirt, with his too-long hair (what there is of it) flying off in all directions, or when he would smile widely without a hint of embarrassment, revealing the gap from a recently pulled front tooth that he hadn't yet gotten around to replacing, I want to drop him off at the nearest shelter. I think I will continue to vacillate between these two reactions for as long as we continue to know each other.

Admittedly, he has been dressing less bizarrely lately, probably in deference to the more conventional types in his assisted-living community (in his old habitat—Greenwich Village—anything went). I admit that I miss the panache that accrues to the red suspenders ever since he exchanged them for a well-worn leather belt, but he does look a lot more distinguished in leather. He has allowed Emily to trim his hair and beard twice since he moved here, but I have no idea if he will ever let her do it again. Now that he dresses a little less colorfully, he looks more like an orthodox rabbi sans yarmulke than my idea of a Biblical prophet. I can't make up my mind whether or not it's an improvement. Still, flying hair, faded tee shirt and wispy beard aside, he is an integral part of my life, and there he will remain until further notice.

Elena

The phone rings. As I check my caller ID, my heart sinks: it is Elena. For many years we were closer than sisters. We lunched, attended afternoon concerts and sneaked in a movie when we had the time. We talked on the phone almost daily and shared confidences during long, intimate lunches. She was the one person I turned to for advice in times of crisis, it was Elena whose shoulder I cried on when Ralph had an affair and when Paul, then in his early thirties, had a breakdown. She was my rock when Ralph died suddenly in the middle of the night.

But six years ago, after gall bladder surgery, she began to change. Her imperiousness, her growing air of entitlement, and an unsettling tendency to attack viciously if her judgment was questioned began to alienate many of her friends. By the time she became seriously ill, a year or two later, she had few friends left. I was among them, but my feelings about her were changing.

Now she is much sicker and in unrelenting pain. She craves a listener, and out of loyalty and our past relationship, I listen. Her calls come almost daily and can last for an hour or more. They are litanies of vilification—of her daughter, of her doctors, of the hospital and sometimes of me. She is too ill to reason with, but I have not been able to abandon her; I am trapped by our shared past.

* * *

We met thirty-five years ago at what was then called a cocktail party. I had caught sight of her from an adjacent room, where I'd been having insignificant conversations with people I didn't know. She was alone, leaning quietly against a wall, her body sheathed in a long, fluid gown of shimmering brown jersey. Light from the setting sun illuminated one side of her face, suggesting a cubist painting. She had a dancer's stance and a slim dancer's body, and her expression held a tinge of melancholy. She was, perhaps, the most beautiful woman I had ever seen. Though I was in my forties at the time, I found myself deep in the throes of an adolescent crush. I asked her name and we talked for a while. I wondered aloud why she seemed so sad. She said that this was her first evening out since having separated from her husband three weeks before. I remembered an attractive man I had just been talking to, who'd mentioned that his divorce had become final that day. I excused myself, searched him out and brought him over to meet her. Within minutes, their conversation had gone from tentative to serious. They later had a brief affair. It was my first successful, if short lived, *shidach*, but its early demise suggested that matchmaking might not be my calling.

Within a very short time Elena and I became close friends. As my marriage was then in one of its more difficult phases, our friendship was built on a foundation of husband bashing. Soon we were sharing life stories. Hers was the more dramatic one.

Born to Russian-Jewish parents in what was then Palestine, she had been forced into an arranged marriage at a very early age. Her husband was an American industrialist. After years of being beaten and humiliated by her increasingly disturbed husband, she left him, taking her son and daughter with her. Her husband died shortly after their divorce, and she was left with nothing.

She became a Flamenco dancer—quite a stretch for a nice Jewish girl—and managed to cobble a living out of that and other jobs, ranging from teaching dance movement at an acting school to running the activities program at a home for the aged. Because she was both smart and enterprising, she managed to make enough to get by. She'd had many affairs and later re-married; this was the husband from whom she had separated just before we met.

Long before her second marriage, her son was diagnosed with schizophrenia and had deteriorated rapidly. Caring for Gabe became the driving force in her life. Totally preoccupied with his care, she banished her daughter Becca to boarding school, something that Becca never forgave her for. Some years after Elena remarried, her husband gave her an ultimatum:

either she puts Gabe into a state institution or he leaves. She chose her son.

Elena told me nothing of Becca's history until years later. In the meantime, our shared problems cemented our friendship. They enabled me to overlook those aspects of her behavior that were less than sterling—her haughtiness towards waiters and supermarket clerks, and her rudeness to taxi drivers, one of whom actually put us out of his cab in the middle of 57th Street. Her derisive attitude toward whomever she thought of as inferior made me extremely uncomfortable, but I tried to overlook it because I found her fascinating and there were so many things we had in common: writing—we had both published books; our connection (mine by marriage) with show business; a love of reading and a deep interest in politics. On this we totally disagreed: she was politically conservative and I leaned left. At first I enjoyed our political joustings, but later they got ugly. Politics became a place we didn't go.

At one point, we went into business together—an on-line mail order art gallery—but we battled about everything: from the pricing of the art to the design of our brochure. Her paperwork was a disaster: being dyslexic, she would scramble prospective buyers' Email addresses and phone numbers, making deciphering them a frustrating guessing game. After a year of this, I knew that to save my sanity, I had to get out. I gave her three months notice and happily left the business. I have had no regrets, even when over the next few years she single-handedly built it into a successful internet business. I was happy for her, but I wondered how on earth she managed to keep her orders straight.

Despite my defection, we were able to salvage our friendship. It continued even when, years later, she began to get really nasty. The contempt she had always shown for her daughter, anyone who crossed her, and whomever she deemed to be of a lower social class, began to emerge in more and more situations.

Now, she is eighty-three, living in the Northeast to be near Gabe, who lives in a residence for the mentally ill, and dying slowly in intractable pain after five major surgeries for an intestinal condition that has defied diagnosis. The decades spent fighting for her son as he made his tortured way through the mental health system have hardened her. Any success she'd previously had in keeping her less admirable traits in check has eroded. She has become completely intolerant of dissent from any quarter and extremely short of temper. She is bent, emaciated and mean.

Her attitude of superiority, combined with a distrust that borders on paranoia, has so angered her doctors that eventually they stopped prescribing the drugs she needs to control her pain, claiming that she was abusing them. There is no doubt in my mind that whatever their reasonable fear of liability should she overdose, some degree of retribution was involved. It is clear that they detest her. This must have taken some doing, considering the oath doctors take to do no harm. Without effective drugs to control her pain, Elena cannot eat. My height, she now weighs ninety-six pounds.

Secretly, I have some sympathy for her doctors. I have accompanied her on several visits, and she usually treated her doctors as rudely as she does checkout clerks. Whenever I tried to calm her down, she included me in her diatribe. Invariably, the visits ended with her being angry at me for not taking her side. There is no dealing with her when she is angry She still has her reasonable moments, but as in the nursery rhyme, when she is bad, she is horrid.

Becca has called me frequently in the last weeks. Her calls, like Elena's, are long, ruminative and redundant. They are still battling, a continuation of their life-long struggle. Elena doesn't dispute that she has treated her daughter badly, but she feels that whatever her resentments, it is Becca's duty to take care of her. Elena's needs are limitless. Becca has tried to meet some of them, but there is no way that she can undertake her complete care without abandoning her own work and family. At one point, Elena was forced to hire round-the-clock help, which made her even angrier at Becca: she can pay for it only if she dips into Gabe's trust fund, which she had intended to be used solely for his continued care after she is gone. I find myself in sympathy with both of them. While dying has its reasonable claims, Elena's are unreasonable. As for Becca, she has her own bitterness to deal with. Every time either of them calls, I am torn in two.

*   *   *

The phone is still ringing. I decide to call Elena back later. All this reminiscing has unsettled me. I think back to my last visit to Elena, six months ago. She wasn't completely bedridden then, but she looked much older and sicker. Appalled at how much she had deteriorated, I suggested that she hire someone to help her.

"Why should I pay a stranger," she replied, angrily, "When Becca is only five minutes away?"

I took a deep breath, knowing I was on dangerous ground.

"Because," I said, "Becca is neglecting her own work and family to take care of you. Also, she's exhausted. And she can't understand why you are always so angry at her, when she's been doing so much for you."

I could see the storm clouds gathering as I spoke.

"How dare you!" she shouted. "You're *my* friend. You should be taking my side!"

"I will not take your side when I think you're wrong!" I said.

"Then go!" she shouted. "Go back home! I can do without you!"

"Can't we discuss this calmly?" I asked.

"Get out!" she screamed, pointing to the door in case I didn't get the message.

And so I left.

On the two-and-a-half-hour trip back to Beverly, in between bouts of wanting to strangle her, I marveled at the strength she was able to summon in defending what she felt was due her. I suddenly thought what a blessing it would be to everyone if she would just give in and die. Then I was overwhelmed with guilt that I would wish anyone dead for my comfort. It was a long ride home.

*   *   *

With a sigh, I dial Elena's number, returning her earlier call. Becca picks up. She has been crying. The night nurse has told her that Elena will probably not survive more than a couple of weeks; All her systems are beginning to fail from weeks of starvation and dehydration. Becca, sobbing, says that despite everything, she will miss her mother terribly. I understand that to mean that once Elena is gone, Becca will have to abandon any hope of reconciliation.

The news that Elena's death may be imminent has galvanized me. Listening is no longer enough; only my presence will do. I will drive up to see her this week in recognition of the years—almost half our lifetimes—of our deep and nourishing friendship, even though this visit may be no better than the last. She has been begging me to come, but I've put it off, thinking I can always see her next week, next month, next summer. Now there is no time; goodbyes must be said.

*   *   *

This story has a postscript. The day after I wrote it, I learned that Becca and her husband had sent a letter to the head of the local hospital, pleading her mother's case. The director, having had no idea of what had been going on, ordered the head of the Palliative Care Unit to readmit Elena immediately.

Whether his motivation was to avoid litigation or to care for a patient who needed help is not clear. I suspect it was a little of both, leaning a bit more heavily toward the former.

For a while, Elena was being medicated and re-hydrated regularly. While she still had some pain, it had lessened, allowing her to resume eating. She had just begun to regain some of her lost weight and her temper, when the hospital reneged again. Unless their decision is reversed, she will ultimately die of starvation. Becca visits her mother seldom to avoid being verbally abused, but checks in with the night nurse frequently. Elena is not happy with this arrangement, and, I hear, is beginning to abuse the nurse. Her phone calls had resumed and I was getting ready to visit her again when she called and cancelled our friendship on the grounds that in discussing her with Becca, I have been disloyal. It is now two months since her last call.

I await the next development.

The Case For Uncertainty

It is time for my yearly physical. I was feeling fine, but now anxiety reigns. It has replaced the delight that usually fills me as I look out on my yard plantings and settle down to breakfast and the New York Times (an addiction never, apparantly, to be conquered).

I was operated on for colon cancer six years ago shortly after Joe's death. It was found to be at an early stage and thus considered ninety-eight percent curable. And to be sure, here I was, coming up on the fifth anniversary of my surgery, expecting to be declared cured. But yesterday, the doctor told me that one of the routine tests she'd ordered over a week ago revealed troubling symptoms that required further investigation. An immediate colonoscopy was ordered. The possibilities range from serious through inconsequential, but once having had cancer, I expect the worst. The surge of fear I experienced upon hearing the news has been tempered by the passage of many hours of deep breathing. I am not afraid of dying. My work with hospice in the past few years has dispelled any fear I ever had. But despite my advanced age, I am not ready to go. I still feel young in spirit and open to new experience, and my capacity for joy is nowhere near exhausted. I want more.

In New York, all my doctors were men, most of them elderly. Here, they are all women, mostly young. This is by chance, not choice, despite my feminist proclivities. It isn't that I trust women less, but I liked the analgesic effect of the paternalistic tone my male doctors employed, though it sometimes irritated me politically. While those supremely confident masters of the medical universe never actually committed to a favorable outcome, their manner strongly suggested it. In contrast, my present physicians are not at all motherly—it would, after all, be difficult to be maternal with a woman so many decades older than they are. My rational self appreciates being made party to their uncertainty; it is surely more honest. Still, there is that secret longing to hear those comforting assurances—at least until the pathology report arrives.

Now I must wait five days, and patience has still not become one of my virtues, despite the lessons of my garden. Also, I am very scared. I suspect that I'm in for a long, long weekend. Well, perhaps it's good for my character, as there are few certainties in life, and it's about time I learned to live with it. Once again I blithely took for granted my good health. Things were going well, and foolishly, I never considered that they might not continue that way indefinitely. Like my father, I am an incurable optimist, the word 'incurable' indicating my belief that optimism without some concession to reality is a disease. My father, who remained jobless through eight years of the Great Depression and died at the age of sixty-four without ever making his mark or his fortune, had the same kind of blind faith in a glorious future, despite his overwhelmingly bad-luck life.

Yesterday's report proves how ridiculous is the certainty that my life will remain untouched by disaster. The reality is that my house could burn down, or termites could devour its underpinnings, or I could die sooner than later. Or, despite yesterday's findings, I might outlive my children, which is unthinkable. Why am I not crazed about global warming, the energy situation, the possibility of atomic destruction, as they might affect my children, if not me? I haven't been wearing blinders; I am reminded each day of the grim possibilities by apocalyptic headlines that tell me everything is getting worse. I suppose it's because I've been living so contentedly—my proximity to Emily and Mike, the probability that the next mail will bring news of a Schubert series in Salem, or that the wind will waft into my garden a wayward seed that will take root and produce an unexpected blossom—that I have blocked out any thoughts that could threaten my smug belief in continuing good fortune.

I am less upset about the colonoscopy than about the test that might follow. If the scope doesn't reveal the origin of the problem, I will have to undergo an endoscopy. This, I am told, involves swallowing a camera embedded in a pill. How big, I wonder, is that pill?

Tomorrow I do the prep.

*   *   *

The day has arrived. I have already received eight phone calls wishing me luck. Emily stopped by to give me a hug. Paul called from New York to offer to come and stay with me if I need him, whether for post-surgical care or emotional support. His mention of surgery gave me my first jolt of the day; I hadn't thought that far ahead. Even Bert, who has no memory to speak of, remembered and sent me an encouraging Email. I am beginning to think about what my death will mean to them, beyond what it means to me.

Mike will drop me off at the hospital and then leave. He will pick me up when it's over. I have always preferred to face medical appointments alone, particularly if they promise to be an ordeal. This is not altruism on my part, but a desire not to be distracted by anyone else's anxiety. At these times I want only to concentrate on mine.

After registering, I was installed in a small cubicle identical to ten or fifteen others. The attending nurse told me to take off everything from the waist down. It was nice to be reminded that only half of my body will be under assault. She then started an IV and left me lying on a not-too-comfortable gurney, surrounded by a closed floor-to-ceiling curtain. After a few minutes of increasing claustrophobia, I called a nurse and asked her to pull back the curtain. My panic subsided and I lay quietly waiting. I watched the doctors and nurses hurrying past my cubicle—everyone seemed to be in a rush—until an orderly came and wheeled me into the small room that might hold my fate. The surgeon was looking at my chart. She greeted me and gave my hand a sympathetic squeeze. Then everything went black.

I awoke after what seemed like seconds later, with no memory of the passage of time or the indignities of the procedure. The doctor was at my side, looking cheerful. There were two small polyps, she said; one was removed for biopsy but looked benign, and the other was not as accessible, and would have to be watched. The pathology report would arrive in a week. And she saw no need for an endoscopy, precluding the need to swallow a camera.

I think of this morning as a dress rehearsal that went well. In theatrical lore, this does not bode well for opening night. The pathology results have still to be determined. But for today, I remain serene. Like Scarlett, I'll think about it tomorrow, at Tara.

*   *   *

It is one week later, and it appears that this will be an ongoing saga. The biopsied polyp was benign, but the other one will have to be monitored. This means that I must continue to have yearly colonoscopies with all the anxiety that accompanies them. Surely by this time, I should have a philosophical attitude about any recurrence. After all, one has to die of *something*. But I want to know who the next president will be, whether anything will be done to reverse the climate change, what will happen in Iraq and Afghanistan and Iran, and between Israel and the Palestinians, whether or not space travel will extend to another galaxy, and who will win Best Actress in, say, 2020. By then, I'd be ninety-three, and who knows in what condition.

Well, old girl, I tell myself, you might as well carpe diem and have a good time. At your age, you can no longer die young.

Sugar On My Mind

My friend Pat gives me a baleful look as I reach across the coffee table for a brownie. We are attending the monthly meeting of what we call, somewhat preciously, a "salon". A year or so ago, Pat and Susan, another friend, had decided to ask a few women if they would like to get together at intervals to talk about issues other than personal gripes. We would each bring something to nibble on; my offering this day is a plate of grapes and some cherries. Jane has brought brownies and Mimi a shrimp dip with crackers, while Susan, the hostess, has supplied coffee and a chili dip with chips. The only things I should be eating are the cherries and the chili dip—without the chips, as I had been diagnosed a few months before with diabetes. We are talking about the latest shenanigans at the White House when I realize that I can no longer hold out against the brownies. I take the biggest one.

Pat confronts me after the meeting.

"You know, Davida" she says in a disapproving tone, "you ought to ask yourself why you're in denial about your diabetes."

Pat can—and does—say anything to me. I am never offended. In this case, I realize that she is worried about what seems to be my cavalier attitude about a serious disease. But the word "denial" strikes me as off the mark. Yes, she is right about my lack of commitment to a low bad-carb diet. Exercise is another matter—we both accept that I won't do any. Some people have the exercise gene; I don't.

I thank Pat for her concern and say that I will indeed ask myself why I am being so careless. But as soon as the word is out of my mouth, I realize that it isn't carelessness. Neither is it ignorance. I've bought a couple of books about diabetes and a chart of the glycemic index for every food extant, and I know the exact carbohydrate value of every forkful I put in my mouth. My blood sugar had gone down nicely for the first few weeks and then started to inch up again. I was slipping, but unconcerned.

So what is my problem? Why the brownie? Why the whole grain breakfast cereal I persist in eating even though it sends my blood sugar into the stratosphere? Why the fresh pineapple that I shouldn't have bought in the first place and shouldn't have finished in one sitting in the second. Why indeed, knowing that I am already showing some of the ancillary damage that could ultimately shorten my life? I have already developed some small amount of neuropathy, and my blood tests show a small decrease in kidney function. Why this unprecedented disregard for my health? Why now, when before this, I've always taken all steps necessary to secure it?

The word 'now' hits a chord, and I suddenly understand. From the age of seventeen I was always dieting, a task made arduous because slender is not part of my Jewish heritage, As I approached middle age, I vowed that if I lived to be eighty, I would stop denying myself everything I'd had to eschew during my adulthood, such as Hershey Kisses (no almonds), whipped cream, lemon meringue pie, raspberry chocolate layer cake, big hunks of cream cheese, tapioca pudding, ice cream, barbequed ribs, bacon and grilled cheese sandwiches, and fried anything. Damn it, I deserve them after all those spartan years. And now that I'm almost eighty, I've developed diabetes, and am being told to give up all the foods I've been looking forward to for forty years.

No, it's not denial, it's not carelessness and it's not ignorance: it's that I've made a deal with my body. I will continue, within reason, to indulge its love of forbidden foods in return for which it may have to give up a couple of years.

To put it baldly, I'll be exchanging a somewhat shorter life span for that brownie and an occasional butterscotch sundae. Seems like a reasonable swap to me.

Wish You Were Here

People usually express surprise when they learn that my birthday is January first. It's as if being born on that particular day is something unusual. I have never understood why. There are three hundred and sixty-five days in every non-leap year, and I would imagine that an equal number of births take place every day of the year, with some leeway for a skewed amount of love-making during widespread blackouts, blizzards and other natural disasters.

My birthday is about to occur again. This one is a landmark: eighty, a number I never expected to reach. None of my progenitors got this far except for Grandma Gottfried, who made it to eighty-four. My mother, the next longest-lived, died at seventy two. I found myself thinking about her as my birthday approached, and realized that if by some magical incantation she suddenly appeared, I would be the elder. I wondered what she would think of the person I have become, and how she would react to the signs of age in my face and body. I imagined her putting her arms around me and saying something loving and complimentary, ignoring the effect that the years have had on me. She would no doubt express amazement at my longevity, something which is a surprise to me as well: I have done nothing in the way of deliberately healthy living during my zero-exercise, gustatorily over-indulgent life.

I have begin to wonder how much longer I will be able to live in my lovely little house. Inevitably, I will get frailer, shorter and less sturdy on my feet. This combination will make it difficult to use a stepstool to get into cabinets

I am just barely tall enough to reach now. I had hoped to die in this house, but lately I'm realizing that it might not be practical. I get a bit depressed whenever I project what my ninth decade might hold, if I am lucky/unlucky enough to live into it. Or maybe my unhappiness is merely due to the fact that no one has yet mentioned my birthday, much less suggested celebrating it.

I had entered my seventh decade with Ralph and my eighth with Joe: dinners for two in three-star restaurants, followed, with Joe, by a Broadway musical, and with Ralph, an Off-Broadway play (always a serious one) followed by a long discussion of its virtues, flaws, and deeper meanings. And of course, a gift—both times an unusual piece of jewelry. Ralph's was a stunning oval ring of Baltic amber with a host of delicate insect fossils captured in its once viscous sap. Joe's was a magnificent pendant, also of amber, set in an antique silver setting. As both amber and silver are my favorite adornments, it was heart-warming to know that both men had paid attention.

*   *   *

Today, with less than two weeks to go, I received two welcome phone calls. Emily, with Ellen, a mutual friend, is planning a birthday brunch on New Years Day, which falls on a Monday this year, and two other friends, Susan and Pat, will be co-hosting a Saturday night bash that same weekend. Two parties in two days! That night in bed, as I contemplate my good fortune, I find myself thinking again of my mother. I ask her in the dark if she could possibly attend at least one of the two, or failing that, give me some sign that she hears my invitation. There is, of course, no reply.

I haven't been given a birthday party since I was twelve, the year of my first menstrual period. My father was of the opinion that parties were only for children, and in his eyes at least, my hormones had catapulted me into the austerity of adulthood. Perhaps because of my own deprivation, I gave birthday parties for my children until, in mid-adolescence, they begged me to stop; I was embarrassing them with their friends. Also, I produced a surprise gala for Ralph every fifth year, though after the third gala I dropped the 'surprise' part, mostly because he caught on. So having two parties for my eightieth seems only fair. Emily calls it a 'birthday festival'.

*   *   *

It is January second, and the festivities are over. No letdown, though; I'm still vibrating with the pleasure of having been the center of attention, something that happens rarely, and probably will again only if I manage to live another ten years.

Susan's Rockport house has several small rooms, many with fireplaces. Each mantelpiece bears a collage of candles, fruit, paintings and artifacts that change with the occasion. On that Saturday night, the room was illuminated by dozens of candles of every size, the dancing pinpoints of light mirroring in miniature the fiercely leaping flames in the fireplace. There were flowers everywhere. One vase was filled with tulips, my favorite, in every posture of their life's journey from upright to languidly drooping.

At my insistence, the invitations had included the words "No gifts, please". I wondered if their absence obligated my friends to say all the wonderful things they said in their speeches. I wish I could remember their exact words, but I do remember that every one of them mentioned love and a generosity of spirit. My children spoke not of love, but of respect. Someday, I'll have to ask them why they left love out, but I'm not yet ready to stick a pin in my happiness balloon.

After the speeches, Pat read a sweetly whimsical poem she'd written about me in the style of a Lear limerick, and Mike sang the hilarious lyrics he'd written to the tune of 'Maria', from West Side Story, substituting my name for hers. By the time the poetry reading and the singing were done, I was in tears. Later, I told my kids that they won't need to hold a memorial service when I die, because I'd just had one.

Partway through the evening, I found myself desperately wanting my mother to be there. I loved her, but ours had been a relationship of unrequited love: my mother was so busy supporting the family during the eight years my father was out of work, and so distracted by the bottomless needs of my mentally ill brother that she hardly had time for me. But I loved her for her sweetness and her gentle spirit, although I never felt that I'd gotten my fair share. In hindsight, I suspect that she was grateful for my being the 'good child', a role I must have unconsciously assumed to win her love. I resented my brother bitterly at the time, but never my mother. My anger towards her emerged only after I had my own daughter and understood viscerally what I had missed, and then dissipated when I had a son who needed more than his fair share from me.

I wondered what she would think about me now. Would she see anything of herself in me, something I have wished for all my adult life? It was odd to think that were she to magically appear, she would be eight years younger.

I had spent a lot of time thinking about her as my birthday approached, feeling deep disappointment that I hadn't come close to being the woman she had been: a model of kindness, her inner strength camouflaged by a dusting of anxiety, a gentle demeanor and the ability to give of herself that had brought her as much love as she gave; the number of friends who attended her funeral was staggering. But to my surprise, I realized that many of the comments my friends made about me that night might just as well have been made about her.

My birthday brunch took place two days later at the beautiful, old, meandering home of friends Ellen and Doug. After a superb meal, positively Roman in its excess, I was presented with a Bose radio. Emily, Mike, Paul, Maria and Bert had pooled their fortunes to get me what had been my heart's desire ever since I'd heard it played at full volume at the home of friends. I was touched that they had been paying attention, just as Ralph and Joe had paid attention decades before.

*   *   *

It is now late January. In the weeks since my 'festival' I seem to have acclimated to being eighty quite comfortably. My concern about being able to manage this house as I age further has settled into a part of my brain that I rarely visit. I now try to concentrate on the joys of my old age (being ambulatory and still able to drive) and ignore its ravages ("Whose body is this, anyway?").

As I write this, there is an ice storm raging. I make the rounds from window to window to see its various faces. Icicles hang off the tree branches like rows of Christmas lights. Neighboring houses have lost their color in the gray light, but their roofs gleam white from the snow that fell earlier. It is now four-thirty and nearly dark, but I have not turned on any lights, the better to appreciate the random patterns that form and re-form on the windows.

Tomorrow, with temperatures predicted to be in the twenties, the streets will likely be treacherous with ice, foreshadowing another day indoors for those of us too old to risk a fall. I am still active and would like to keep it that way. I stay off icy sidewalks, wear galoshes in inclement weather, and always layer when it's below freezing. In these later years, I have learned to treasure my physical well being above all else. For this, I credit my quintessentially Jewish Grandma Becky, who taught me what was really important in life. She would gently counter my childhood complaints with "As long as you've got your health".

Postscript

I do not fear death, nor do I worry about its ever-increasing imminence; I have had intimate relations with it on too many occasions to be afraid. Besides, I've had other things to concern myself with. The deficit, for instance. It has lately been on my mind, though it is unlikely to affect me personally, as having entered my ninth decade, I have less of a future than I used to. I don't know why it matters to me that everybody else's grandchildren—I have none—may have to face privation because of it. With my gene pool just one more puddle drying on the tarmac of history, I really shouldn't be concerned. And then there is my financial situation. In the grip of periodic panics triggered by the frequent drops in the Dow Jones Industrial Average, out comes my calculator, and for the hundredth time I do the mathematics that predict how long my savings will last. It is always with great relief that I learn that my nest egg, husbanded carefully, is likely to last a lot longer than I will. As for my mortality, I have tried to live by the words of Claude Pepper, the late, then octogenarian senator from Florida. When asked about his agenda for the next session of Congress, he replied that he never planned that far in advance. "At my age," he said, "I don't even buy green bananas".

I have spent my life dancing as fast as I can, and I plan to continue as long as my legs hold out. Despite the evidence that everybody dies, I remain unable to visualize my own non-being, and thus secretly hold to the belief that I will break precedent and go on forever. Still, to be on the safe side, I buy my bananas ripe.

If I've ever had any regrets about my life, they no longer exist. I could, for example, regret the need, due to both finances and aging, for me to leave New York, that incomparable and endlessly diverting city. But I have bonded with my house and my community more strongly than I ever thought possible.

I could regret a large part of my marriage, which was in some ways far more difficult than most. But there were aspects of it so nurturing of necessary parts of myself that I am grateful for the way it helped me grow, both intellectually and emotionally.

I could regret having had children, whose early years, because of their many medical problems and my working full time, made my life an exhaustion of visits to professional after professional. But their present lives, filled with love and landmark achievements, have given me so much joy that it was worth every trip.

I could regret my six years with Joe, because more than half of them were spent fighting his lymphoma, the disease that finally killed him. But there were long remissions, and we took advantage of every minute of respite. Those years of receiving his unconditional love were so healing for me that I cannot imagine having lived my life without them.

I could regret my present solitude. But I seem to have grown into it as if it is my birthright. I feel such delight when I sit alone in my beloved artichoke of a house, writing, reading or listening to music, that I now wonder how I was able to get through those frenetic years. Being alone at this time of my life is heaven realized.

I have been more than compensated for the unhappy times by the multitude of blessings I've received from my family, my friends and the two men I've loved, all of whom I have chronicled as honestly as I could in this book.

Davida Rosenblum
Beverly, Massachusetts,
March, 2008